GROUND STUDIES FOR PILOTS
Volume 3

Volumes in the Series

Volume 1: Radio Aids
Volume 2: Plotting and Flight Planning
Volume 3: Navigation General and Instruments
Volume 4: Meteorology
and
Aviation Law for Pilots

GROUND STUDIES FOR PILOTS

Fifth Edition
Volume 3

NAVIGATION GENERAL
and INSTRUMENTS

R. B. Underdown
FRMetS MRAeS
formerly Director of Ground Training and latterly Principal,
College of Air Training, Hamble

OXFORD
BLACKWELL SCIENTIFIC PUBLICATIONS
LONDON EDINBURGH BOSTON
MELBOURNE PARIS BERLIN VIENNA

Copyright © S. E. T. Taylor and H. A.
Parmar 1970, 1979
Amendments for fourth Edition copyright
© R. B. Underdown 1986, 1988
Fifth Edition
Copyright © R. B. Underdown 1993

Blackwell Scientific Publications
Editorial Offices:
Osney Mead, Oxford OX2 0EL
25 John Street, London, WC1N 2BL
23 Ainslie Place, Edinburgh EH3 6AJ
238 Main Street, Cambridge,
  Massachusetts 02142, USA
54 University Street, Carlton
  Victoria 3053, Australia

Other Editorial Offices:
Librairie Arnette SA
2, rue Casimir-Delavigne
75006 Paris
France

Blackwell Wissenschafts-Verlag
Meinekestrasse 4
D-1000 Berlin 15
Germany

Blackwell MZV
Feldgasse 13
A-1238 Wien
Austria

First published in Great Britain by Crosby
  Lockwood & Son Ltd 1970
Reprinted 1972
Second edition 1974, reprinted 1976, 1978
Third edition, in three volumes, 1979
Reprinted by Granada Publishing 1981,
1983
Fourth edition published by Collins
  Professional and Technical Books 1986
Reprinted with updates by BSP
  Professional Books 1988, 1990
Fifth edition published by
Blackwell Scientific Publications 1993

Set by Best-set Typesetter Ltd., Hong Kong
Printed in Great Britain by Hartnolls Ltd,
Bodmin, Cornwall

DISTRIBUTORS

Marston Book Services Ltd
PO Box 87
Oxford OX2 0DT
(*Orders*: Tel: 0865 791155
      Fax: 0865 791927
      Telex: 837515)

USA
  Blackwell Scientific Publications, Inc.
  238 Main Street
  Cambridge, MA 02142
  (*Orders*: Tel: 800 759-6102
          617 225-0401

Canada
  Oxford University Press
  70 Wynford Drive
  Don Mills
  Ontario M3C 1J9
  (*Orders*: Tel: 416 441−2941)

Australia
  Blackwell Scientific Publications Pty Ltd
  54 University Street
  Carlton, Victoria 3053
  (*Orders*: Tel: 03 347-5552)

British Library
Cataloguing in Publication Data
A Catalogue record for this book is
available from the British Library

ISBN 0-632-03434-3

Library of Congress
Cataloging in Publication Data
Underdown, R.B.
    Ground studies for pilots/
    R.B. Underdown. − 5th ed.
      p.   cm.
    Includes index.
    Contents: − v. 3. Navigation general
    and instruments
    ISBN 0-632-03434-3 (v. 3)
    1. Navigation (Aeronautics)   2. Aids
    to air navigation.
  I. Title.
TL586.U48   1993
629.132′51 − dc20   92-43150
                                 CIP

Contents

Preface   vi

Part 1 MAPS AND CHARTS   1
  1 Mathematics Reminders   3
  2 Form of the Earth   18
  3 Convergency, Conversion Angle, Departure   28
  4 Projections General   41
  5 Mercator's Projection   51
  6 Lambert's Conical Orthomorphic Projection   65
  7 Polar Stereographic Projection   76
  8 Transverse and Oblique Mercator Projections   82
  9 Grid Technique   90

Part 2 AIRCRAFT INSTRUMENTS   101
  10 Airspeed Indicator (ASI)   103
  11 Altimeters   110
  12 Vertical Speed Indicators (VSI and IVSI)   124
  13 Machmeter   130
  14 Gyroscope   140
  15 Direction Indicator (DI)   149
  16 Artificial Horizon   164
  17 Turn and Slip (Balance) Indicator   171
  18 Air Temperature Measurement in Flight   178
  19 Inertial Navigation   183
  20 Electronic Displays and Systems   194

Part 3 MAGNETISM AND COMPASSES   215
  21 Magnetism: General and Terrestrial   217
  22 Aircraft Magnetism 1   223
  23 Aircraft Magnetism 2   241
  24 Direct Reading (Standby) Compasses; P-type, E2-type   259
  25 Turning and Acceleration Errors   264
  26 Remote Indicating Compass   270

Part 4 SOLAR SYSTEM   283
  27 Solar System: Time   285

Answers to Multi-choice Test Questions   307
Glossary of Abbreviations   308
Index   312

Preface

Following the United Kingdom's signature of the Treaty of European Unity in February 1992 paving the way for a common European Market from January 1993, new syllabuses for pilots' licences have been introduced. The European Civil Aviation Conference, through wide consultations within and between its member states, has produced the harmonised syllabuses setting the required standards.

To meet these revised standards, the text of *Ground Studies for Pilots*, which is published in four volumes:

Volume 1 *Radio Aids*
Volume 2 *Plotting and Flight Planning*
Volume 3 *Navigation General and Instruments*
Volume 4 *Meteorology*

and their companion volume, *Aviation Law for Pilots*, has been completely revised. This volume includes aircraft instruments, magnetism and compasses together with all of the subjects commonly referred to as 'Navigation General' – Form of the earth, maps and charts, the solar system and time. New material is included on air data computers and the electronic displays and systems (EFIS) of modern aircraft such as flight management systems and flight directors. Much-appreciated assistance, by supplying technical data and illustrations for this edition, has been given by British Airways, Smiths Industries, RACAL Avionics Ltd, GEC Avionics, GEC Plessey, Collins Division of Rockwell International, Rosemount Inc. and British Aerospace. Particularly I would like to acknowledge the valuable help provided by my former colleagues Max Johnson and Tony Palmer for their most helpful suggestions and for reading the script.

I am grateful to HMSO for permission to reproduce the pages from the Air Almanac to form the basis for examples and questions. Specimen examination questions for pilots' licence examinations are available by post from the Civil Aviation Authority, Printing and Publication Services, Greville House, 37 Gratton Road, Cheltenham, Glos, GL50 2BN.

Roy Underdown
Hamble

Part 1
MAPS AND CHARTS

Chapter 1
MATHEMATICS REMINDERS

Mathematics plays an important part in the professional pilot's ground training syllabus: a solid background of elementary mathematics with an ability to shift figures quickly not only helps a student with his exams, but is a necessity in understanding a great deal of the syllabus material. If you have done it all before and have forgotten much of it, or are just feeling shaky about it, in this short chapter we remind you of some of the pertinent maths processes without offering any text book proofs or heavy explanations. As the CAA allow the use of pocket electronic calculators in their examinations, a revisionary treatment of their use is also included.

Assuming a certain facility with fractions and decimals we will start with:

Ratio and proportions

A ratio is the mathematical relationship between two quantities. It indicates the number of times one quantity is contained in another quantity of the same kind, and is either expressed as a fraction, x/y or simply $x:y$.

Example

An aircraft's maximum speed is 180 kt whereas its cruising speed is 150 kt. Then the ratio of the cruising speed to the maximum speed is $\frac{150}{180}$, that is, $\frac{5}{6}$. Working in reverse, if the ratio between any two quantities and the value of one of them is known, then the value of the other may be found. In the above example, when the ratio of 5/6 and the cruising speed are known, the maximum speed is expressed in the relationship

$$\frac{5}{6} = \frac{150}{\text{max. speed}}$$

Thus
$$\text{max. speed} = \frac{150 \times 6}{5} = 180$$

Here is another application. Divide 84 in the ratio 3:4. Add 3 and 4 to give 7, divide 84 in seven parts, that is, each part is equal to 12. Then 3 parts is equal to 36 and 4 parts is equal to 48, the two shares adding up to the original figure of 84.

On many occasions we handle ratios without being conscious of it. The Greek letter π that we use in maths is the ratio of the circumference of a circle to its diameter. When we talk of a one million chart we mean a ratio of 1:1 000 000. An aircraft's mach number is the ratio of its true airspeed to the local speed of sound.

When two ratios are equal, then the four quantities comprising these ratios are said to be in proportion and the whole term may be expressed in the form $a:b::c:d$. The numbers 3, 4, 18 and 24 form a proportion. The ratio $\frac{3}{4}$ is equal to the ratio $\frac{18}{24}$. If we know any three of these terms the fourth may be found very simply. For example in an expression similar to that above, the first term is 4, the third 12 and the fourth 36. Then the second term, b, stands in relationship to the rest as

$$\frac{4}{b} = \frac{12}{36}$$

Then
$$12b = 4 \times 36$$

$$b = \frac{4 \times 36}{12} = 12$$

If one quantity B depends on another quantity A so that when the value of A increases, the value of B similarly increases, then B is said to be directly proportional to A and is expressed as $B \propto A$. Conversely, if the value of B decreases as the value of A is increased, B is said to be inversely proportional to A and is written as $A \propto 1/B$. In the above example, the terms $4:12::12:36$ are in direct proportion. If 4 kg of fuel takes you one ground nautical mile and 8 kg takes you two ground nautical miles then the terms are in direct proportion. Alternatively, if one workman takes one full day on a job whereas two would do it in half a day, the two quantities are in inverse proportion. Problems involving direct and inverse proportions are solved as follows.

Example
If an aircraft travels 25 nm in 4 min, what distance will it cover in 16 min? The distance covered in 1 minute is the ratio $\frac{25}{4}$ nm.

∴ in 16 minutes the distance travelled $= \frac{25}{4} \times 16$ nm

$$= 100 \, \text{nm}$$

Example
A survival dinghy carries sufficient emergency rations to last four survivors five days. How many days will the rations last if there were six survivors aboard?

No. of survivors is increased in the ratio $\frac{6}{4}$

∴ no. of days is decreased in the ratio $\frac{4}{6}$

Hence the total number of days $= \frac{4}{6} \times 5 = \frac{20}{6} = 3\frac{1}{3}$

Some examples

(1)   What ground distance in nm is represented by 7.296 in on a half-million map? 1 in on the map represents 500 000 in on the ground.

$$\therefore 7.296 \text{ in represents } \frac{500\,000 \times 7.296}{6080 \times 12}\text{nm}$$

$$= 50 \text{ nm}.$$

(2)   In the time that an aircraft A travels 240 nm, another aircraft B travels 270 nm. How far has B travelled when an aircraft A has gone 320 nm?
When A travels 240 nm, B travels 270 nm.

$\therefore$ ratio B to A is $\frac{270}{240}$ or $\frac{9}{8}$

When A has gone 320 nm,
B has travelled $\frac{9}{8} \times 320 = 360$ nm.

(3)   If the tabulated data for an aircraft gives:

Aircraft weight (tonne)	300	288
fuel flow (kg/h)	12 500	11 900

What is the fuel flow if weight is 296 tonne?

Solution
12 tonne less gives fuel flow 600 kg/h less.
So, 4 tonne less $(300 - 296)$ will give $\frac{4}{12} \times 600$ less $= 200$
Required flow $= 12\,500 - 200 = 12\,300$ kg/h.

Percentages

A percentage is simply a fraction with a denominator of a 100, the words per cent meaning 'per hundred'. The fraction $\frac{69}{100}$ expresses 69 as a percentage and may be rewritten 69%. Any other fraction may be expressed as a percentage by multiplying it by 100. Thus, $\frac{6}{10}$ when expressed as a percentage is

$$\frac{6}{10} \times 100 = 60\%.$$

A decimal fraction may be converted to a percentage by moving the decimal point *two* places to the right. For example, $0.039 = 3.9\%$ and $5.4 = 540\%$.

Example
A pilot flying at 6000 ft increases his altitude to 7400 ft. What is the percentage increase of the altitude?

The ratio of the increase is $\dfrac{1400}{6000}$

and the percentage increase $= \dfrac{1400}{6000} \times 100 = 23.3\%$ (correct to 1 decimal place)

To express quantity *a* as a percentage of another quantity *b*, multiply the fraction *a/b* by 100.

Example
Express 120 kg of fuel as a percentage of 760 kg of fuel.

$$\frac{120}{760} \times 100 = 15.79\% \text{ (correct to 2 decimal places)}$$

Practice problems
(1) Due to head winds an aircraft is required to increase its normal route fuel from 10 000 kg to 11 845 kg. What is the percentage increase in fuel?

$$\frac{1845}{10\,000} \times 100 = 18.45\%$$

(2) If the route fuel is 23 670 kg and 7% of this is added as a contingency measure, how much fuel is carried?
Start fuel 23 670 kg

$$7\% \text{ of start fuel} = \frac{7 \times 23\,670}{100} \text{kg}$$

$$= 1656.9 \text{ kg}$$

∴ Fuel + contingency = (23 670 + 1657) kg = 25 327 kg.

(3) When flying at a given mach number, if the TAS at FL 380 is 400 kt and at FL 320 is 415 kt, what percentage increase in the TAS is achieved by flying at the lower flight level?

$$\frac{15}{400} \times 100 = 3.75\%$$

(4) On a Mercator chart a true ground distance of 274 nm measures 271 nm. What is the percentage error?

$$\frac{3}{274} \times 100 = 1.09\%$$

(5) Full tanks on an aircraft hold 44 000 kg of fuel. If a company requires a contingency reserve of 10% of fuel to destination and alternate to be carried on all flights, what is the maximum contingency reserve with full tanks?

$$44\,000 \text{ kg} = 110\%$$

$$\text{so contingency reserve} = \frac{10}{110} \times 44\,000 \text{ kg}$$

$$= 4000 \text{ kg}$$

Algebra

We will now revise the type of problem that crops up, which we know some students have lost their youthful ability to solve readily. A typical solution by simple equation is given in the following example:

How far can an aircraft go from base at a G/S out of 450 kt and back at 400 kt, if fuel flow out is 6600 kg/h and back is 6100 kg/h, with usable fuel on board (FOB) of 40 000 kg?

Distance divided by G/S out gives *time* on the outward leg.
This time multiplied by fuel flow gives *fuel used out*.
Ditto for the homebound leg.
The total of the two fuels equals the FOB.

Algebraically, where x is the distance in nm, this gives

$$40\,000 = \left(\frac{x}{450} \times 6600\right) + \left(\frac{x}{400} \times 6100\right)$$

$$= \frac{44x}{3} + \frac{61x}{4}$$

Multiply both sides by 12 (derived from 3 × 4)
$$480\,000 = 176x + 183x = 359x$$
$$\therefore \quad x = 1337\,\text{nm}$$

Indices

A quick reminder.
To multiply – add the indices: $a^m \times a^n = a^{m+n}$.
To divide – subtract the indices: $a^m \div a^n = a^{m-n}$.
To raise to a power – multiply the indices: $(a^m)^n = a^{mn}$.
To find a root – divide the indices: $\sqrt[n]{(a^m)} = a^{m/n}$
And oddments:

$$\sqrt{a} = a^{\frac{1}{2}}$$
$$\sqrt[3]{a} = a^{\frac{1}{3}}$$

$$\frac{1}{\sqrt{a}} = a^{-\frac{1}{2}}$$

$$a^2 b^{-2} = \frac{a^2}{b^2}$$

Example

If scale is 1:1 000 000 how many kilometres does 1 cm represent?

Solution

$$1\,000\,000 = 10^6$$
$$1\,\text{km} = 1000\,\text{m}$$
$$= 10^3 \times 10^2\,\text{cm}$$
$$= 10^5\,\text{cm}$$

so, $1\,\text{cm} = \dfrac{10^6}{10^5} = 10^1\,\text{km}$

$$= \underline{10\,\text{km}}$$

Properties of a circle

A few facts:

(a)   Circumference of a circle $= 2\pi r$ (where r is the radius).

(b)   Length of an arc $= \dfrac{N}{360} \times 2\pi r$

(where N is the number of degrees in the angle subtended by the arc at the centre of the circle).

(c)   A perpendicular bisector of a chord from the centre of a circle divides the chord in two equal parts (Fig. 1.1).

(d)   Equal chords are equidistant from the centre of a circle.

(e)   Angles in the same segment of a circle are equal. (In Fig. 1.1, $X_1 = X_2$.)

(f)   The angle at the centre of a circle equals twice the angle at the circumference (Fig. 1.1).

Angle YOZ is twice the angle YX_1Z or YX_2Z.

(g)   The angle in a semi-circle is a right angle.

In Fig. 1.2 the straight line AB divides the circle in two equal parts. Segment ADCB is therefore a semi-circle and the angle ACB is a right angle. So is the angle ADB.

 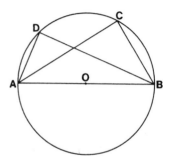

Figs 1.1, 1.2   Properties of a circle – angular values

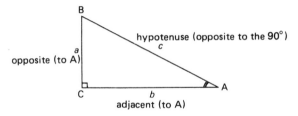

Fig. 1.3   Names of sides of a right-angled triangle

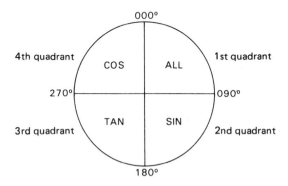

Fig. 1.4   Trigonometrical ratios positive/negative

Trigonometry

Consider the right-angled triangle ABC in Fig. 1.3.

$$\text{Sin A} = \frac{\text{opp}}{\text{hyp}} = \frac{a}{c}$$

$$\text{Cos A} = \frac{\text{adj}}{\text{hyp}} = \frac{b}{c}$$

$$\text{Reciprocal Sec A} = \frac{\text{hyp}}{\text{adj}} = \frac{c}{b}$$

$$\text{Tan A} = \frac{\text{opp}}{\text{adj}} = \frac{a}{b}$$

These ratios are constant for a given angle. When an angle exceeds 90°, the required ratio is first given a sign according to Fig. 1.4. Here the ratios and their reciprocals are *positive* in the given quadrants. Elsewhere they are negative. Then the angle is reduced to less than 90° before the tables are entered, by applying 180° or 360°, viz:

When the angle θ is in the *second* quadrant, it becomes (180° − θ).
When the angle θ is in the *third* quadrant, it becomes (θ − 180°).
When the angle θ is in the *fourth* quadrant, it becomes (360° − θ).

Example

Find the sine of 210°.

210° is in the third quadrant, ∴ equivalent acute angle = 210° − 180° = 30°.
Sine of 30° is 0.5 and the sign is −*ve*; therefore the value is −0.5
In a triangle ABC, ∠C = 90°, *a* = 32.3, *b* = 25.9. Find ∠A.

$$\text{Tan } A = \frac{a}{b} = \frac{32.3}{25.9}$$

$$= 1.247$$

$$A = 51°17' \text{ (from nat tan tables).}$$

Note

When using a scientific calculator it is not necessary to reduce an angle to the first quadrant. The calculator is programmed to do this and to allocate the appropriate sign for the function required.

For solving triangles other than right-angled triangles there are two standard formulae:

(a) $\quad \dfrac{a}{\sin A} = \dfrac{b}{\sin B} = \dfrac{c}{\sin C}$

(b) $\quad a^2 = b^2 + c^2 - 2bc \cos A$

This formula may be rewritten as
$$b^2 = a^2 + c^2 - 2ac \cos B$$
$$c^2 = a^2 + b^2 - 2ab \cos C$$

(1) In a triangle ABC, *a* = 421.9, *c* = 321.6, ∠A = 65°12′, find ∠C
Answer: 43°47′.

Solution

Two sides and one of the opposite angles are given, therefore we will use the simpler formula (a) above.

$$\frac{a}{\sin A} = \frac{c}{\sin C} \quad \text{or} \quad \frac{\sin C}{c} = \frac{\sin A}{a}$$

Thus, $\qquad \sin C = \dfrac{c \sin A}{a}$

$$= \frac{321.6 \sin 65°12'}{421.9} = \frac{321.6 \times 0.9078}{421.9} = 0.6920$$

$$= 43°47' \text{ (from nat sine tables).}$$

(2) In a triangle ABC, *a* = 12.8, *b* = 15, *c* = 9.9, find ∠C

Solution

Using the formula from (b) above

$$c^2 = a^2 + b^2 - 2ab \cos C$$

$$-2ab \cos C = c^2 - a^2 - b^2$$

$$2ab \cos C = a^2 + b^2 - c^2$$

$$\cos C = \frac{a^2 + b^2 - c^2}{2ab}$$

$$\cos C = \frac{12.8^2 + 15^2 - 9.9^2}{2 \times 12.8 \times 15}$$

$$= \frac{163.84 + 225 - 98.01}{384} = \frac{290.83}{384} = 0.7574$$

$$= 40°45' \text{ (from nat cos tables)}$$

Using a scientific calculator

Very basic, hand-held, electronic calculators are permitted in CAA examinations, where the CAA will be issuing solar-powered models.

Non-programmable scientific calculators *without navigational functions and without an alpha-numeric data bank* may be used in all CAA papers except for CPL navigation.

It is advisable in practice to:

(a) have a spare calculator in case of a malfunction;

(b) always make a rough mental estimate of the size of answer expected – incredibly wrong answers can be obtained by touching the wrong key;

(c) read off the answers only to a practical accuracy – just because the calculator works to 8 figures, it does not mean you should produce ETAs to milliseconds!

Here is a selection of typical calculations that will be met. The sequences described will probably be satisfactory on the majority of pocket calculators but if different results are obtained, it will be necessary to check with the appropriate instruction manual supplied with the calculator.

Rate/quantity/time

Conventionally in aviation, most rates (speeds) are expressed per hour, but elapsed times are usually given in minutes. To reconcile this difference, 60 will always appear in the calculation.

Note

Scientific calculators will almost invariably provide a method of converting degrees and minutes of arc to decimals of a degree. This may also be used to convert hours and minutes of time to decimals of an hour. In the following examples, the display that will appear on the calculator is given immediately below the key which is to be touched.

e.g. *Key*   Clear (C/CE)   Touch C/CE to clear previous work

                        =

  Display   0   0 will be shown on the display

Example
Convert 3 h 21 min to a decimal.

Key   Clear (C/CE)   3.21   DMS
Display   0   3.21   3.35

Answer: 3.35 hours.
Reversing the process may require the use of an inverse key (INV):

Key   Clear   3.35   INV   DMS
Display   0   3.35   3.35   3.21

Answer: 3 h 21 min

Some examples

(1)   Find the time taken in minutes to fly 125 nm at 284 kt.
    (a)   Assess size of answer – just under 30 minutes
    (b)   On the calculator:

Key   C/CE   125   ÷   284   ×   60   =
Display   0   125.   125.   284.   0.440...   60.   26.40...

Answer: $26\frac{1}{2}$ minutes (to nearest $\frac{1}{2}$ minute).

(2)   Fuel flow 8450 kg/h. Find the fuel required for a flight of 2 h 37 min.
    Assess answer size – $2\frac{1}{2} \times 10\,000 = 25\,000$ kg.

Solution
    2 h 37 min = 157 min

Key   C/CE   157   ÷   60   ×   8450   =
Display   0   157.   157.   60.   2.61...   8450.   22\,110...

or, using the DMS key:

Key   C/CE   2.37   DMS   ×   8450   =
Display   0   2.37   2.61   2.61   8450.   22\,110...

Answer: 22 110 kg (to the nearest 10 kg).

(3)   Flying 1487 nm takes 1 h 27 min; what is the ground speed?
    Assess size – $1500 \div 1\frac{1}{2} = 1000$

Solution
    1 h 27 min = 87 min

Key   C/CE   1487   ÷   87   ×   60   =
Display   0   1487.   1487.   87.   17.09   60.   1025.5...

Answer: 1026 (to the nearest knot).
or, using the DMS key:

Key	C/CE	1487	÷	1.27	DMS	=
Display	0	1487.	1487.	1.27	1.45	1025.5 . . .

Calculations involving square roots

Touching the square root key ($\sqrt{\ }$) will cause the calculator to display the square root of whatever is on the display at that time, so to get the required result may necessitate rearranging the sequence of working. Try a simple example such as $4\sqrt{9}$. It will need keying as follows:

Key	C/CE	9	$\sqrt{\ }$	×	4	=
Display	0	9.0	3.0	3.0	4	12

Answer: 12

Some examples

(1)   The reception range of VHF signals in nm is given by the formula
$$\text{Range} = 1.25(\sqrt{h_1} + \sqrt{h_2})$$
where h_1 is aircraft altitude in feet, and
     h_2 is aerial elevation in feet.
Calculate the reception range when the aircraft altitude is 25 000 feet and aerial elevation is 1150 feet.

Key	C/CE	25 000	$\sqrt{\ }$	M+	1150	$\sqrt{\ }$	M+	MR
Display	0	25 000	158.1	158.1	1150	33.9	33.9	192.0
Key	×	1.25	=					
Display	192.0	1.25	240.0					

Answer: 240 nm.

(2)   The true airspeed (TAS) in knots can be calculated from the formula
$$\sqrt{(°C + 273)} \times 39 \times M$$
where °C is the ambient temperature in degrees Celsius, and
     M is the mach number (TAS as a proportion of the speed of sound).
     Calculate TAS when ambient temperature is −35°C and the mach number is 0.82

Key	C/CE	35	+/−	+	273	=	$\sqrt{\ }$	×	39
Display	0	35.	−35.	−35.	273.	238.	15.4	15.4	39.
Key	×	0.82	=						
Display	601.6	0.82	493.3						

Answers: 493 kt (to the nearest knot).

Calculations using trig. functions

It will be necessary to present the calculator with the angle expressed as a decimal of a degree. So if the angle is only known in degrees and minutes, proceed as follows, say, to find cos 115°38′.

First ensure that the calculator is working in the *degree mode* and not in any other form of angular measure, such as radians.

Key   C/CE   115.38   DMS   cos
Display   0   115.38   115.6   −0.432 . . .

Note that the calculator allots the correct sign when the angle is not in the first quadrant.

Some examples

(1) Given that crosswind component $= W \sin \theta$

headwind component $= W \cos \theta$

where θ is the angle between the runway and wind direction, and W is the windspeed, find the components when W/V is 210°M/45 kt and the runway direction is 190°M.

Solution (Rough estimate: Headwind only a little under 45 kt, and crosswind component much smaller)

$$\theta = 210° - 190° = 20°$$
$$\text{Headwind} = 45 \cos 20°$$
$$\text{Crosswind} = 45 \sin 20°$$

Key   C/CE   45   ×   20   cos   =
Display   0   45.   45.   20.   0.93   42.2 . . .

Headwind = 42 kt (to nearest kt)

Key   C/CE   45   ×   20   sin   =
Display   0   45.   45.   20.   0.34   15.39 . . .

Crosswind = 15 kt (to nearest kt)

(2) Scale on a chart varies as the secant $(1 \div \cos)$ of the latitude. If the scale at 15°N is 1:3 000 000, what will be the scale at 45°N?

Solution (Rough estimate: scale is increasing, so with greater latitude scale denominator will be decreasing)

$$\text{Scale at equator} = \frac{1}{3\,000\,000 \times \sec 15}$$

$$\text{Scale at 45°N} = \frac{1 \times \sec 45}{3\,000\,000 \times \sec 15}$$

$$= \frac{1}{3\,000\,000 \sec 15 \cos 45}$$

Key   C/CE   3 000 000   ÷   15   cos
Display   0   3 000 000   3 000 000   15.   0.96 . . .
Key   ×   45   cos   =
Display   3 105 828.5   45.   0.707 . . .   2 196 152.4

Answer: Scale 1:2 196 152 (to nearest whole number).

(3)   A typical chart calculation to find the spacing of 5° meridians on a chart at 45°N where the scale is 1:3 000 000.
The expression to evaluate will be:

$$\frac{5 \times 60 \times \cos 45 \times 1\,852\,000}{3\,000\,000}\,\text{mm}$$

(Rough estimate: $\dfrac{100\,\cancel{300} \times 0.7 \times 2 \times \cancel{10^6}}{\underset{1}{\cancel{3}} \times \cancel{10^6}} = 140$)

Key	C/CE	5	×	60	×	45	cos	×	1 852 000
Display	0	5	5	60	300	45	0.707	212.1	1 852 000
Key		÷		3 000 000			=		
Display	3.92...08*		3 000 000		130.95 ...				

Answer: 131.0 mm (to nearest 0.1 mm).
*Notice that when the number becomes large the display is in the exponential form, i.e. $3.92 \ldots \times 10^8$

Converting longitude (arc) to time
15° of longitude is equivalent to 1 hour of time, so:

Time (hours) × 15 = Longitude (degrees)

or   Longitude (degrees) ÷ 15 = Time (hours)

Use will again be made of the calculator's ability to convert sexagesimal measure (degrees/minutes or hours/minutes) to a decimal form (degrees or hours).

Some examples
(1)   Give the equivalent in time of 136°50′ of longitude.

Solution   (Rough estimate: 135/15 = 9)

Key	C/CE	136.50	DMS	÷	15	=	INV	DMS
Display	0	136.5	136.8	136.8	15.	9.12	9.12	9.0719

Answer: 9 h 07 m 19 s or 9 h 07 m (to nearest minute).

(2)   Give the equivalent in arc of 3 h 13 m 15 s.

Solution   (Rough estimate: 15 × 3+ = 45+)

Key	C/CE	3.1315	DMS	×	15	=	INV	DMS
Display	0	3.1315	3.22	3.22	15	48.31	48.31	48.1845

Answer: 48°18′45″ or 48°19′ (to nearest minute).

Expressions using brackets
Most scientific calculators have provision for dealing with brackets. There are usually separate keys for opening and closing brackets. Some examples will demonstrate their value.

(1)   Evaluate the right-hand side of the expression given in the paragraph on algebra:

$$\frac{x}{450} \times 6600 + \frac{x}{400} \times 6100$$

Key	C/CE	6600	÷	450	+	(	6100
Display	0	6600.	6600.	450.	14.66 . . .	14.66 . . .	6100.
Key	÷	400	)	=			
Display	6100.	400.	15.25	29.916 . . .			

Answer: 29.92x (Check 29.92 × 12 = 359).

(2)   Calculate the distance to the Point of No Return using

$$R = \frac{EOH}{O + H}$$

where E = safe endurance in hours
      O = GS OUT in knots
      H = GS HOME in knots
given E = 4 h 38 m, G = 352 kt, and H = 436 kt

Solution   (Rough check mentally: $\dfrac{4\frac{1}{2} \times 400 \times 400}{400 + 400} = \dfrac{720\,000}{800} = 900$)

Solve in sequence EOH ÷ (O + H) = R

Key	C/CE	4.38	DMS	×	352	×	436		
Display	0	4.38	4.63	4.63	352.	1630.9	436.		
Key	÷		(		352	+	436	)	=
Display	711 086.93	711 086.93			352.	352.	436.	788.	902.3

Answer: 902 nm (to nearest nm).

(3)   Using the formula for a plane triangle of:

$$a^2 = b^2 + c^2 - 2bc \cos A$$

find angle A when $a = 720$, $b = 417$ and $c = 375$

Solution
Transpose the equation to give:

$$2bc \cos A = b^2 + c^2 - a^2$$

and $\cos A = b^2 + (c^2) - (a^2) \div (2bc)$

Key	C/CE	417	×	417	+	(	375	
Display	0	417.	417.	173 889.	173 889.	173 889.	375.	
Key	×	375	)	−	(	720	×	
Display	375.	375.	140 625.	314 514.	314 514.	720.	720.	
Key	720	)	÷	(	2	×	417	
Display	720.	518 400.	−203 886.	−203 886.	2	2	417	
Key	×	375	)	=	INV	COS		

Display 834.   375.   312 750.   −0.651   −0.651   130.68
Key   INV   DMS
Display 130.68   130.4109

Answer: A = 130°41′09″.

Chapter 2
FORM OF THE EARTH

The earth

In maps and charts the cartographers attempt to reproduce, as faithfully as possible, a part or a portion of the earth's surface. Therefore, before we study the individual projections, it is essential that we first take a look at the form of the earth itself and see how a position fixing graticule of latitude and longitude is created.

The earth is not a true sphere. It is flattened slightly at the poles and its shape is variously described as an 'ellipsoid', 'oblate spheroid' or in desperation simple a 'geoid' which means 'earthlike'. This flattening of the poles is known as *compression* and it is the ratio of the difference between the equatorial diameter and the polar diameter to the equatorial diameter. It is expressed as

$$\text{compression} = \frac{\text{equatorial diameter} - \text{polar diameter}}{\text{equatorial diameter}}.$$

If we put the appropriate figures in the formula we can soon find the value of this ratio. The equatorial diameter is 12 748.6 km and the polar diameter 12 705.6 km, the ratio becomes:

$$\frac{12\,748.6 - 12\,705.6}{12\,748.6} = \frac{43}{12\,748.6} = \frac{1}{296} \text{ or } \frac{1}{300} \text{ near enough.}$$

What all this means in practice is that if we built a model of the earth on a reduced scale (called the *reduced earth*) so that its equatorial diameter was 300 mm, then the model's polar diameter would be 299 mm.

This shows that in producing maps and charts for normal usage a refinement for the earth's shape is neither necessary nor profitable. As for navigation charts, no errors of any significance occur through lack of refinement, and therefore, the remainder of the discussion on maps and charts is based on the assumption that the earth is a perfect sphere.

On any plain sphere, in order to establish a reference system it is necessary to adopt a convention defining the directions and a location-fixing system of co-ordinates. These are established as follows:

The poles

The poles are situated on the earth's suface at the ends of the rotational axis. The north pole is that end of the earth's rotational axis about which the earth

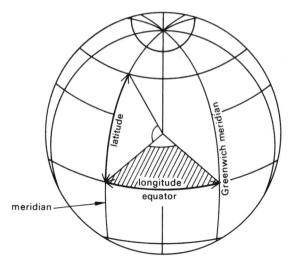

Fig. 2.1   Latitude and longitude

rotates anti-clockwise when viewed from above it. The south pole is the opposite end of the rotational axis to the north pole. The two poles locate the extreme north and south points.

The equator

The equator is a great circle (discussed later) with its plane perpendicular to the earth's axis. Since the earth's axis defines the north–south direction, a plane perpendicular to it must define the east–west direction. Thus, the plane of the equator lies in the east–west direction. All points on the equator are equidistant from the poles and it divides the earth into the northern and southern hemispheres.

Latitude

A latitude is defined as the *arc of the meridian* (see Fig. 2.1) intercepted between the place and the equator. It is measured in degrees, minutes and seconds north or south of the equator. One degree (1°) equals 60 minutes (60′) and one minute equals 60 seconds (60″). The choice of the equator as a datum of measurement is a natural one, on account of its having the largest circumference of all the parallels of latitude.

The planes of all other latitudes lie parallel to the plane of the equator. The arc of the circle from the equator to either pole being a quarter of a circle, the maximum possible latitude is 90° north or south, (see Fig. 2.2) – The spacing of the parallels of latitudes along the meridians is perfectly uniform. This means that the arc distance between, say, 10°N and 20°N is exactly equal to the arc distance between 70° and 80° or any other two parallels having a difference of 10°. This being so, the distance between any two parallels up a meridian may be calculated quite simply. A meridian together with its anti-meridian completes one full circle, that is, 360°. The circumference of any circle is given in the formula, circumference = $2\pi r$, where r is the radius. For the earth, the arc distance between any two parallels may be given in the relationship

$$\frac{\text{difference in latitude}}{360} \times 2\pi r$$

From the above, and taking the radius of the earth to be 3441 nm, the distance between two latitudes one degree apart is

$$\frac{1}{360} \times 2 \times 3.14 \times 3441\,\text{nm} = 60\,\text{nm} \qquad \text{along a meridian.}$$

Finally, all parallels of latitude indicate an east–west direction. Thus, if you are flying along a parallel of latitude, you are flying a 090° or 270° track.

Longitude

A longitude is defined as the shorter *arc of the equator* (see Fig. 2.1) intercepted between the Greenwich meridian and the meridian of the place. It is measured in degrees, minutes and seconds east or west of the Greenwich meridian. The anti-meridian of Greenwich is the maximum longitude possible, i.e. 180°E/W.

The term *meridian* may be described as a semi great circle which runs north–south from pole to pole. Meridians, together with their anti-meridians complete the great circle. Every point on the earth has its own meridian passing through it. All meridians indicate north–south direction, the true north reference datum being along any meridian towards the north pole.

It will be noticed that with regard to the meridians we have no natural datum to start the count with and consequently, the meridian of Greenwich is arbitrarily taken as the datum. It is also called the *prime meridian.*

The meridians are also placed uniformly along the parallels, the distance between any two meridians *along the equator* being

$$\frac{\text{difference in longitude}}{360} \times 2\pi r$$

For a one degree difference in longitude along the equator, the distance between the meridians is

$$\frac{1}{360} \times 2 \times 3.14 \times 3441\,\text{nm} = 60\,\text{nm}$$

which, you will notice, is identical to the distances between parallels along a meridian.

However, unlike the distance between two latitudes along a meridian, the distance between two given meridians along a latitude away from the equator does not remain constant at 60 nm for a 1° change of longitude. This is

Fig. 2.2 Basic distances on the earth

because, as can be seen in Fig. 2.2, the meridians converge towards the poles. They are a maximum distance apart at the equator and converge into a point at the poles.

But taking another glance at Fig. 2.2 it will be noticed that the lengths of the parallels of latitude also reduce (it reduces in proportion) once away from the equator. The circle of the equator, having the largest circumference gives the longest distance, whereas the latitude of 90°N/S is a mere point.

Therefore, the distance between the meridians along any parallel depends on the length of the parallel itself. This quantity which varies from being maximum (that is, one unit) at 0° to a value of 0 at 90° in fact varies as a cosine curve. Accordingly, the variation in the lengths of the latitude follows a cosine relationship. Let us examine this.

The length of the equator, that is, the circumference of the earth is 360 × 60 nm = 21 600 nm. At 30°N/S the circumference is (21 600 × cos 30°) nm = 18 706 nm. Along this parallel, 360 meridians at one degree intervals are placed uniformly at a distance of

$$\frac{18\,706}{360}\,\text{nm} = 52\,\text{nm}.$$

Putting this another way, one degree at the equator contains 60 nm, and one degree at 30°N/S contains (60 cos 30°) nm = 52 nm.

Similarly, the circumference or the length at 60°N/S is

$$(21\,600 \times \cos 60)\,\text{nm} = 10\,800\,\text{nm}$$

and the distance between each meridian one degree apart is

$$\frac{10\,800}{360}\,\text{nm} = 30\,\text{nm}$$

Or, $(60 \cos 60°)\,\text{nm} = 30\,\text{nm}$ and this one fact, that the distances on the earth at 60°N/S are exactly one half of those at the equator, is worth remembering. To summarise so far:

(a)   All parallels of latitude are parallel to the plane of the equator and indicate the east–west direction.

(b)   The spacing of the parallels along the meridian is given by

$$\frac{\text{difference of latitude (d lat)}}{360} \times 2\pi r$$

(c)   One degree difference of latitude along a meridian measures 60 nm anywhere between the equator and the poles.

(d)   One degree difference of longitude (d long) measures 60 nm at the equator. Away from the equator this distance reduces at the rate of the cosine of the latitude and is found from the formula

distance between two meridians one degree apart = 60 cos lat.

(e)   All meridians indicate north–south direction.

Definitions

A few more definitions, terminologies and the facts now.

Great circles

If you draw the largest possible circle on a tennis ball, the circle's circumference will be the same as the circumference of the ball, its radius will be the same as the radius of the ball and in fact, it will divide the ball in two equal parts. What you have just drawn is a great circle.

A great circle is defined as a circle on the surface of a sphere whose centre and radius are those of the sphere itself, thus the plane of the great circle passes through the centre of the sphere, dividing it into two equal parts. Note these fundamentals arising from the concept of a great circle.

(a)   Since it has the greatest radius possible, it has the least curvature and nearly approaches being a straight line.

(b)   And, since a straight line between any two points is the shortest distance between those two points, we can say that the shorter arc of a great circle passing through any two points on the earth's surface represents the shortest distance between those two places.

(c)   Only one great circle can be drawn through any two given points *unless* those two points are diametrically opposite in which case an infinite number of great circles can be drawn. An example is the meridians. A meridian, together with its anti-meridian is a great circle and any

Fig. 2.3   Rhumb line track

number of meridians can be drawn between the two poles (which are diametrically opposite).

(d) The equator is a great circle.

(e) The meridians (semi great circles) cut the equator at a constant angle of 90°. Elsewhere, a great circle cuts the meridians at a changing angle. This can be visualised by drawing a straight line in Fig. 2.2 at any place other than along the equator. To fly the shortest distance between the two places we must fly the great circle track, but the changing angles makes such a flight quite difficult, unless flying due north/south along a meridian (Fig. 2.3).

(f) A radio wave detected by an aircraft's receiver will have followed the shortest distance across the earth's surface. We must remember this when plotting such a radio signal on a chart on which a straight line is not a great circle.

Small circles

A small circle is any circle on the surface of the earth whose centre and radius are not those of the earth itself. Any parallel of latitude, other than the equator, is a small circle.

Rhumb line

A rhumb line (R/L) is a regularly curved line on the surface of the earth which cuts all meridians at the same angle, Fig. 2.3. From this definition it

will become apparent that an aircraft flying a constant track will be following a rhumb line track. The other points to note are these.
(a)   Only one rhumb line can be drawn through any two points.
(b)   A rhumb line does not represent the shortest distance between two places, but it is convenient to follow.
(c)   The meridians and the equator are the only examples of great circles which are also rhumb lines.
(d)   All latitudes and longitudes intersect each other at 90°. Therefore, all parallels of latitude are rhumb lines. When flying along a latitude, you are flying a rhumb line track, make no mistake about it.

Change of latitude (ch lat)
This is the same as 'difference of latitude (d lat)' and the terms are interchangeable. It is defined as the arc of meridian intercepted between the parallels of the two places and is named north or south according to the direction of the change. Thus, a flight from 5°N to 20°N represents a ch lat (or d lat) of 15°N whereas a flight in the reverse direction changes its latitude by 15°S.

Change of longitude (ch long)
This, again, is the same as 'difference of longitude (d long)' and is defined as the smaller arc of the equator intercepted between the meridians of the places. It is named east or west according to the direction of the change. A change from 178°W to 178°E is a change of 4°W and the converse is true. If you can't visualise the other side of the globe, look in an atlas and make yourself familiar.

Distances
Now that we have established a convention for directions and a position locating graticule we will turn our attention to the various units of distance measurement.

Nautical mile
Strictly, a nautical mile at any place is the length of an arc of the meridan subtending an angle of one minute at the centre of curvature of that place (Fig. 2.4). ICAO's definition of a nautical mile is that it is a measure of distance of 1852 metres.

Any distance on the surface of the earth formed by an angle originating at the earth's centre is the great circle distance. Now, it will be remembered that a latitude is also similarly defined, that is, one minute of latitude is the arc distance on the surface subtended by an angle of one minute at the earth's centre. This fact makes it possible to calibrate the meridians in nautical miles i.e. 1' of latitude is one nautical mile and 1° is 60 nm when measured along the meridians.

Fig. 2.4   Nautical mile

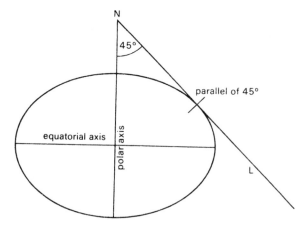

Fig. 2.5   Form of the earth

However, because of the ellipticity of the earth the actual distance of one nautical mile on the surface of the earth varies. In fact, because of this, the earth's centre is variously defined as 'geographical centre', 'geocentric' and so forth, according to the purpose of the definition. To illustrate the effect of the ellipticity, the shape of the earth in Fig. 2.5 is grossly exaggerated. In this figure the earth's axis is extended northward to point N so that a straight line, NL, drawn from N makes an angle of 45° to the axis. It can be shown by geometry that the point where this straight line is tangential to the surface of the earth defines the parallel of 45°. Because of the shape of the earth, that is where the parallel of 45° lies; if the earth was a perfect sphere, 45° would lie exactly half way between the equator and the pole.

The distance from the equator to 45° is 2700 nm (45 × 60 nm) and there is the same difference between 45° and the pole. Consequently, as can be seen in Fig. 2.5 a nautical mile nearer the equator is smaller than that at the pole.

One nautical mile at the equator measures 1843 m, at 45°N/S, 1853 m, at the poles, 1862 m. As already mentioned, the international nautical mile as defined by ICAO measures 1852 metres.

If a sophisticated electronic navigation system is based on a constant length of a nautical mile as 1852 metres, it will suffer an error unless there is a built-in allowance for the figure of the Earth and also an increasing error with increase of altitude. (At 60 000 ft, 1857 metres subtends the same angle as 1852 metres at sea level.)

Kilometre

A kilometre is 1000 metres. A metre is 1/10 000 000th part of the average distance along the earth's surface from the equator to either pole. A kilometre therefore equals 1/10 000th part of the average distance along the earth's surface between the equator and the pole. For practical purposes it is taken as 3280 feet.

As the distance between the equator and either pole is 5400 nm and also 10 000 km, it follows that 54 nm = 100 km.

Statute mile

Established by the Royal Decree of Queen Elizabeth I, the standard length of the statute mile (sm) is 5280 feet.

The approximate conversions from one unit to another are as follows.

$$66 \, \text{nm} = 76 \, \text{sm}$$
$$41 \, \text{nm} = 76 \, \text{km}$$
$$41 \, \text{sm} = 66 \, \text{km}$$
$$1 \, \text{nm} = 1.15 \, \text{sm}$$
$$1 \, \text{nm} = 1.85 \, \text{km}$$

Questions

If you have assimilated the contents of this chapter you should be able to answer these questions.
(1) A pilot wishes to fly from A(50°N 16°E) to B(51°N 15°E). He has a choice of the following two routes:
(a) fly along the parallel 50°N until the meridian 15°E is intercepted and then fly up the 15°E meridian to his destination; or
(b) fly along the meridian 16°E until the parallel of 51°N is intercepted and then fly along the 51°N parallel to his destination.
Is there any advantage between the two routes? Give a reason for your answer.
(2) Give an example of a rhumb line which is also a great circle.
(3) Define (a) a great circle; (b) a rhumb line.
(4) Which parallel of latitude is also a great circle?
(5) Which small circles are also rhumb lines?

(6) What is the distance from Calcutta (30°N 90°E) to New Orleans, USA (30°N 90°W) over the north pole?

Answers

(1) Route (b) is shorter in the ground distance on account of the earth's convergency.

(2) Any meridian together with its anti-meridian is a great circle and since it cuts itself at zero degrees (a constant angle) it is also a rhumb line (see p. 23).

(3) See the text.

(4) The equator.

(5) Any parallel of latitude.

(6) 7200 nm.

Chapter 3
CONVERGENCY, CONVERSION ANGLE, DEPARTURE

In this chapter we continue our study of familiarisation with the earth.

Convergency

We have already seen that a great circle cuts successive meridians at different angles because the meridians converge towards each other to the poles. This inclination between any two meridians is called *convergency*, and it equals the angular difference between the measurements of the great circle at each meridian.

The inclination of the meridians or convergency between two meridians X and Y (in Fig. 3.1) may be found by various methods, as follows:

(1) By transferring on the chart the meridian X to X' (or the other way round) to pass through position B, and measuring the angle formed by the two meridians Y and X' at B (marked convergency angle in the figure).

(2) By measuring the angle that the straight line joining A and B makes at positions A and B and calculating the difference. In above figure, $\angle C = 118 - 062 = 056°$

(3) By mathematical calculation, using formula

$$\text{Convergency} = \text{ch long} \times \text{sine lat.}$$

The formula is derived from the reasoning that the meridians cut the Equator at 90° and therefore, they are parallel to each other and the angle of inclination between them is 0. At each pole every meridian on the face of the Earth meets in a point. The convergency or inclination of any two meridians here therefore amounts to the change of longitude between them. For example, two meridians 1° apart will make an angle of 1° at the Poles. Therefore, at any intermediate latitude, the convergency must equal change of longitude × sine of the latitude.

This formula is correct only when two places A and B are on the same latitude and when the change of longitude is not excessive. If A and B are at different latitudes, the sine of mid-latitude between them may be used in the formula, giving sufficiently accurate results for our purpose. Convergency between places 180° longitude apart and at the same latitude is always 180°.

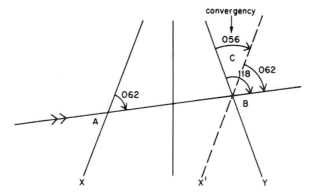

Fig. 3.1   Convergency

Great circle – rhumb line relationship

A straight line drawn on a conformal chart having correct convergency (that is, chart meridians inclining at the same angle as the meridians at the same place on the Earth) will be a great circle. The associated rhumb line will appear as a curve (Fig. 3.2). (An important point is illustrated here also: the rhumb line, or to be precise the tangent to it, at the central meridian is parallel to the great circle; when using charts with converging meridians in practice, the Rhumb Line Track is the same as the mean Great Circle Track, measured at the central meridian between departure and destination meridians.)

However, on a chart which projects meridians as straight lines parallel to each other, a straight line will be a rhumb line and not a great circle (since it will cut all the meridians at the same angle). The example is the Mercator's projection, and on such charts the great circles must appear as curves (Fig. 3.3).

If you observe Figs 3.2 and 3.3 you will notice that in either hemisphere the rhumb line, as regards the great circle, always appears towards the equator, a point useful to remember when plotting radio position lines.

The angular difference between the great circle and the rhumb line is called conversion angle (see *Ground Studies for Pilots Volume 2, Plotting and Flight Planning*) and its value is half the value of the convergency.

To prove that Conversion Angle (CA) = $\frac{1}{2}$C (convergency)
AB and CD are two meridians (Fig. 3.4) and the straight line EF is a great circle.

$$\angle FEG \text{ is Conversion Angle and} = \angle EFH$$
$$= \angle JFK$$

Transfer AB to A_1B_1 to pass through position F. Then $\angle CFA_1$ is Convergency angle.

A rhumb line makes the same angle at each meridian,

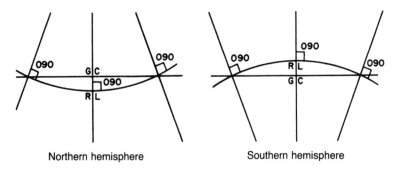

Fig. 3.2   Comparison between great circle and rhumb line on conformal chart with correct convergency

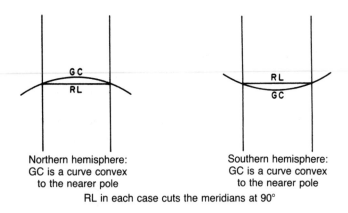

Northern hemisphere:
GC is a curve convex
to the nearer pole

Southern hemisphere:
GC is a curve convex
to the nearer pole

RL in each case cuts the meridians at 90°

Fig. 3.3   Comparison between great circle and rhumb line on Mercator chart

$$\therefore \angle AEF + \angle FEG = \angle CFA_1 + \angle A_1FK - \angle JFK$$

But $\angle AEF = \angle A_1FK$

and transferring $\angle JFK$ to the left hand side of the equation,

$$\angle FEG + \angle JFK = \angle CFA_1$$

or $\qquad CA + CA = C$ (and assuming the CAs are equal)

$\qquad\qquad 2CA = C$ or Conversion angle = half the convergency.

Great circle and rhumb line bearings

Problems of the following nature are solved by application of the above theory.

(1)   A bears 055° RL from B. What is the RL bearing of B from A? Since here we are only dealing with rhumb line bearings, B's bearing from A must be reciprocal of A's bearing from B. Therefore the answer is 235°.

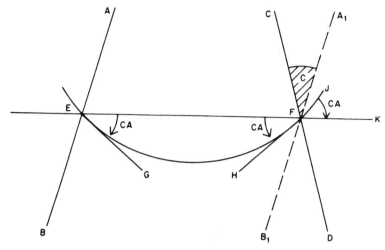

Fig. 3.4   Convergency and conversion angle

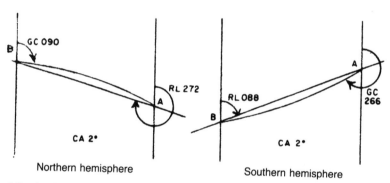

Fig. 3.5   Applying conversion angle

(2)   A bears 090° GC from B. Convergency = 4°. What is the GC bearing of B from A in the Northern and Southern hemispheres?
It is always advisable to draw up a simple sketch as shown in Fig. 3.5:
Convergency given is 4°; therefore CA = 2°
A's RL bearing from B = 092; and B's RL bearing from A = 272°
∴ B's GC bearing from A = 274°
Southern Hemisphere: CA = 2°; A's RL brg = 088°; B's RL brg. from A = 268°
∴ B's GC bearing from A = 266°

(3)   GC bearing of B from A is 095°; RL bearing of A from B is 273°
(a)   What is the CA?
(b)   In which hemisphere are we?
(c)   What is the GC bearing of A from B?

Fig. 3.6   Finding great circle bearing

Solution

(a) CA is the angular difference between GC and RL
     ∴ CA = 095 + 180 = 275 − 273
              = 2°

(b) In Fig. 3.6 above, for the Northern Hemisphere, the RL bearing of A
     from
     B = 095 + 2 + 180
        = 277°
     and therefore the aircraft cannot be in the Northern hemisphere. The
     sketch for the Southern hemisphere illustrates the facts as given.

(c) Since the RL bearing of A from B is 273, the GC bearing
     = 273 − 2 (CA)
     = 271°.

A further illustration (see Fig. 3.7):
Calculate the convergency between A (48°30′N 28°12′E) and B (55°00′N
10°00′E). If the Rhumb line Track between A and B is 300°, what is the
initial Great Circle Track?

Solution

$$\text{Convergency} = \text{ch long} \times \sin \text{mean lat}$$
$$= 18°12′ \times \sin 51°45′$$
$$= 18.2° \times 0.7853$$
$$= 14.3°$$

The GC and RL Tracks are the same at the mid-meridian, that is, in this
problem, at 19°06′E.

The total convergency between A and B is 14°, therefore the convergency
between the mid-meridian and the meridian of A must be 7°; with the RL
Track of 300°, the GC Track from A is 300° + 7° = 307°, and the simple
sketch clarifies the solution.

In our experience we have found that some students initially find this topic
a bit difficult to understand and apply. But you will soon get conversant with
it: ample exercises are given here to help you. These exercises are graded so
that they become progressively more involved from the simplest one until all
principles are covered. When attempting the problems, know the different

Fig. 3.7   Finding initial great circle track direction

ways in which convergency/conversion angle may be found and keep the two formulae firmly in mind. Also remember that the convergency formula has three elements in it: convergency, longitude and latitude. Knowing any two of these the third one can be found. For example:

$$\text{difference of longitude} = \frac{\text{convergence}}{\text{sin mean lat}}$$

Exercise 1

(1)   Give ch long (change of longitude) between
  (a)   10°E and 20°E
  (b)   10°E and 160°W
  (c)   8°W and 8°E
  (d)   160°W and 158°E
  (e)   175°E and 168°W.

  Answers: (a) 10°E; (b) 170°W; (c) 16°E; (d) 42°W; (e) 17°E

(2)   If the RL bearing of A from B is 070°, what is the RL bearing of B from A?

  Answer: 250°.

(3)   If the RL bearing of B from A is 300°, what is the RL bearing of A from B?

  Answer: 120°.

(4)   GC bearing of Q from P is 060°, CA = 4°; if the two places are in the northern hemisphere what is the
  (a)   RL bearing of Q from P?
  (b)   RL bearing of P from Q?
  (c)   GC bearing of P from Q?

  Answers: (a) 064°; (b) 244°; (c) 248°.

(5) The GC bearing of X from Y is 315°; CA = 4°; if the two places are in the northern hemisphere what is the
   (a)   RL bearing of X from Y?
   (b)   RL bearing of Y from X?
   (c)   GC bearing of Y from X?

Answers: (a) 311°; (b) 131°; (c) 127°.

(6) X and Y are in the southern hemisphere. X bears 120° RL from Y. If the CA is 2° what is the
   (a)   GC bearing of X from Y?
   (b)   RL bearing of Y from X?
   (c)   GC bearing of Y from X?

Answers: (a) 122°; (b) 300°; (c) 298°.

(7) The GC bearing of M from N is 040°; the RL bearing of M from N is 042°;
   (a)   what is the conversion angle?
   (b)   in which hemisphere are the two places?
   (c)   what is the RL bearing of N from M?
   (d)   what is the GC bearing of N from M?

Answers: (a) 2°; (b) northern hemisphere; (c) 222°; (d) 224°.

(8) The GC bearing of A from B is 340°; the RL bearing of A from B is 345°;
   (a)   what is the conversion angle?
   (b)   in which hemisphere are the two places?
   (c)   what is the RL bearing of B from A?
   (d)   what is the GC bearing of B from A?

Answers: (a) 5°; (b) southern hemisphere; (c) 165°; (d) 170°.

(9) The GC bearing of B from A is 280°; the RL bearing of A from B is 096°;
   (a)   what is the conversion angle?
   (b)   in which hemisphere are the two places?
   (c)   what is the GC bearing of A from B?

Answers: (a) 4°; (b) northern hemisphere; (c) 092°.

(10) The RL bearing of P from Q is 050°; the GC bearing of Q from P is 228°;
   (a)   what is the conversion angle?
   (b)   in which hemisphere are the two places?
   (c)   what is the GC bearing of P from Q?

Answers: (a) 2°; (b) southern hemisphere; (c) 052°.

Exercise 2

(1) The GC bearing of A from B is 160°; if the CA = 2°, what is the
    (a) GC bearing of B from A in the northern hemisphere?
    (b) GC bearing of B from A in the southern hemisphere?

Answers: (a) 344°; (b) 336°.

(2) The GC bearing of P from Q is 130°, the GC bearing of Q from P is 318°.
    (a) what is the conversion angle?
    (b) in which hemisphere are the two places?
    (c) what is the RL bearing of Q from P?

Answers: (a) 4°; (b) northern hemisphere; (c) 314°.

(3) If the GC bearing of N from M is 280° and the GC bearing of M from N is 094°, what is the RL bearing of M from N?

Answer: 097°.

(4) A and B are on the parallel of 30°N and A is at 8°W. If the GC bearing of B from A is 087° what is B's longitude?

Answer: 4°E. (Hint: all parallels of latitudes indicate E−W direction and all latitudes are rhumb lines.)

(5) A's position is 41°26′S 175°W. The convergency between A and B is 7°. If B is due west of A and sin of 41°26′ is 0.7,
    (a) what is the GC bearing of B from A?
    (b) what is B's longitude?

Answers: (a) 266$\frac{1}{2}$°; (b) 175°E.

(6) A's position is 54°S 160°E; the convergency between A and B is 21°. If B is due east of A and the sin of 54 is 0.8,
    (a) what is the GC bearing of B from A?
    (b) what is B's longitude?

Answers: (a) 100$\frac{1}{2}$°; (b) 174°W.

(7) X is at 40°N 12°E; Y is at 40°N 06°E. If you are given that sin 40° = 0.64,
    (a) find the GC bearing of X from Y
    (b) find the GC bearing of Y from X.

Answers: (a) 088°; (b) 272°.

(8) The earth convergency between two positions on the same parallel 8° of longitude apart, is 7.2°. On the same parallel, X is at 173°W and Y is at 176°E.
    (a) what is the GC bearing of X from Y in the northern hemisphere?
    (b) what is the GC bearing of Y from X in the southern hemisphere?

Answers: (a) 085°; (b) 265°.

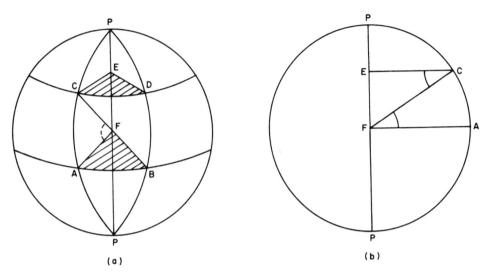

Fig. 3.8   Departure

(9)   A and B are both on the parallel of 30°. The longitude of A is 10°W. The GC bearing of A from B is 266°(T). What is the longitude of B?

Answer: 6°E.

(10)   A flight is made from VOR A (51°N 01°W), local variation 8°W, to VOR B (51°N 06°W), local variation 9°W. The radials are maintained throughout the flight. If the drift is 7° starboard give (a) heading (M) immediately on departure and (b) heading (M) immediately before arrival at B. Given, sin 51° = 0.8.

Answers: (a) 273(M); (b) 270(M). (Hint: the aircraft is flying a great circle path.)

Distance along a parallel or departure

Because the meridians converge, it is clear that change of longitude is only a measure of distance on the Equator, the only parallel which is a Great Circle. The change of longitude on the Equator from 15°W to 20°W, say, is 300 nm but a similar change of longitude at 70°N is nothing like that distance. But there is a very definite relationship.

In Fig. 3.8(a) AB is the arc of the Equator = change of longitude.

CD is the arc of parallel, of which the distance is required.

(It will be noticed that the distance CD becomes progressively smaller nearer to the Pole, but the change of longitude does not alter).

F is the centre of the Earth; PP the Earth's axis.

∠AFC is the angle of the latitude CD

∴ Triangles ECD and ABF are parallel and equiangular

(1)
$$\frac{CD}{AB} = \frac{CE}{AF}$$

In Fig. 3.8(b)

$$\frac{CE}{CF} = \cos \text{ latitude}$$

∴ CE = CF cos Lat

(2)   = AF Cos Lat (CF and AF being radii of the Earth)

Substituting (2) in (1)

$$\frac{CD}{AB} = \frac{AF \cos \text{lat}}{AF}$$

or, CD = AB cos lat

Thus, distance CD = change of longitude × cosine latitude

The distance made good along a parallel (that is, in an East/West direction) is called *Departure*.

If the distance and latitude are given, by rearranging the formula Departure = ch long × cos lat, we can find the change of longitude.

$$Dep = \text{ch long} \times \cos \text{lat}$$

$$\therefore \text{ch long} = \frac{Dep}{\cos \text{lat}} = Dep \times \sec \text{lat}$$

although on a hand-held calculator, it will probably be easier to use ch long = Dep ÷ cos lat

Or, given dep and ch long, latitude could be found:

$$\cos \text{lat} = \frac{Dep}{\text{ch long}}$$

Above three variations of the formula are summarised below for convenience:

(1)   Departure = ch long × cos lat

(2)   ch long = Dep ÷ cos lat

(3) $$\cos \text{lat} = \frac{Dep}{\text{ch long}}$$

Examples

(1) What is the rhumb line distance between A (53°23′N 01°19′W) and B (53°23′N 07°47′W)?

$$\text{Departure} = \text{ch long} \times \cos \text{lat}$$
$$= 06°28' \times \cos 53°23'$$
$$= 388' \times 0.5964$$
$$= 231.4 \text{ nm}$$

(2) An aircraft takes off from 40°20'N 178°38'E and flies an RL track of 090°. What is its longitude after it has travelled 219 nm?

$$\text{ch long} = \text{Dep} \times \sec \text{lat}$$
$$= 219 \times 1.3119$$
$$= 287.3'$$
$$= 4°47'$$
$$\therefore \text{ new longitude} = 176°35'W$$

(3) After flying 448 nm along a parallel of latitude an aircraft changes its longitude by 8°21'. What is the latitude?

$$\cos \text{lat} = \frac{\text{Dep}}{\text{ch long (in minutes)}}$$
$$= \frac{448}{501}$$
$$= 0.8942$$
$$= 26°36'N \text{ or } S$$

The following practice problems are graded to become progressively more involved. Students taking the CPL exam are normally given the appropriate trig. function values with the questions. The CAA will issue a basic solar-powered calculator at the examination. (For solutions using electronic calculators see p 13 onwards).

A reminder before you start: departure is in nm, therefore if you are solving for distance between two places, first convert ch long from degrees to nm by multiplying it by 60. Similarly, when you are looking for ch long, the departure formula will give you the answer in nm; therefore, divide the answer by 60 to get ch long.

Practice problems

(1) Two places on the equator are 8° long apart. If the cosine of 0° is 1, what is the distance between the two places?

Answer: 480 nm.

(2) Two places on 30°S are 8° long apart. What is the distance between them? Given, cos 30° = 0.87.

Answer: 417.6 nm.

(3) Two places on the parallel of 60°N are 8° long apart. What is the distance in nautical miles between them? (Cos 60° = 0.5.)

Answer: 240 nm.

(4) Two places are 360 nm apart on the equator. What is the difference of longitude (d long) between them? (Sec 0° = 1.)

Answer: 6°.

(5) Two places, 360 nm apart are on 60°S. What is the d long between the two places? (Sec 60° = 2.)

Answer: 12°.

(6) What is the departure between A (36°N 10°W) and B (36°N 20°W)? (Cos 36° = 0.8.)

Answer: 480 nm.

(7) Give the distance in nm between A (41°S 120°W) and B (41°S 125°30'W). (Cos 41° = 0.75.)

Answer: $247\frac{1}{2}$ nm.

(8) Give the RL distance between A (51°27'N 00°19'E) and B (51°27'N 13°07'W). (Cos 51°27' = 0.62.)

Answer: 499.7 nm.

(9) An aircraft flying along the parallel of 81°24' changes its longitude by 55°13'. What distance in nm has it flown? (Cos 81°24' = 0.15.)

Answer: 496.9 nm.

(10) If the departure is 230.6 nm along the parallel of 46°31', what is the change of longitude? (Sec 46°31' = 1.45.)

(11) A is at 35°S 140°W; B is on the parallel of 35°S and 370 nm due east of A. What is B's longitude? (Sec 35° = 1.22.)

Answer: $132°28\frac{1}{2}'$ (to the nearest $\frac{1}{2}$ min).

(12) An aircraft takes off from 47°30'S 178°30'W and flies a rhumb line track of 270° for 224 nm. What is its new position? (Sec 47°30' = 1.48.)

Answer: 47°30'S 175°59'E (to the nearest minute).

(13) How long will it take to go round the earth along the parallel of 75°N at the ground speed of 540 kt? (A computer may be used for GS/time conversion, cos 75 = 0.26.)

Answer: 10 h 24 min.

(14) A flight is planned from 40°S 110°E to 40°S 102°E. Give the distance in kilometres if the flight is taking place along the rhumb line track. (Cos 40° = 0.766.)

Answer: 681.5 km.

(15) What is the rhumb line distance from Calcutta (30°N 90°E) to New Orleans, USA (30°N 90°W)? (Cos 30° = 0.866.)

Answer: 9352.8 nm. (Compare this with the GC distance found in the exercise in chapter 2.)

The above problems are appropriate for both the CPL and the ATPL syllabuses. The following additional problems may be attempted by the ATPL students.

Additional problems

(1) Departure = 243 nm; ch long = 4°45'; what is the latitude?

Answer: 31°30'N/S.

(2) At what latitude would a distance of 1066 nm cause a change of longitude of 23°59'?

Answer: 42°12'N/S.

(3) Two aircraft, A and B, leave position X (51°N 02°E) for Y (56°N 08°W). Aircraft A on the take-off travels due north until the 56°N parallel is intercepted and then follows that parallel to 8°W longitude. Aircraft B on take-off travels a track of 270°(T) until the longitude of 8°W is intercepted and then flies due north to 56°N. Which of the two aircraft flies the shorter distance and by how many nautical miles?

Answer: Aircraft A travels 42 nm (to the nearest nm) less than aircraft B.

(4) An aircraft takes off from 48°05'N 01°W and flies a track of 270°(T) for 2 h 15 min. It then alters its track to 000°(T). Later, it alters its track on to 090°(T) and having flown on this track for 1 h 40 min it recrosses the original meridian of 01°W. If its ground speed was constant at 440 kt throughout the flight what was the flight time on the second leg (Tr 000°(T))?

Answer: 1 h 40 min. Hints: (a) find the ch long on 48°05'N leg; (b) with this ch long find the latitude for the third leg; (c) you now have two latitudes to give the northing.

(5) A flight of 2148 km is being made on a track of 270°(T) along the parallel of 69°N. If the LMT of arrival at the destination is the same as the LMT of departure, what is the flight time?

Answer: 3 h 36 min. (Hint: first find the ch long, then relate this to the speed of the sun's travel which is 15°/hr.)

Chapter 4
PROJECTIONS GENERAL

Now that we understand the various properties of the earth itself, we are ready to discuss the matter of projections. The object of making a map or a chart is to represent the spherical earth, or at least a part of it, on a flat surface, so that we can record and locate the positions on the earth.

The cartographer works from a model earth (the earth reduced in size to the required scale and called the *reduced earth*), marked out with the graticule, originally with a light source at some given point within the globe which projects the graticule on to a paper. The paper may be wrapped round the globe like a cylinder, or it may sit on the globe in the form of a cone or it might be just a plane surface, tangential to the globe at a given parallel. Finally he enters the details of ground features as required.

When a projection contains only a graticule of latitude and longitude with perhaps very few geographical features, it is called a *chart*. A map, on the other hand contains both the graticule and an abundance of ground features.

The cartographer's reduced earth contains all the properties present on the earth. Thus, it would possess the following features.

(a) The scale: it would be both correct and constant. It will be correct because the model earth is a reproduction of the earth on a given scale. It will also be constant, that is, anywhere on the reduced earth a one inch span of the dividers will measure the same distance.
(b) The shapes will be correct.
(c) Areas will be shown correctly.
(d) The bearing measurements anywhere on the reduced earth will be identical to the measurements on the earth.
(e) Great circles will be straight lines, just as on the earth.
(f) Meridians and parallels will intersect each other at 90°.
(g) Adjacent sections fit perfectly together.

Projections on flat surfaces

Any attempt at reproducing a spherical shape on to a flat surface must produce inevitable distortions. Thus, on a flat surface we must expect distortions of the ideal properties of the reduced earth as mentioned above. For example, over a flat surface area the scale can never be simultaneously correct and constant. Further, the scale is only correct (that is, it remains at the selected value) at a point, e.g. polar stereographic projection, or along a line, Mercator or Lambert.

Similarly, correct shapes are never possible on any map: but this is only a technical distinction. In practice, shapes very close to true shapes can be produced on certain projections in limited areas. Correct areas can be shown at the expense of the shapes.

These are only some of the examples of the limitations. But in spite of them, by systematically arranging the graticule it is possible to control the distortions and produce a projection which meets the requirements very satisfactorily. Achieving a particular property is at the expense of other properties.

Classifications of projections

Projections are classified in a variety of ways and there is no need to get depressed if you do not recognise the title of a projection in your atlas. Here are some of the methods of classification.

(1) According to the method of construction

(a) Geometric or perspective. A flat surface, cylinder or a cone is placed conveniently on the surface of the reduced earth and a light source, again conveniently placed (at the centre or at one of the poles of the reduced earth) projects the graticule. An example is the polar stereographic.

(b) Geometric, modified. The basic geometric projections may be improved by modifying them mathematically. This is normally done to achieve a certain property. Mercator and transverse Mercator projections are examples.

(c) Mathematical. Some projections are produced entirely by mathematical methods, although the basic concept might be drawn from the geometric projection. Lambert's orthomorphic projection is an example here.

(2) According to properties

(a) Equal area projections. On these projections areas are shown in the correct proportions. As the spherical surface is flattened out to give equal areas, the scale, shapes and bearings will all be distorted. A square on the reduced earth may appear as a rectangle or even a parallelogram: as long as the area shown is in the correct proportion, its shape does not matter. As aviators, however, we shall not be concerned with these, but it is useful to know that equal area and orthomorphism (correct bearings) cannot exist together. An example of an equal area is the Bonne's projection seen in any atlas.

(b) Orthomorphic or conformal projections. On these projections the bearings are represented correctly. It will be appreciated that for the bearings to be correct the shapes must be correct, and on projections of this type the shapes of *small areas* are preserved. We will come back to orthomorphism pretty soon.

(c) Equidistance projections. In this type of projection the cartographers strive to achieve a constant scale as it occurs on the earth. Again, we shall not be concerned with these projections.

(3) According to the orientation of the paper
The geometric projections described in 1(a) above are also called True Projections and the sheet on which the graticule is to be projected is called the *developable surface*.

(a) Cylindrical projections – Mercator.
(b) Conical projections – Lambert.
(c) Zenithal projections: the plane of the projection is tangential to the earth's surface – polar stereographic.

Projections used in aviation
In aviation we generally use maps and charts for two purposes, that is, navigation plotting and map-reading (topographical maps). In each of these we look for the following properties.

Plotting charts
(a) *Orthomorphism (Conformality)*. This is perhaps the primary requirement of a plotting chart. On this chart the bearings measured are correct.
(b) *Rhumb lines*. If the rhumb lines on the chart are straight lines, we would be able to fly a constant track. Although not a primary requirement, it would be very convenient.
(c) *Distances*. On any chart used for in-flight plotting, we should be able to measure the distances easily.
(d) Lastly, the adjacent sheets should fit to give continuity.
The charts in common use are Mercator's, Lambert's and polar stereographic projections.

Topographical maps
(a) Here we are primarily interested in the shapes which should be shown fairly correctly.
(b) Scale on the map should be fairly constant and any scale error distributed evenly over the area.
(c) Adjacent sheets should fit accurately.
Transverse Mercator is used for producing topographical maps of regions having their greatest extent north–south, e.g. UK, Malaysia. Lambert's projection with two standard parallels is suitable for regions having their greatest east–west extent, e.g. USA. Regions roughly circular would advantageously employ oblique stereographic projections whereas in the equatorial regions Mercator's projection is ideal.

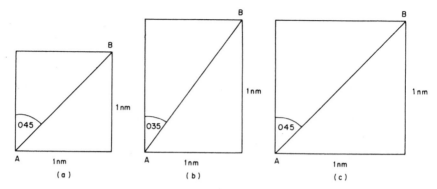

Fig. 4.1   Scale on a chart

Orthomorphism

The word *orthomorphism* is derived from the Greek words *orthos* which means right, or correct, and *morphic* meaning form or shape. The adoption of this title is rather unfortunate as it is bound to confuse those of us who are products of the modern comprehensives and not therefore scholars of classical Greek. So, right from the start we would like to make it clear that on an orthomorphic projection, the bearings measured are correct. The shapes are inevitably tied up with bearings and we will talk about these when discussing individual projections. The American equivalent of the word orthomorphism is *conformal*. The following considerations go into the construction of an orthomorphic chart.

As we said earlier, as soon as we commence the process of flattening a spherical surface, distortion of shapes takes place, accompanied by inherent distortion of the scale. On the reduced earth the scale is correct. On a flat chart, the distortion must cause variation of the scale. Accepting the limitation that the scale varies from point to point, it is possible to adjust this variation so that on the resultant graticule the scale is the same (though not necessarily correct, that is, equivalent to the reduced earth) along the meridian and parallel through any given point. The scale will have varied at the point next to it, but here again, for a very short distance round it, it will be the same. In other words, the scale may vary from point to point, but the scale around a point remains the same for short distances.

To achieve orthomorphism two requirements must be met. One is that if the chart is to be orthomorphic, the scale at any point measured over a very short distance is the same in all directions, although it may vary from point to point. The validity of this requirement is illustrated in Fig. 4.1.

Fig. 4.1(a) represents a square to the scale of $1'' \equiv 1$ nm on the reduced earth. This means that $1''$ on the reduced earth measures 1 nm on the earth. On this square the bearing of B from A is 045°.

Suppose that on a certain projection this square appears as a rectangle as in Fig. 4.1(b). The east–west scale on this projection is $1'' \equiv 1$ nm. This scale is

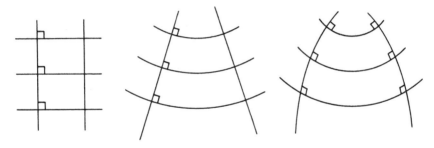

Fig. 4.2   Meridians and parallels intersect at 90°

the same as on the reduced earth and is therefore correct. But 1 nm in the north–south direction is represented by 2″ on this projection and consequently the bearing of B from A is wrong. The scale through point A is not the same in all directions and therefore the chart is not orthomorphic.

On yet another projection, Fig. 4.1(c), the east–west scale is 2″ to 1 nm. This is not correct scale, but the scale north–south is also 2″ to 1 nm. Thus, the scale from point A is the same in all directions and the bearing of B as measured at A is again correct.

It must be emphasised that the above illustration is a very much exaggerated view; the points we are talking about are very close to each other.

The second requirement of orthomorphism is that the meridians and parallels on the projection must intersect each other at right angles, just as they do on the earth. The meridians and parallels on the earth define the north/south and east/west directions and these directions must be reproduced on the chart for the correct measurements. Also, when the meridians and parallels are arranged to intersect at right angles, the shape of a small area about that point is correct which means that the bearings must be correct. It must be noted that the meridians and parallels need not be straight lines in order to intersect at right angles, see Fig. 4.2.

To summarise the two requirements of orthomorphism:
(a)   At any given point on the chart the scale must be the same in all directions, although it may vary from point to point.
(b)   The meridians and parallels on the chart must cut each other at right angles.

Scales

The scale is the ratio of a distance measured on the chart to the corresponding distance on the earth's surface. It is given in the formula

$$\text{scale} = \frac{\text{chart length (CL)}}{\text{earth distance (ED)}}$$

(both CL and ED must be expressed in the same units).

On the reduced earth the scale is constant and correct everywhere. Thus, if the radius of the model globe was, say, 637.5 mm compared with the actual earth radius of 6375 km, its scale as a representative fraction would be

$$\frac{637.5}{6375 \times 10^6} = 1:10\,000\,000$$

This would mean that 1 unit on the model globe would be equal to 10 million units on the earth.

For projections where the scale may be varying from point to point, it may not be possible to give a scale which is applicable to the whole coverage. You will find that on some projections (polar stereographic) the scale is given for a point, or a particular parallel (Mercator and Lambert). The maps and charts on which the scale error is extremely small are commonly called *constant scale* maps/charts. On these charts distances may be measured directly with a graduated rule. The scale itself may be represented in a variety of ways, the representative fraction being the most commonly used method in aviation.

Representative fraction

This expresses the ratio of a unit of length on the map to its corresponding number of similar units on the earth, e.g. $\frac{1}{1\,000\,000}$. This may also be written in another form, $1:1\,000\,000$. In either case the scale tells us that a distance of 1 unit on the chart represents a distance of $1\,000\,000$ units on the ground. It also tells us that 1 mm on the chart equals $1\,000\,000$ mm ($= 1$ km) on the ground. In other words, the scale expressed as above has no inherent unit of its own; you provide a convenient unit and the result will be the same provided the same unit is used in both denominator and numerator.

Another point we need to note is that since we are dealing with a fraction of 1, the larger the figure in the denominator the smaller the scale we will have. The scale $1:250\,000$ is larger than a scale of $1:5\,000\,000$. On large-scale charts comparatively less ground distance is covered and consequently more ground details can be inserted.

Graduated scale line

These show the actual lengths on the map corresponding to various distances on the earth. A graduated scale line is found on charts which are considered to have a constant scale throughout the sheet. On some charts (Lambert's six million) more than one such line is found. For more accurate distance measurement a variable scale may be used, but this is beyond the scope of our present studies. It is worth noting that a ruler calibrated in millimetres enables distances to be read off directly in kilometres on a $1:1\,000\,000$ scale map.

Statement in words

This method, generally used on Ordnance Survey maps gives the corresponding values of two different units of length, one on the map and the other on the earth, e.g. the OS motorist's route planning map at 1:625 000 revised every autumn is described as 'about 1 inch to 10 miles'. The one in a quarter million scale (1:250 000) Topographical Air Charts of the UK, which are based on the OS Routemaster series, are approximately $\frac{1}{4}$ inch to the mile. The 1:50 000 Ordnance Survey maps which replace the former 'one inch to the mile' (1:63 360) and have metrication of contours, are '2 cm to 1 km'.

In addition to the above it must be noted that the meridians, being semi great circles, provide a natural nautical mile scale. One degree change of latitude along a meridian measures 60 nm on the earth and therefore the meridians are usually graduated in nautical miles. These graduations are very useful for measuring distances.

Scale factor

We stated earlier that one of the steps in the construction of a projection is to reduce the earth to a chosen scale. It is this scale that is generally printed on the chart. We also stated that on any flat chart the scale is bound to depart from the chosen scale of the reduced earth. In detailed study of the scales, it is sometimes more convenient to calculate how much the scale differs from the chosen scale at a given place, rather than the actual scale there. This difference from the reduced earth (RE) scale is called the *scale factor*, and it is expressed as a ratio of the chart length to the reduced earth length

$$\text{scale factor} = \frac{\text{chart length}}{\text{reduced earth length}}$$

It can be seen from the above relationship that the scale factor will be 1 wherever the scale on the chart is identical to the scale of the reduced earth. Thus, when the ratio is not exactly 1 the difference between it and 1 is the amount the scale differs from the reduced earth scale. For example, if the scale factor at a point has a value of 1.0123, this means that a measurement of 1 unit at this point will be in error by 0.0123 and the percentage error will be 1.23%.

Alternatively, knowing the scale factor or percentage error at a point, we can work out the actual scale at that point. It must always be remembered that scale is correctly expressed as a representative fraction and not by just the denominator (i.e. not 'half-million chart' but '1 in half-million chart') and the scale factor must be applied to the representative fraction. For example, if the reduced earth scale is 1:1 000 000 and the scale factor at point A is 1.2 then the scale at A is equal to

$$\frac{1}{1\,000\,000} \times 1.2 = 1:833\,333$$

and note that the scale at point A is larger than the reduced earth scale.

Scale problems

Problems involving scales are often set in the exams. We give you here a few worked examples followed by plenty of practice problems. You may find the following conversion factors (in addition to the ones given in an earlier chapter) useful in working out your scale problems.

$$1 \, nm = 72\,960 \text{ inches (UK)}$$
$$1 \text{ International } nm = 1852 \, m = 72\,913 \text{ inches}$$
$$1 \, sm = 63\,360 \text{ inches}$$
$$1 \, km = 39\,370 \text{ inches}$$
$$1 \, km = 100\,000 \, cm$$
$$1 \text{ inch} = 2.54 \, cm$$
$$1 \text{ metre} = 39.37 \text{ inches (or 3.28 ft)}$$

Worked examples

(1)   How many km to a cm are represented by a scale of $1:2\,500\,000$?

$$1 \, cm \text{ represents } 2\,500\,000 \, cm \text{ or } \frac{2\,500\,000}{100\,000} km = 25 \, km$$

(2)   You have a chart, scale 4 inches to 1 statute mile. Express this as a representative fraction.

$$\text{Scale} = \frac{CL}{ED} = \frac{4 \text{ inches}}{1 \times 5280 \times 12}$$

$$= 1:15\,840$$

(3)   If 100 nm are represented by a line 7.9 inches long on a chart, what is the length of a line representing 50 km?

$$7.9 \, in = 100 \, nm = 185.2 \, km$$
$$\therefore 50 \, km = \frac{50 \times 7.9}{185.2}$$
$$= 2.13 \text{ inches}$$

(4)   If the scale is $1:250\,000$ what is the distance in millimetres on the chart between 32°11′N 06°47′E and 30°33′N 06°47′E?

Since both positions are situated on the same meridian the distance between the two in nautical miles is the arc of the meridian in number of minutes ($1° = 60$ minutes) intercepted between the two, viz, change of latitude in minutes.

$$\text{Thus the distance in } nm = \begin{array}{r} 32°11′ \\ -30°33′ \\ \hline 1°38′ \end{array} \text{ or } 98 \, nm = 181.5 \, km \text{ (calculator)}$$

Now we proceed to solve the problem in the usual way – 1 mm on the chart represents 250 000 mm on the earth,

$$\therefore 181.5 \, km \text{ will be represented by } \frac{181.5 \times 1\,000\,000}{250\,000} mm$$

$$= 726.8 \, mm$$

Chart symbols, conventional signs and relief

You learn all this from the maps and charts you come across in your flying activities from the word go. Civil Aviation Authority Aeronautical Information Circular entitled Aeronautical Charts provides comprehensive information on various maps and charts available and the ICAO approved symbols. On radio navigation charts, the legend is available. Many maps print the key on the side of the map. The only word of warning is spot elevations: these are indicated by a dot with a figure by the side. Before using any chart, look around the margin to check if spot elevations are given in feet or metres. 123 metres, for example, is about 404 feet – quite a difference. Relief on the topographic charts is usually shown by contours with a spot elevation. The closer together are the contours, the steeper the hills. Layer tinting is another method of showing relief. The depth of the colour as keyed at the side of the map indicates the gradient, again with a spot elevation to show the highest spot in the area.

High ground can be a killer and a knowledge of all conventional signs is important. Although map-reading may appear daunting at first when you bear in mind that you will be flying the aeroplane and keeping a good look-out, be reassured that it will come naturally provided you do your pre-flight preparation conscientiously.

Practice problems

(Answers to multichoice test questions are on p 307)

(1) Which of the following two charts has a larger scale? (a) 1:1 000 000; (b) 1:250 000
Answer: Chart (b).

(2) Which is the larger scale, 1:1 303 000 or 17.8 nm to one inch?
Answer: 17.8 nm to one inch.

(3) If the scale is 1:500 000, how many statute miles on the ground are represented by one inch on the map?
(a) 6.85   (b) 7.89   (c) 12.7

(4) A Mercator's chart has a scale of 1:1 461 000 at 50°N. How many nautical miles are represented by one inch at 50°N on this chart?
(a) 23.06   (b) 37.11   (c) 20.02

(5) If on a chart, 30 statute miles are represented by 30 centimetres, what is the scale of the chart?
(a) 1:160 934   (b) 1:159 033   (c) 1:185 318

(6) On a chart, scale 1:1 000 000, how many inches does a ground distance of 286 kilometres measure?
(a) 11.26   (b) 18.12   (c) 20.87

(7) A line 6 inches long drawn on a chart measures 105 nm. What is the scale of the chart?
(a) 1:1 275 982   (b) 1:1 088 000   (c) 1:688 975

(8)   On a chart having a scale of 1:2 000 000, how many kilometres are represented by a line 3.7 inches long?
(a) 116.79   (b) 101.42   (c) 187.96

(9)   On a chart having a scale of 1:250 000, at what distance apart in inches would two positions A (20°33'N 150°08'W) and B (21°37'N 150°08'W) appear?
(a) 16.22   (b) 30.35   (c) 18.67

(10)   On a chart, a line 8 inches long represents 200 statute miles. What is the length of a line in centimetres representing 326 kilometres?
(a) 17.87   (b) 20.58   (c) 12.9

(11)   At what distance apart in mm would two pinpoints taken at a 20 minute interval appear on a chart, scale 1:1 000 000 if the ground speed was 180 kt?
(a) 96.5   (b) 111.1   (c) 108.2

(12)   If the scale of a chart is 1:6 000 000, how many kilometres are represented by a line 5.2 inches long?
(a) 7.9248   (b) 79.248   (c) 792.48

(13)   Position A on latitude 46°44'S is due north of position B which is on latitude 49°39'S. If the distance between the two on a constant scale chart is 6.01 cm, what is the scale of the chart?
(a) 1:3 243 072   (b) 1:1 949 087   (c) 1:5 392 679

(14)   An aircraft takes 15 min 12 s to cover the distance 6.6 cm between A and B on a chart having a scale of 1:2 000 000. Calculate the aircraft's ground speed in knots.
(a) 281.3   (b) 132   (c) 244.7

(15)   The distance flown by an aircraft in 40 seconds at a ground speed of 480 kt is shown on a chart by a straight line, 1.4 inches long. Give the scale of the chart in centimetres to kilometres.
(a) 1 cm to 2.778 km   (b) 1 cm to 3.89 km   (c) 1 cm to 38.9 km.

Chapter 5
MERCATOR'S PROJECTION

Gerhard Kramer, a Flemish mathematician, was fifty-seven years old when he published his cylindrical orthomorphic projection in 1569. It was modish to have a Latin surname to be distinguished from the unscholarly plebeians, hence Mercator. The copies of his chart still exist but he left no clue as to how he calculated the spacing of the graticule. Thirty years later Edward Wright of Cambridge published the tables for the construction of the projection in his book *Certaine Errors in Navigation*. Accurate tables, called meridional parts tables did not become available until a hundred years later when calculus opened up a new dimension in mathematics. Perhaps the most used projection in the world, Mercator was particularly popular in Britain because, they say, the then British Empire on this projection looked bigger than the rest of the world. We will now consider the three stages in its development.

Geometric cylindrical

A roll of paper in the form of a cylinder is placed round the reduced earth, its axis being coincident with the axis of the generating globe. Thus, the cylinder

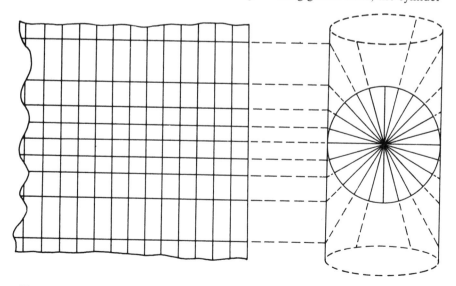

Fig. 5.1   Cylindrical projection

is tangential to the reduced earth at the equator, see Fig. 5.1. A light source placed at the centre of the generating globe casts shadows of the graticule on to the developable surface. The resultant graticule is rectangular in shape.

The primary feature of all normal cylindricals is the property of straight and parallel meridians, equally spaced, at right angles to the equator. ('Normal' cylinder means a cylinder having its axis coincident with the axis of the reduced earth.) Thus, the first step in drawing up any normal cylinder is to rule in the meridians against the equator or any other parallel.

The next step is to insert the rest of the parallels. The spacing of these parallels gives the individuality to the cylinder. However, note from Fig. 5.1 that all parallels are of equal length, the length of any parallel on the cylinder being the same as the reduced earth, that is, $2\pi R$.

The scale of such a geometrical projection must be worked out separately in east–west and north–south directions.

East–west scale

$$\text{Scale} = \frac{\text{CL}}{\text{ED}}$$

$$= \frac{\text{length of any parallel } \phi \text{ on the projection}}{\text{length of the same parallel } \phi \text{ on the RE}}$$

$$= \frac{2\pi R}{2\pi R \cos \phi}$$

$$= \frac{1}{\cos \phi} = \sec \phi$$

North–south scale
The scale factor in the north–south direction on this projection can be calculated by calculus, and it is $\sec^2 \phi$.

Properties
The great difference in the rate of change of the scale in the two directions as we saw above renders the distance measurement a highly complex business. In addition, the scale variation from a point being different in different directions, the chart is not orthomorphic. These two major disadvantages rule out its use for plotting or as a topographical map.

Simple (equidistant) cylindrical
This is the second stage in the development of a cylinder. Whereas the ancient mariners were not to be fooled by the geometric cylindrical, they loved this one as it looked so *earth-like*. It was widely used by the navigators before the arrival of the real science of map projection and Mercator, and in consequence discovered many remote islands.

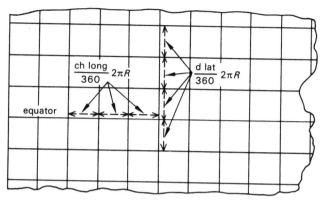

Fig. 5.2   Simple (equidistant) cylindrical projection

Construction

This is a straightforward mathematical projection in which the calculated distances are plotted on the map sheet to give the graticule. The equator is marked in as a straight line. It is then divided correctly for the meridian spacing

$$\left(\frac{\text{ch long}}{360} \times 2\pi R \right)$$

and the meridians drawn in as straight and parallel lines at right angles to the equator (Fig. 5.2). The meridians are then divided to give the parallel spacing at *correct* reduced earth scale

$$\left(\frac{\text{ch lat}}{360} \times 2\pi R \right)$$

and the parallels draw in. The scale in the east–west direction on such a chart is sec ϕ, found in the same way as for the geometric. The scale factor in the north–south direction is obviously 1, since the scale has been made constant and correct by construction.

Properties

Distance measurement in directions other than due north–south or due east–west is complicated. It is not orthomorphic as it does not meet one of the two requirements of orthomorphism. The chart is no longer in use.

Orthomorphic cylindrical or Mercator's projection

This is the one we are interested in most, as its whole purpose is to produce a conformal graticule on which a rhumb line will be exactly represented by a straight line. In this projection the spacing of the parallels is deliberately

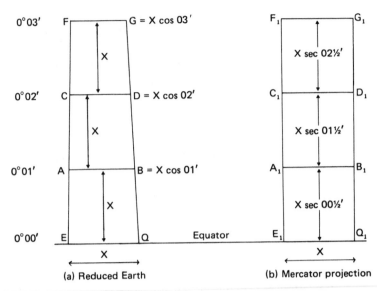

Fig. 5.3   Mercator's projection

chosen in such a way that with increase of latitude, the rate of expansion of scale in the north–south direction proceeds at the same rate as the expansion of scale in the east–west direction (which is secant of latitude). See Fig. 5.3. Thus, at any one point the scale will have expanded by the same amount, will have reached the same value and will in fact be the same in all directions.

As in other normal cylindricals the scale factor in the east–west direction is sec φ because converging meridians have become straight and parallel. Thus, the rate of expansion required in the north–south direction will be such as to give the scale factor of sec φ at any latitude. Putting this the other way, the meridians will be stretched apart as they depart from the equator at a rate proportional to the secant of the angle of latitude. The actual process of calculating the spacing involves the use of calculus and meridional parts tables are available. Our primary interest in the study of Mercator is in understanding its properties.

Properties

Orthomorphism
Yes, the chart is orthomorphic by construction. It meets both the requirements of orthomorphism.

Where on the chart is the scale correct?
The cylinder is tangential to the equator of the reduced earth. Therefore, it is only here that the two lengths are identical, to give the correct scale. Thus the answer is, only at the equator.

How does the scale vary?

Away from the equator, the scale varies as secant of the latitude. The same chart length at 30°N will measure a larger distance than at 60°N. For this reason the scale of a Mercator is given as a representative fraction for a stated latitude, e.g. 1:1 000 000 at 51°N.

Convergency

Convergency is defined as the inclination between two meridians. On Mercator the meridians are straight lines parallel to each other. Consequently, the angle of inclination is 0° throughout. Thus, the convergency on the chart is *constant*, and because it is constant, it cannot be correct anywhere on the chart except at the equator where the earth convergency is also 0°.

Great circles

Great circles on the earth cut meridians at different angles. These must be curves on this chart where the meridians are parallel to each other. They curve *concave* to the equator. However, the equator and all the meridians together with their anti-meridians are great circles by definition, and they appear as straight lines. (They are rhumb lines as well.)

Rhumb lines

All straight lines drawn on this chart are rhumb lines because they cut all the meridians at the same angle.

Shapes

As the projection is orthomorphic, shapes of small areas are not distorted. The shapes of large areas in high latitudes where the scale expansion becomes very rapid are considerably distorted. An example is the shape of Greenland on this projection. A circle at the equator will appear egg-shaped at, say, 60°N. This effect of the scale expansion in high latitudes stretches its property of orthomorphism until it finally cannot be used for plotting.

Areas

Mercator's projection is not an equal area projection. Areas are greatly exaggerated in the high latitudes. South America which is ten times the size of Greenland actually appears smaller than Greenland on this projection.

Fits

The sheets with the same meridian spacing will fit accurately in north–south and east–west.

Mercator as a plotting chart

Mercator meets all the requirements we would look for in a plotting chart. It is orthomorphic, rhumb lines are straight lines and it has a satisfactory scale in the lower and intermediate latitudes.

Limitations of Mercator

Due to the expanding scale, the chart cannot be used for plotting purposes in high latitudes, say, above 70°/75°N/S. The rapidly expanding scale makes accurate distance measurements difficult, and eventually the bearings are distorted. The poles cannot be produced on the chart.

Disadvantages of the Mercator

(1)   The major one we have already met – radio bearings are great circle bearings which must be converted to rhumb lines before plotting.
(2)   On a long route, the rhumb line can add appreciably to the distance. It is then usual to plot the latitude and longitude of a series of points which constitute the great circle and join these points by rhumb lines forming a composite RL track. This used to be common practice over the Atlantic and Pacific; nowadays, with increasing aircraft speeds, long routes are no problem and the Lambert's projection can be used giving distances very close to great circle distances.
(3)   The chart cannot be used in polar regions.

Measurement of distances

Since the scale on the chart varies from place to place, care must be exercised in taking distance measurements. Always use the latitude scale (up a meridian) using a convenient section which straddles the middle of the line you are measuring. Keep that section for the whole of the line. For large distances, say in excess of 300 nm, section out the line to be measured and take a mean latitude cover for each section. Then measure each section separately and add up for total distance. Short distances readily spanned by the divider can be measured in one attempt over the mid-latitude of the line concerned.

To form a local graticule

A local graticule of the Mercator can be constructed as follows:
   Say you wish to produce a graticule covering 55°N to 57°N, 100°W to 105°W.

(1)   Choose a scale for longitude, say 1 inch ≡ 1° longitude.
(2)   Draw a base line AB and mark off longitudes at a distance of 1 inch per degree.
(3)   Construct the meridians as parallel lines perpendicular to the base line.
(4)   From the point of origin A draw an angle *from the base line* equal to the mean of the required parallels (see Fig. 5.4), and let this intersect the adjacent meridian at C.
(5)   From A, with radius AC, draw an arc CD.
(6)   At D, draw the line of latitude, parallel to the base line.
(7)   Repeat the process as required.

   The points to watch are that the angle is from the base line and not from north on the protractor; and relate the degrees of longitude to the degrees of latitude – one degree spacing in our sketch, but such a scale for 5° spacing of longitude for example must refer to a similar 5° spacing of latitude.

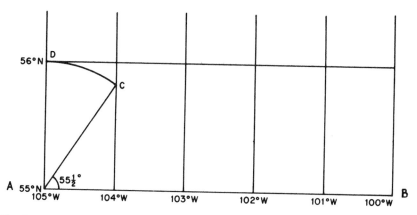

Fig. 5.4   Constructing a local graticule

Fig. 5.5   Plotting a bearing on a Mercator

Plotting radio position lines

As all radio bearings are great circles, they must be converted to rhumb lines before plotting on a Mercator. This is readily done by applying conversion angle either from the formula $CA = \frac{1}{2}$ch long × sin mean lat, or from the abac scale printed and explained in the left-hand corner of the chart, and demonstrated in *Ground Studies for Pilots Volume 2, Plotting and Flight Planning.* Apply to the nearest whole degree, and bear in mind that the RL always appears towards the equator. A thumbnail sketch is always useful (see Fig. 5.5).

Conversion angle is applied *where the work is done.*

Example

You are in DR position 30°N 20°W and receive a QTE from a station in 35°N 23°W of 123°. The work of measurement has been done at the station; the conversion angle must then be applied to this measurement: the GC bearing is 123°, add CA of 1°, and plot this RL of 124° from the station.

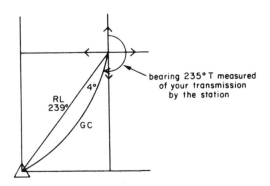

Fig. 5.6   Plotting a QDM on a Mercator (S. Hem)

Now if the circumstances had been similar to the one quoted above, but you decided to measure the bearing of the station yourself from the aircraft, then what you measured is the subject for conversion; in other words, you have done the work. Say your heading is 350° (T), and you took a relative bearing of the station on the ADF of 315°.

Relative bearing	315	GC
Add heading true	350	
	665	
	−360	
True bearing	305	GC − this is the work done
Conversion angle	− 1	to bring it nearer to equator
True bearing	304	RL
	−180	to get to the station for plot
Plot	124°	

Consider this example in the southern hemisphere (Fig. 5.6). QDM is 050°, variation at the station 5°E, CA = 4°.

Apply the station's variation to the QDM to give a heading to steer with zero wind of 055°(T)

	055	
	+180	to get to the station
	235	the actual work done
CA	+ 4	to bring it nearer to equator
Plot	239°	

Practice paper: Mercator North
Note: use CA throughout as 1° when its value is 0.5 or more.
Construct a Mercator graticule from 20°N to 25°N, 10°W to 15°W using the

scale of 1 inch ≡ 1° longitude. Then answer the following questions based on it:

(1) Estimate RL track angle and distance from A (20°N 14°W) to B (24°30′N 10°30′W).

(2) Would RL track angle from 25°N 14°W to 29°30′N 10°30′W be more, same or less than answer in 1 above? Why?

(3) What is the scale of your chart at the equator?

(4) What is GC bearing of (a) A from B; (b) B from A?

(5) Is the convergency of the chart correct?

(6) Is the convergency of the chart constant?

(7) Where is the convergency of a Mercator chart constant?

(8) Where is the convergency of a Mercator chart correct?

(9) Why is a Mercator chart of little or no navigational value in high latitudes?

(10) Give the track from F (22°30′N 15°W) to K (22°30′N 10°W) which will give the shortest distance.

(11) Is your chart orthomorphic? Why?

(12) Measure on your chart the GC bearing of M (25°N 13°W) from N (20°N 13°W).

(13) An aircraft in DR position 20°20′N 14°50′W on heading 050°(T) obtains a relative bearing of 355° from station at 23°12′N 10°W. What would you plot?

(14) An aircraft in DR position 24°30′N 15°W gets QDM 126° from station at 20°N 10°W. Station variation 9°E. What would you plot?

Answers

(1) 036°; 329 nm.

(2) Less – expanding scale (meridians converge on the earth).

(3) 1 in = 60 nm at the equator; therefore scale is 1:4 377 600.

(4) (a) 217°; (b) 035°.

(5) No.

(6) Yes.

(7) All over the chart.

(8) At the equator.

(9) Scale expansion.

(10) Shortest distance is along GC track which is 089° (initial) 090° (mean) and 091° (final).

(11) Yes, the two basic requirements of orthomorphism are met, that meridians and parallels intersect at 90° and the scale at a point is the same in all directions.

(12) 000°.

(13) 226°.

(14) 314°.

Practice paper: Mercator South

Note: use CA to the nearest whole degree.

Construct a Mercator graticule from 20°S to 50°S, 30°E to 60°E (showing the meridans and parallels at 5° intervals) using scale 1 inch ≡ 5° longitude, and answer the following questions.

(1) Two lines are drawn from 35°E to 55°E, the first at 22°S, the second at 47°S.
    (a)   Which represents the longer distance?
    (b)   Which has the smaller scale?
    (c)   What is the scale of this chart at the equator?

(2) How many km are expressed by 1 cm at the equator?

(3) Point A is at 50°S 60°E; point B is at 25°S 35°E.
    (a)   What is RL track and distance from A to B?
    (b)   Would RL track angle from 75°S 60°E to 50°S 35°E be greater or lesser than (a) above? Give a reason.
    (c)   What is the initial GC track from (*a*) A to B; (*b*) B to A?
    (d)   What is the mean GC track from A to B?

(4) What track to nearest degree will give the shortest distance between (a) 47°S 30°E and 47°S 55°E? (b) 47°S 30°E and 20°S 30°E?

(5) Express the scale of this chart at 35°S as a representative fraction.

(6) An aircraft in DR position 40°S 55°E receives QDM 321° (station variation 18°W) from X (30°S 30°E). What would you plot?

(7) An aircraft in DR position 49°S 46°E on heading 090°(T) gets ADF bearing (relative) of 268°, QC 0, from station at 25°S 45°E. What would you plot?

Answers

(1) (a)   Line drawn at 22°S.
     (b)   22°S.
     (c)   1:21 888 000.

(2) 218.9 km.

(3) (a)   322°; 1950 nm.
     (b)   Greater – expanding latitude scale.
     (c)   (a) 314°; (b) 150°.
     (d)   322° – GC and RL are same at mid-meridian.

(4) (a)   Initial 099°; mean 090°; final 081°.
     (b)   000°.

(5) 1:17 929 000. The scale is found in two ways – (a) measure the distance at mid-position on the chart (along a meridian) by dividers open one inch. Convert this distance as representative fraction. (b) By calculation. The latter method is more accurate and is explained in the following pages.

(6) 116°.

(7) 178°.

Scale problems on Mercator

In tackling any problems on Mercator in which scale is involved we have only to remember that the scale varies as secant of latitude.

(1)   If the scale at equator is $1:608\,776$, what is the scale at 56°N?

The scale expands at the rate of secant of latitude, therefore scale at 56°N = scale at equator × sec 56°

$$= \frac{1}{608\,776} \times \sec 56°$$

As the numerator of the RF must be 1, the equation is rewritten:

$$= \frac{1}{608\,776 \times \cos 56}$$

$$= 1:340\,427$$

It is noted here, by the way, that the denominator at 56°N is a smaller figure than at the equator. This indicates scale expansion; 1 inch at 56°N will measure lesser earth distance.

(2)   Scale at 56°N is $1:1\,000\,000$. What is the scale at 46°N?

$$\text{Scale at equator} = \frac{1 \times \cos 56°}{1\,000\,000}$$

$$= \frac{1}{1\,000\,000 \times \sec 56}$$

$$\therefore \text{Scale at 46°N} = \frac{1}{1\,000\,000 \times \sec 56 \times \cos 46}$$

$$= 1:1\,242\,332$$

(3)   Scale at 50°N is $1:608\,000$. What is the scale at 60°N?

$$\text{Scale at 60°N} = \frac{1}{608\,000 \times \sec 50 \times \cos 60}$$

$$= 1:472\,930$$

(4)   An aircraft flies from CLINTON, 43°37′N 81°30′W to NIAGARA, 43°07′N 79°00′W. The distance between the meridians of CLINTON and NIAGARA on a Mercator chart is 15 in. What is the scale of the chart at 45°N?

Change of longitude = 2°30′ represented by 15 in on the chart.
$\therefore$ 1° ch long = 6 in

and since the meridians on a Mercator are straight lines parallel to each other

1° at the equator   = 6 in; or,
60 nm at the equator = 6 in
$\therefore$ 10 nm at equator = 1 in

and at 45°N the scale of the chart is

$$= \frac{1}{10 \times 6080 \times 12 \times \cos 45}$$

$$= 1:515\,900$$

Practice problems: Mercator's projection

Exercise 1 (CPL and ATPL)

(1) If the scale at the equator is 1:6000000, what is the scale at 45°S? (Sec 45° = 1.41, cos 45° = 0.71.)

Answer: 1:4260000.

(2) If the scale at the equator is 1:1427000, what is the scale at 58°N? (Sec 58° = 1.88, cos 58° = 0.53.)

Answer: 1:756310.

(3) If the scale at 60°S is 1:3000000, what is the scale at the equator? (Sec 60° = 2.0, cos 60° = 0.5.)

Answer: 1:6000000.

(4) If the scale at 30°N is 1:2450000, what is the scale at the equator? (Sec 30° = 1.15, cos 30° = 0.87.)

Answer: 1:2817500.

(5) If the scale at 30°N is 1:3500000, what is the scale at 40°N? (Cos 30° = 0.87, sec 30° = 1.15, cos 40° = 0.77, sec 40° = 1.30.)

Answer: 1:3099250.

(6) If the scale at 60°N is 1:2000000, what is the scale at 40°N? (Cos 60° = 0.5, sec 60° = 2, cos 40° = 0.77, sec 40° = 1.30.)

Answer: 1:3080000.

(7) The scale at the equator is 1:4000000. The distance as measured on the chart by a straight line between A (60°N 70°W) and B (60°N 80°W) is 9.2 inches. (Cos 60° = 0.5, sec 60° = 2.0.)
 (a) What is the scale at 60°N?
 (b) What is the chart length in centimetres along the equator representing 60 nm?
 (c) What is the earth distance in kilometres between A and B?

Answer: (a) 1:2000000; (b) 2.778 cm; (c) 555.6 km.

(8) On a Mercator, two meridians one degree apart are spaced at a distance of 7.62 cm. What is the scale on this chart at 48°N? (Sec 48° = 1.49, cos 48° = 0.67.)

Answer: 1:977664.

(9) On a Mercator the straight line distance between two positions A (40°S 08°E) and B (40°S 08°W) is 88 cm. What is the chart length in millimetres between 12°W and 13°W at the equator?

Answer: 55 mm.

(10) At 60°N a distance of 30 cm on the chart measures a ground distance of 390 nm. What is the scale of the chart at the equator?

Answer: 1:4810000. (Hint: to avoid awkward figures, work in kilometres.)

Exercise 2 (ATPL)

(1) If the scale at 40°N is 1:500000, where is the scale of 1:450500?

Answer: 46°21′N/S.

(2) If the scale at 42°N is 1:1000000, where is the scale of 1:500000?

Answer: 68°11′N/S.

(3) In problem 2 above, is it possible to have a scale of 1:2000000 anywhere on the chart?

Answer: No. (Hint: compare it with the scale at the equator.)

(4) On a Mercator one degree of change of longitude measures 3.03 cm. In which latitude is the scale 1:2000000?

Answer: 56°59′N/S.

(5) On a Mercator the spacing between the meridians of 160°W and 170°W is 26 cm. What is the scale at 56°N?

Answer: 1:2392000.

(6) On a Mercator the distance between meridians 172°W and 159°W is 9 inches. At what latitude would you find the scale of 1:3000000?

Answer: 61°41′N/S.

(7) If the scale at 60°N is 1:2000000, where is the scale of 1:1000000?

Answer: 75°31′N/S.

(8) If the scale at 57°20′N is 1:1091000, what is the meridian spacing, one degree apart, in centimetres?

Answer: 5.5 cm.

(9) The scale on a Mercator at 42°S is 1:500000. What is the distance in inches between two places A (42°S 112°E) and B (42°S 115°42′E) on the chart?

Answer: 24.1 inches.

(10)   A Mercator has a scale of 1:1 000 000 at the equator. On this scale, two positions A and B both on 54°N are shown 10 inches apart. What is the difference in longitude between them?

Answer: 2°17.1′.

Chapter 6
LAMBERT'S CONICAL ORTHOMORPHIC PROJECTION

This projection devised by Johannes Lambert and first published around 1772 is variously known as

Lambert's conical orthomorphic projection;
Lambert's 2nd projection;
Lambert's conformal.

It is an improvement on Mercator's projection: its scale is very nearly constant and great circles are almost straight lines. The difficulty caused by rhumb lines not being straight lines is overcome either by superimposing a square grid on it or by simply flying mean tracks. With the ICAO's blessing this projection is now progressively replacing Mercator as a plotting chart.

The projection is entirely mathematical and the resulting graticule has some similarity to the geometric conic with two standard parallels. In fact, this projection is based on the conic conception and therefore we shall first look into the properties of a simple conic projection.

Simple conic projection

A cone is placed over the reduced earth so that it is tangential to a predetermined parallel of latitude. This parallel is called its *standard* parallel. A standard parallel on any projection is that parallel which is drawn to the same scale as the scale of this parallel on the reduced earth. A Mercator's standard parallel is the equator.

In Fig. 6.1 a cone EAXBQ is placed on the reduced earth, tangential along the parallel AB, which is its standard parallel. Parallel AB is also the *parallel of origin* of the chart. Its radius from X, the apex of the cone, is XB and is given by the formula $R \cot \phi$ (where R is the radius of the reduced earth and ϕ is the standard parallel). The formula can be proved quite simply.

AB is the standard parallel which is described by angle OXB, ϕ. OB is the radius of the reduced earth, R. (It can be seen that the lat angle QOB = $\angle$OXB.)

In triangle XOB

$$\frac{XB}{OB} = \cot \phi; \quad \therefore \ XB = OB \cot \phi$$

$$= R \cot \phi \ (OB \text{ is the radius}).$$

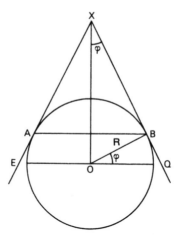

Fig. 6.1 Simple conic projection

Construction

The following steps describe the method of drawing up a simple conic.

(a) Draw the central meridian.

(b) From vertex X draw in the standard parallel as a segment of a circle, radius XB being $R \cot \phi$.

(c) From the vertex draw the meridians cutting the standard parallel at uniform spacing. This spacing is calculated from

$$\frac{\text{ch long}}{360} \times 2\pi R \cos \phi.$$

(d) Mark off the positions for placing the remaining parallels along the central meridian. As the length of the meridian is $2\pi R$, the spacing is

$$\frac{\text{ch lat}}{360} \times 2\pi R.$$

Thus, all parallels are at a constant distance from each other just as they are on the reduced earth. Draw in the parallels to complete the graticule.

Properties

Scale

The scale is correct along the standard parallel and all the meridians. It is too large along the other parallels, increasing with distance away from the standard parallel.

Orthomorphism

As all the meridians are drawn as straight lines to the parallels from a common point, they cut each parallel at 90° and one requirement of orthomorphism is met. But as the scale variation from a point is not the same in all directions, the chart is not orthomorphic.

Convergency
As the meridians are drawn as straight lines, the convergency is constant throughout the chart.

Constant of the cone (n)
What determines the actual value of the convergency on a conical chart? It will be seen in Fig. 6.2 that when the cone covering the surface of the reduced earth is unwrapped, the paper containing the graticule is not a full circle but only a sector of a circle. In Fig. 6.2, AB is the standard parallel, starting from the Greenwich meridian and going round the earth and back to the Greenwich meridian. But the angle through which it represents the earth's 360° is in fact less than 360° and this is the measure of its convergency.

The ratio of the angle subtended by the arc AB to the length of the same latitude on the earth is called the constant of the cone. Its value varies from 0 for a Mercator (Mercator may be considered as an extreme case of a cone, having an apex angle of 0°) to the value 1 on polar stereographic (which may be considered the other extremity of the cone, having an angle of 180° at the apex). For a simple cone it will therefore remain between 0 and 1, the actual value being dependent on the chosen standard parallel.

The value of the constant of the cone, n, may be ascertained from a comparison of the length of the standard parallel to the actual length on the earth.

The length of a parallel on the earth is equal to $2\pi R \cos \phi$. As the standard parallel is correct to scale:

$$2\pi R \cot \phi \times n = 2\pi R \cos \phi$$

and
$$n = \frac{2\pi R \cos \phi}{2\pi R \cot \phi}$$

$$= \frac{\cos \phi}{\cot \phi}$$

but
$$\cot \phi = \frac{\cos \phi}{\sin \phi}$$

∴
$$n = \frac{\cos \phi \sin \phi}{\cos \phi}$$

$$= \sin \phi$$

where ϕ is the standard parallel.

Thus, the convergence on this projection is the sine of the standard parallel. For a standard parallel of say 50°N, the chart convergence is sin 50° = 0.7660 and the angular inclination between two meridians 10° apart anywhere on the chart will measure 7.660°.

Fig. 6.2   Constant of the cone

The geometric conic can be mathematically modified by placing the parallels using the *orthomorphic* formula instead of placing them at a constant distance. This would produce a strict orthomorphic projection. But in our syllabus we are primarily interested in the orthomorphic based on the two standard parallel conic and we will talk about this now.

Conic with two standard parallels

As the title of the projection suggests, two parallels are drawn correctly to scale by means of a secant cone which is a cone imagined to cut the reduced earth's surface along two parallels of latitude as shown in Fig. 6.3.

Consequently, the scale between the two standard parallels contracts and the scale outside the standard parallels expands, see Fig. 6.3. The meridians are drawn in as straight lines radiating from the cone's vertex. The spacing of the parallels along the meridians gives true scale along the meridians.

The chart is not orthomorphic as the scale variation requirement is not met. However, since we have two parallels on the projection giving correct scale, the accuracy of the mapped area as well as the coverage itself is better than the simple conic. Countries having an east–west extent rather than a north–south one may be mapped on this projection. Maps of the UK (ch lat 10°) have been successfully made on this projection for atlases. However, the projection is not much used, as the modification given below is preferred.

Lambert's orthomorphic projection with two standard parallels

We saw earlier that on a conic with two standard parallels there is a scale contraction between the standard parallels and expansion outside them. Thus, the scale along the parallels varies from one parallel to the next whereas the scale along the meridians remains constant. To make the chart orthomorphic, the meridian scale must be modified in such a way that at any point along a meridian the scale is equal to the scale of the parallel pass-

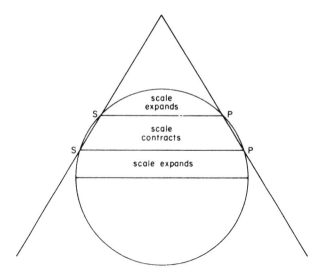

Fig. 6.3 Secant cone

ing through that point. Lambert achieved this by use of his orthomorphic formula. The radius of each parallel is calculated from this formula and drawn in as an arc of a circle from a common centre (the apex). The two standard parallels are then divided to give a uniform meridian spacing using the formula so well known to us by now,

$$\frac{\text{ch long}}{360} \times 2\pi R,$$

and the meridians are inserted as straight lines.

Properties

Orthomorphism
The projection is orthomorphic by construction.

Where is the scale correct?
The scale is correct along the two standard parallels. This means that the scale is the same as on the reduced earth.

How does the scale vary?
It contracts in between the two standard parallels and expands outside the standard parallels, Fig. 6.4.

Thus a span of say one inch on the dividers measuring 5 nm along a standard parallel will measure more than 5 nm inside the two parallels, the maximum distance being measured (approximately) at a point midway between the two. This is the chart's parallel of origin. Similarly, outside the standard parallels it will measure less than 5 nm. In terms of representative

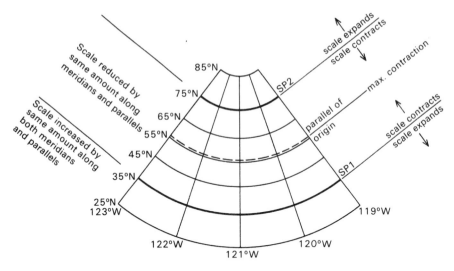

Fig. 6.4   Scale variation on a Lambert's

fractions, if the scale was given as, say, 1:250 000, this is true for the two standard parallels. The denominator will be greater than 250 000 inside the two standard parallels and smaller to the outside.

Outside the standard parallels, the expansion towards the poles is not in the same proportion as towards the equator. The rate of expansion towards the poles is slightly higher than towards the equator. However, this distinction is of technical interest only. In fact, on some large-scale charts e.g. 1:1 000 000 in spite of the foregoing discussion the scale error is so small that for all practical purposes the chart is considered to be a constant scale chart. The printed graduated scale line on one million training charts emphasises the point. This scale variation does become important as the chart scale becomes smaller. On a six million chart different graduated scale lines for different latitudes may be given and distance measurements must be carried out like Mercator.

Convergence
On Lambert's the value of convergence between two given meridians is given in the formula:

$$\text{convergence} = n \times \text{ch long}$$

where n is the sine of the parallel of origin. Parallel of origin, or n, is a factor in the orthomorphic formula upon which the mathematical adjustment is based. Parallel of origin occurs in a position slightly displaced towards the pole from the parallel midway between two standard parallels. Its position is shown in Fig. 6.4. Value of n, however, is printed on the chart, but in the absence of this information, as pointed out above, the sine of the mid-latitude of the two standard parallels may be used for calculating the convergence.

Example

Find convergence on a Lambert's projection between 119°W and 123°W at 43°N, given 55°N is the parallel of origin (Fig. 6.4).

$$C = \text{ch long} \times n$$
$$= 4 \times 0.8192$$
$$= 3.2768°$$

Referring back to Fig. 6.4, it will be noticed that the convergence between the same two meridians, that is 119°W and 123°W at any other latitude, say, 40°N will still be the same value of 3.2768°. In other words, on a Lambert's, convergence is constant, its value depending on the value of n.

Next question is, is convergence correct? Well, if convergence is constant, it cannot be correct, because the earth's convergency varies as sine of the latitude. In the above example at parallel of origin (55°N) the earth convergency is

$$C = \text{ch long} \times \text{sin lat}$$
$$= 4° \times 0.8192$$
$$= 3.2768°$$

which is the same value as on Lambert's. The reason is, on a Lambert's the *convergence is shown correct only at the parallel of origin*. At 40°N the earth convergency:

$$C = \text{ch long} \times \sin 40°$$
$$= 4° \times 0.6428$$
$$= 2.5712°$$

whereas on Lambert's the convergence at 40°N is still 3.2768°, which is too high. Similarly, towards the pole from the parallel of origin, the chart convergency is too low.

To summarise, chart convergence is constant but not correct anywhere on the projection except at the parallel of origin. Towards the equator the chart convergence is too high; towards the poles it is too low.

Great circles

Say, a straight line is drawn on the earth, joining position A (55°N 123°W) to position B (55°N 119°W). The convergency between A and B on the earth is $4 \times 0.8192 = 3.3°$. On a chart, if a straight line is to be a great circle, the two positions must produce the same chart convergence as on the earth. Thus, a line joining A and B on the chart will be a great circle. Elsewhere on the chart, the convergence between any two places will be different from that on the earth and such a straight line will not be a great circle. A great circle, away from the parallel of origin appears as a curve, concave to the parallel of origin. As the difference between earth convergency and chart convergency increases with distance from the parallel of origin, so must the deviation between a straight line and great circle. However, for practical purposes, a straight line drawn on a Lambert may be considered to be a great circle. See Fig. 6.5.

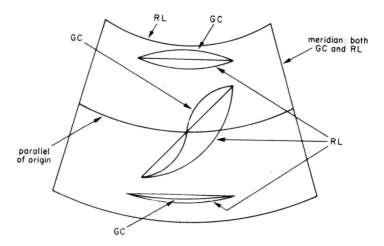

Fig. 6.5   Rhumb lines and great circles

Further, since the convergence on the chart is different from that on the earth (except at the parallel of origin) a radio wave travelling a great circle path will make different angles on the earth and on the chart at a given meridian. Let us take an example. A radio wave leaves position 43°15′N 07°30′W on a bearing of 078° and crosses 10°E at 44°36′N.

The angle made by the radio wave at 10°E on the earth is

$$C = \text{ch long} \times \text{sin mean lat}$$
$$= 17.5° \times \sin 4355\tfrac{1}{2}$$
$$= 17.5° \times 0.6936$$
$$= 12.14°$$
∴   Bearing on the earth $= 078° + 12.14°$
$$= 090.14°$$

On a Lambert with parallel of origin, say, at 58°N, the bearing:

$$\text{convergence} = \text{ch long} \times \text{n}$$
$$= 17.5° \times \sin 58$$
$$= 14.84°$$
and the bearing measured $\qquad = 078° + 14.84°$
$$= 092.84°$$

Rhumb lines
Rhumb lines cut all meridians at the same angle. Therefore they will appear as curves concave to the pole, taking on the same curve direction as the parallels which are themselves rhumb lines by definition. Meridians are both GCs and RLs, so is the equator.

Fig. 6.5 shows the relationship between a straight line, rhumb line and a great circle.

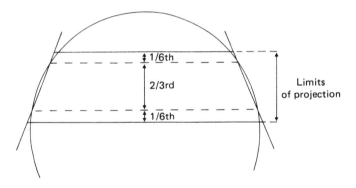

Fig. 6.6   Standard parallels

Shapes

Provided the north–south coverage is not excessive and a careful choice of the standard parallels is made, shapes are sensibly preserved over the whole area.

Fits

Sheets will fit north/south and east/west if the scale and the standard parallels are the same. Also, a particular sheet of chart you are using need not have standard parallels on it. It may be a section of a larger projection.

Spacing of the standard parallels

If the scale of a projection is so adjusted that the maximum scale reduction on it equals approximately the maximum scale expansion, the overall scale error will be small. If the overall error does not exceed anywhere about 1% or so, the chart is considered to be a constant scale chart.

By placing the standard parallels about two-thirds of the total north–south coverage, that is, about 1/6th from the northern and the southern limits of the coverage, an even distribution of the scale error is achieved over the complete projection. The standard parallels on the Lambert's orthomorphic projection are placed according to this rule, see Fig. 6.6.

Limitations of Lambert's projection

As explained earlier, the limitation of the projection lies in the north–south coverage. A good scale will be available and orthomorphism will remain intact as long as the ch lat between the two standard parallels is not too large. The greater the latitude difference between the two standard parallels the greater the scale error and distortion of the shapes. And if the shapes are greatly distorted, so are directions, with a loss of orthomorphism.

Uses of Lambert's projection

This projection is increasingly being used as a plotting chart. Its other uses are as topographical charts, radio aid charts, airways charts and meteorological synoptic charts.

Plotting on Lambert's projection

(1) When measuring a track, use the mid-meridian between two points, and use this track angle to calculate the heading. This will be the mean great circle track, and also the rhumb line track as the measurement at the mid-point of a tangent to the curving RL track will almost be the same as the straight line GC track.

(2) As always, use the latitude scale for measuring distance, *keeping the habit of* measuring in the area where the line is.

(3) When finding W/V, the track and GS method is simpler. This method must be used when finding winds on a track which has a large E–W component (maximum convergency is experienced). If the air plot method is used, measure the wind angle from the meridian nearest the fix.

(4) Bearings given by the station (QTE, QDM, QDR) and VOR bearings are measured at the station and plotted from the station meridian. Therefore, no correction for convergence is called for. Where the work is done at the aircraft (ADF bearings), bearings are measured with reference to the meridian at the aircraft's position involving the aircraft's heading. Such bearings must be corrected for convergence *before* obtaining the reciprocal to plot from the station. Alternatively, the aircraft's DR meridian may be transferred to the station position, and the bearings plotted from the transferred meridian without correction for convergence.

Examples

Hdg	045		Hdg	045
Rel Brg	100		Rel Brg	100
GC Brg	145(T)		GC Brg	145(T)
Convergence	+ 2 (Towards eq)			−180
	147		Plot	325° from station position
	−180			with reference to the
Plot	327° from station position			aircraft's transferred
				meridian.

Practice problems: Lambert's chart

(1) Aircraft in DR position 43°N 81°W obtains QDM 173°, from station A (39°N 84°W) where variation is 36°E. What would you plot?

Answer: 029°.

(2) Aircraft on heading 270°(T) in DR position 46°N 84°W obtains relative bearing 239° from station 40°N 81°W. What would you plot?

Answer: 331°.

(3) Aircraft in DR position 69°30′S 65°W obtains QDM 277° from station at 71°S 70°W. Variation at a/c position 19°W; mean variation 22°W, variation at station 25°W. What would you plot?

Answer: 072°.

(4) Aircraft in DR position 72°S 66°W on heading 359°(T) obtains relative bearing 335°, from station at 68°S 70°W. What would you plot?

Answer: 158°.

(5) Aircraft on heading 090°(T) in DR position 69°S 68°W
   (a) obtains relative bearing 090° from station at 72°S 68°W. What would you plot?
   (b) obtains relative bearing 359° from station 69°S 64°W. What would you plot?
   (c) obtains QDM 045° from station 69°S 64°W. Variation 20° at the station, 24° at the aircraft, mean variation 22°, all variations are easterly. What would you plot?

Answers: (a) 360°
         (b) 265°
         (c) 245°.

Chapter 7
POLAR STEREOGRAPHIC PROJECTION

This is a zenithal perspective projection, with a light source at one pole and the plane of projection tangential to the other pole (Fig. 7.1). It is conformal.

Since all 360° on the earth around the Pole are represented on paper by 360°, the constant of the cone, n, is 1, if you care to consider it that way.

Construction
On the sheet on which the graticule is to be drawn, select a convenient point to represent the pole, i.e. the point which is tangential to the model earth in the basic concept of the projection.

From the point, draw in radial lines representing meridians at an angular spacing equal to the actual ch long.

With the Pole as centre, draw the circles of parallels. As may be seen from Fig. 7.1, where x is the co-latitude of each parallel, the radius of each parallel is calculated from the formula:

$$\text{Radius} = 2R \tan \tfrac{1}{2}\text{co-lat}$$

where R is the radius of the model earth. This model earth radius in practice is derived from the earth's actual radius of 250 000 000 inches divided by the scale required.

Appearance of the graticule
It will be noticed that a coverage of more than 90° of latitude can be achieved; see the graticule shown overleaf in Fig. 7.2.

Properties

Scale
The scale is correct at the pole. The distances measured very close to the pole are very nearly correct distances. Away from the pole the scale expands at the rate of $\sec^2 (x/2)$, where x is the co-latitude (90° − lat). Thus, although near the pole the scale may be considered to be constant, elsewhere distance measurements must be made with reference to the latitude scale as on a Mercator.

Although the scale varies from point to point, at any given point the scale is the same in all directions and this valuable asset will be recognised as one

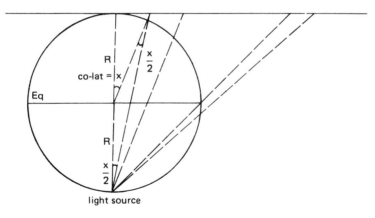

Fig. 7.1   Principle of projection

of the requirements of orthomorphism. We will now see how the scale varies north–south and east–west from a point.

First, the scale along a parallel will be considered. To get an idea of the scale expansion, we can simply compare the length of a parallel projected on the chart with the length of the same parallel on the earth.

The radius of a parallel on the polar stereographic is given as $2R \tan(x/2)$. Multiply this by 2π, that is, $2\pi \times 2R \tan(x/2)$, and this is its circumference, or the total length. The total length of a parallel on the earth is $2\pi R \cos \phi$, where ϕ is the given parallel. As $2\pi R$ occurs on both sides, we can compare $2\tan(x/2)$ with $\cos \phi$.

				Projection	Earth
lat, ϕ	x	$\dfrac{x}{2}$	$\tan \dfrac{x}{2}$	$2\tan \dfrac{x}{2}$	$\cos \phi$
80°	10°	5°	0.087 49	0.174 98	0.173 65
70°	20°	10°	0.176 33	0.352 65	0.342 02
60°	30°	15°	0.267 94	0.535 90	0.500 00

The ratio of the projected length to the length on the earth is the measure of the scale expansion or the exaggeration. Let us take 60° as an illustration.

$$\text{Exaggeration} = \frac{0.535\,90}{0.5} = 1.071\,80$$

(Note: the expansion we worked out just now is the same as that obtained directly from use of the scale factor mentioned above, that is, $\sec^2 (x/2)$.) This shows that anywhere along 60° the scale expansion occurs at the rate 1.071 80.

We will now take any point on 60°N and calculate the scale from this point for an extremely small distance in the north–south direction. Extremely small though they must be, being limited to conventional mathematics, we will calculate the distance along the meridian from 60°02′N to 59°58′N.

The expansion along a meridian may be given by the relationship:

$$\frac{\text{length of the meridian between two parallels}}{\text{length of the meridian between the same parallels on earth}}$$

We know that the length of a meridian on the earth is

$$\frac{\text{ch lat}}{360} \times 2\pi R;$$

the length on the projection is simply the difference between the radius of the two parallels.

$$\frac{\text{dist. on projection}}{\text{dist. on the earth}} = \frac{2R\left(\tan\dfrac{x'}{2} - \tan\dfrac{x''}{2}\right)}{2\pi R \dfrac{\phi' - \phi''}{360}}$$

$$= \frac{\tan\dfrac{x'}{2} - \tan\dfrac{x''}{2}}{\dfrac{\pi(\phi' - \phi'')}{360}}$$

We will work the numerator first and for sake of accuracy, use 9 figures.

$$\phi' = 60°02'; \; x' = 29°58' \frac{x'}{2} = 14°59'$$

$$\phi'' = 59°58'; \; x'' = 30°02' \frac{x''}{2} = 15°01'$$

Numerator
$$\begin{aligned}
\tan 15°01' &= 0.268\,260\,988 \\
\tan 14°59' &= 0.267\,637\,442 \\
\text{subtract} &= 0.000\,623\,546
\end{aligned}$$

Denominator $\phi' - \phi'' = 4' = 0.066\,66°$

$$\frac{\pi \times 0.066\,66}{360} = 0.000\,581\,771$$

$$\frac{\textit{Numerator}}{\textit{Denominator}} = \frac{0.000\,623\,546}{0.000\,581\,771}$$

$$= 1.071\,80$$

This compares with the result we got earlier and clearly shows that the scale at 60°N is the same in all directions. If you now do the same exercise for another parallel, say, 60°02′, you will work in entirely different sets of figures but the conclusion will be the same.

Because the scale expansion away from the poles is at the rate of sec^2 (half co-lat), the scale factor will have increased to 2 at the equator.

Orthomorphism
Since scale varies in the same proportion just noted in all directions from a given point i.e. along the meridians and parallels, and since meridians and parallels cut each other at right angles, the chart is orthomorphic.

Convergency
On the chart this is the value of ch long, or 1 (one) degree of ch long is shown on the chart by 1° angular difference. On the earth this difference exists only at the Poles, and only there on the chart is convergency correct. Elsewhere on the earth, convergency reduces towards the equator, where it is 0; so chart convergency is constant at 1, correct only at the Poles, too large away from the Pole.

Great circle
This cannot be a straight line, since convergency is not correct. However, when plotting in high latitudes not too far away from the Pole where convergency is correct, a GC is taken to be a straight line for practical purposes. As distance from the Pole increases, a GC in fact curves concave to the Pole, and finally the equator, itself a GC, will appear as a distinct curve. Rather an academic point for a chart used for aviation in the polar regions, perhaps. A straight line drawn on a polar stereographic chart is sometimes referred to as a stereodrome.

Rhumb line
This is a curve concave to the Pole. Parallels of latitude are demonstrative.

Equal area
Only very nearly for small areas; from the properties of scale and convergency already mentioned, it is clear that the chart cannot be equal area.

Plotting radio bearings
Because a straight line approximates to a GC, QTEs, QDMs, radio bearings *et al.* may be plotted direct from the meridian of the station, after the usual resolution into the bearing True which the station measured.

ADF bearings, though, measured from the aircraft's meridian, must be resolved into an angle to be plotted from the station's meridian. Convergency must be applied before the reciprocal is found, its value being ch long.

Problems
Since convergency is 1, the sums are of no real profundity, only off-putting because the chart is not widely familiar. Simple sketches which are easily drawn for this projection provide a quick appreciation of how best to solve a particular problem.

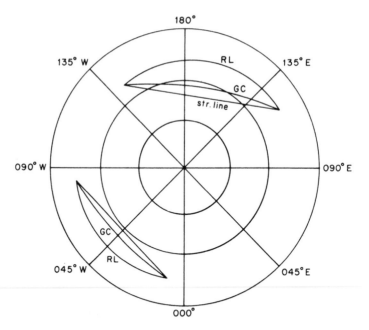

Fig. 7.2   Rhumb lines and great circles

(1)   What is the approximate GC bearing of B (71°N 50°E) which would be found by measuring the direction of A (71°N 90°E) on a straight line joining A to B? (See Fig. 7.3.)

   The mean approximate GC bearing must be measured at the mid-meridian, as in Fig. 7.3. Both places are on the same parallel.

> Convergency between A and B is ch long   = 40°
> ∴convergency between mean meridian and A = 20°
> and GC bearing of B from A = 270 + 20   = 290°

(2)   What is the highest latitude a straight line from A (70°N 00°E/W) to B (70°N 80°W) will attain?

The distance, pole to A is 20 × 60 = 1200 nm; call it PA.
The distance, pole to B is similarly 1200 nm; call it PB.
Let C be the bisector of the line AB.
Join PC (pole to the point C).
Then distance PC represents the highest latitude – draw a little sketch.

∠PAC is 50° (angle BPA = ch long = 80°; ∴∠CPA is 40°, which makes ∠PAC = 50°) and knowing the distance PA,

$$PC = (1200 \sin 50°)\, nm$$
$$= 919\, nm \quad \text{from the pole.}$$

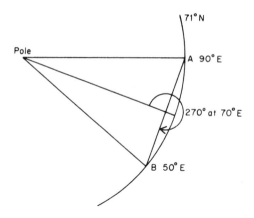

Fig. 7.3   Finding great circle bearing

Converting this into degrees and minutes, 919 nm is equivalent to 15°19′ and the latitude of C = 90° − 15°19′ = 74°41′N.

(3)   What is the convergency between A (75°N 60°W) and B (75°N 10°W):
   (a)   on the earth
   (b)   on the Polar stereographic?

   Answer (a) 48°29′; (b) 50°.

Chapter 8
TRANSVERSE AND OBLIQUE MERCATOR PROJECTIONS

These are modified cylindrical projections like a Mercator's but differing from Mercator in that the cylinder is presumed to be tangential anywhere but at the equator.

In the case of the transverse Mercator the cylinder is presumed to be tangential to a chosen meridian and its anti-meridian, while in the oblique Mercator the cylinder is tangential to any great circle (other than the equator or a meridian and its anti-meridian). It is convenient to take the projections separately.

Transverse Mercator

In the transverse Mercator, the meridian to which the cylinder is tangential is called the Central Meridian (CM). The point where CM and the equator intersect is called the point of origin (Fig. 8.1).

Principle of construction

A cylinder is presumed to be wrapped round the reduced earth (model globe reduced to the scale), being tangential to a chosen meridian with a light source at the centre of the earth. The graticule resulting from such arrangement is modified mathematically to give orthomorphism. In practice, the chart is constructed mathematically throughout. A point to be projected on the chart is resolved in terms of N/S (N or S of the equator) and E/W (E or W of the central meridian) co-ordinates and these co-ordinates (normally in inches) are then plotted on the graticule.

Suppose point A in Fig. 8.1 is to be plotted on transverse Mercator graticule (Fig. 8.2). A GC is drawn up in the first instance from G passing through A to intersect CM at 90° at C. 0 is the point of origin and G is a point on the equator, 90° removed from 0. Now, if you think of the curve GAC in terms of a meridian on a Mercator, with pole at G, you will appreciate that when the cylinder is unwrapped A will appear at A^1. Similarly if there was another point B on the same GC it will appear at B^1. If you are wondering why on an ordinary Mercator no such GC are plotted initially, the reason is that point A on an ordinary Mercator would be on a meridian which is

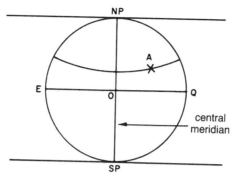

Fig. 8.1   Principle of projection

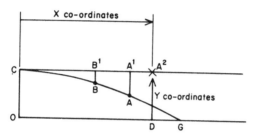

Fig. 8.2   Means of construction

already a GC by definition, whereas A on this projection is on a parallel of latitude which only represents rhumb line distances.

The shifting of A on the earth to position A^1 on the chart causes expansion of the scale in the N/S direction (exactly as the meridians expanded in E/W direction on an ordinary Mercator). This expansion must be compensated by extending the distance CA^1 to CA^2 to obtain orthomorphism. This extension is calculated mathematically. The co-ordinates to be plotted are: CA^2 (called X co-ordinates) and DA^2 (called Y co-ordinates).

Graticule

The appearance of the graticule for a transverse Mercator based on the 80°W meridian and its anti-meridian 100°E is shown in Fig. 8.3. Note that the central meridian appears as a straight line. It is a GC by definition. The two meridians 90° removed from the CM also appear as straight lines (10°E and 170°W in the figure). They are GC by definition as well as by construction. (In Fig. 8.2 notice that the curve of GC is projected as a straight line perpendicular to the CM.) The equator appears as a straight line – in three places, in between the two Poles and at two extremities where the projection provides full N/S coverage. Other parallels appear as ellipses, almost circles

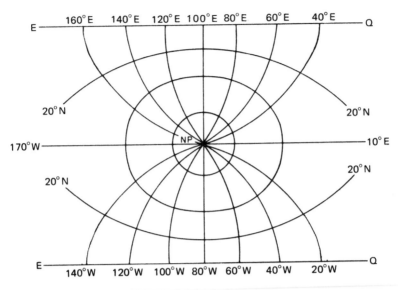

Fig. 8.3   Transverse Mercator graticule

near the Poles. Since on this projection both the meridians and the parallels (with exceptions as shown above) appear as curves perhaps this feature clearly distinguishes this projection from the ones we studied previously. This particular feature, however, may not be discernible on small sheets.

Just as on a Mercator, on this projection a point 90° removed from the point of origin in an E/W direction on the equator cannot be projected.

Properties

Orthomorphism
Yes, the meridians and the parallels cut each other at 90° and the scale variation from a given point is the same in E/W direction as in N/S direction by construction. This makes the chart orthomorphic.

Scale
The scale is correct along the datum meridian and its anti-meridian. Expands away from the datum meridian at the rate of secant of the great circle distance.

Convergency
Convergency is correct at the equator and the Poles. Elsewhere it is incorrect and as the meridians are curved, no simple formula can be given for chart convergence. However, up to 900 miles from the datum meridian the error is very small and may be neglected for all practical purposes.

Great circles
Any straight line which cuts the central meridian at 90° is a great circle by construction. Elsewhere, great circles are curves concave to the datum

meridian and anti-meridian giving complex curves. For practical purposes any straight line drawn near the datum meridian may be taken to represent a GC.

Rhumb line
All meridians and parallels are rhumb lines. Examine how they appear in Fig. 8.3. Elsewhere a rhumb line is a curve concave to the nearer pole.

Shapes
These are correct for small areas.

Fits
You can attach another chart to your chart if the track goes beyond your chart coverage, but only in the N/S directions and provided both charts have the same central meridian and the same scale. There is a rolling fit in E/W directions for two charts of the same scale.

Uses
The projection is quite accurate up to about 300 nm of the datum meridian. This makes it ideal for use as topographical maps of countries having large N/S extent (Korea, Finland, UK). The projection is not suitable for use as plotting chart due to curving meridians and parallels, except in the polar regions where the meridians are still straight lines.

Oblique Mercator

If the standard Mercator chart is treated as the special case of a modified cylindrical projection with the cylinder tangential to the equator, and the transverse Mercator just described in preceding paragraphs as the special case with the cylinder tangential to a chosen meridian (and its anti-meridian), then the oblique Mercator is the general case with the cylinder tangential to any other great circle. In aviation, the chosen great circle will frequently represent a particular great circle route between two important air terminals.

Principle of construction
A cylinder is presumed to be wrapped around the reduced earth of the required scale and tangential to the chosen datum great circle (Fig. 8.4). A convenient point on this great circle is selected as the datum point from which the mathematical modification of the graticule will be made to give orthomorphism.

From the datum point the x, y co-ordinates of all graticule intersections are then determined as:

(1) x co-ordinate – the perpendicular great circle distance from the datum great circle;
(2) y co-ordinate – the distance from the perpendicular (1) to the datum point.

The oblique Mercator graticule is then constructed by plotting the y co-

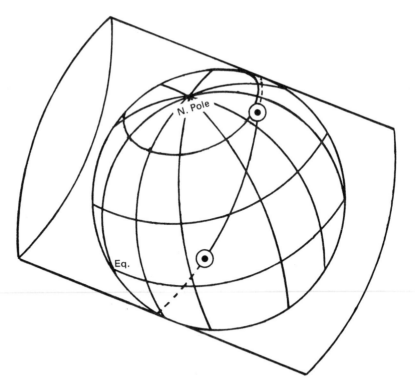

Fig. 8.4   Construction of oblique Mercator

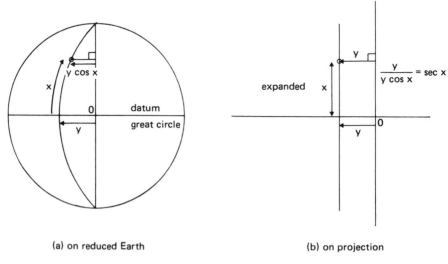

(a) on reduced Earth

(b) on projection

Fig. 8.5   Plotting x and y co-ordinates

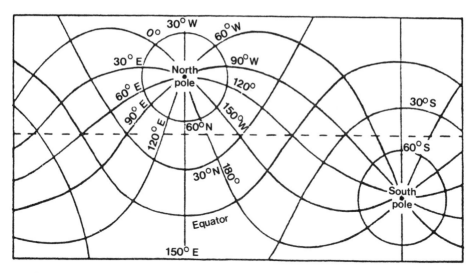

Fig. 8.6   Oblique Mercator graticule

ordinate and the mathematically expanded x co-ordinate (calculated by using the meridional parts for a sphere) on a rectangular grid (Fig. 8.5). The resulting projection is then orthomorphic by construction.

Graticule

The appearance of the graticule over a large area is illustrated in Fig. 8.6, which is applicable to a datum great circle AB of which the pole is located at 40°N 30°W and as such, has its vertex at 50°N 150°E and crosses the equator at 120°W and 60°E. Only the meridian passing through the pole of the datum great circle is a straight line. All other meridians are curves concave to the datum great circle. Their spacing along the datum great circle is the same as the spacing on the reduced earth. Parallels of latitude are complex curves, intersecting the meridians at 90°. Their spacing along the datum meridian is the same as it is on the reduced earth. The equator is sinusoidal and symmetrical about the datum great circle.

Properties

Orthomorphism
The meridians and parallels intersect at 90° and the scale has been made the same in all directions about a point by the method of construction. The chart is therefore orthomorphic (conformal).

Scale
The scale is correct along the datum great circle. Away from the datum great circle, scale varies as secant 'x' where 'x' is the great circle distance (converted to arc) away from the datum great circle.

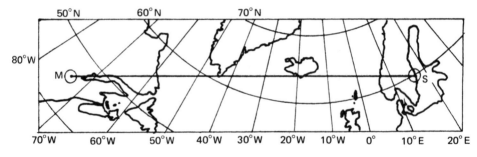

Fig. 8.7   Oblique Mercator route chart

Convergency
May be assumed to be reasonably correct close to the datum great circle, i.e. within a distance of about 700 nm, where the scale error is small.

Great circles
These are curves concave to the datum great circle. Great circles intersecting the datum great circle at 90° will be straight lines.

Rhumb lines
These are complex curves.

Shapes
Correct for small areas.

Uses
The main advantage of this projection is that it enables one uninterrupted projection coverage to be produced for a long great circle route at a practically constant scale. In Fig. 8.7 a strip chart shows that part of the great circle route from Montreal (M) to Stockholm (S).

If a strip chart on oblique Mercator projection for, say, 500 nm (i.e. 8°20′ of great circle distance) on either side of a required great circle route is constructed, it is difficult by mere visual inspection to distinguish it from a Lambert's or a Polar Stereographic. Within the scope of such a chart area it is realistic to assume for all practical purposes that great circles are straight lines and that scale and convergency are correct.

Test questions
(1)   The transverse Mercator projection is
    (a)   conformal and convergency is correct everywhere
    (b)   conformal and convergency is correct along all lines (great circles) at 90° to the central and anti-meridians
    (c)   not conformal and convergency is not correct anywhere.
(2)   The oblique Mercator projection
    (a)   is constant scale
    (b)   has scale increasing away from the datum great circle

    (c)   has scale decreasing away from the datum great circle.

(3) All meridians and parallels intersect at 90° on
    (a)   the transverse Mercator but not on the oblique Mercator
    (b)   the oblique Mercator but not on the transverse Mercator
    (c)   both the transverse and oblique Mercators.

(4) On an oblique Mercator, scale error is negligible for practical aviation purposes (i.e. less than 2%) within a distance from the datum great circle of
    (a)   70 nm
    (b)   700 nm
    (c)   1700 nm.

(5) A transverse Mercator projection would be most suitable for a topographical map of
    (a)   Chile
    (b)   Canada/USA border
    (c)   Mediterranean coastlines.

(6) An oblique Mercator projection is most suitable for
    (a)   long rhumb line routes
    (b)   long great circle routes
    (c)   long routes in quadrantal directions (NE, SE, SW, NW).

Chapter 9
GRID TECHNIQUE

In previous chapters we discussed Mercator, Lambert, Polar Stereographic and Transverse Mercator projections. Each one has certain advantages and disadvantages. Mercator is ideal for flying constant track angles but this involves flying RL distances. Further, radio bearings cannot be plotted directly. These two disadvantages practically disappear on Lambert and Polar Stereographic, but the pilot has to contend with changing tracks due to convergency of the meridians on the chart. Ideally we want a chart on which a straight line is a great circle, scale is considered constant and the meridians do not converge. No projection could provide all these properties together. However, by gridding a Lambert or a Polar Stereographic (and a Transverse Mercator in polar regions) we could combine all these on a single chart.

The first step towards gridding a chart is to select a suitable meridian as the *Datum*. The grid meridians are then drawn up parallel to and at a constant distance from the datum meridian. We now have two sets of directions on the chart: geographical meridians indicating true north and grid meridians indicating grid north (Fig. 9.1).

Convergence of meridians
It will be noticed in Fig. 9.1 that only one grid meridian (i.e. datum) coincides with true meridian; away from the datum there is an angular difference between the two, the difference increasing with distance from the datum. This angular difference between True North and Grid North is called Convergence.

Relationship between TN and GN
Where the track starts at the datum meridian, the Grid track and True track will be the same initially. The grid track, however, will remain the same throughout the flight. Where a flight commences elsewhere e.g. from A to B in Fig. 9.1, it is necessary to establish the relationship between grid and true tracks. Positions A and B are reproduced in Fig. 9.2, showing the disposition of directions grid and true north. The grid track in both cases is 090° and if the convergence at A and B is, say, 5°, true track at A is 085° and at B 095°. This relationship may be expressed in the following formula, the convention being,

Fig. 9.1   Grid meridians

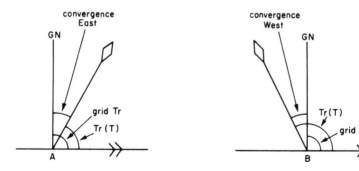

Fig. 9.2   East and west convergence

Where true north lies to East of Grid North, Convergence is East
Where true north lies to West of Grid North, Convergence is West

Direction True $\begin{array}{c} + \text{ Convergence E} \\ - \text{ Convergence W} \end{array}$ = Direction Grid

and, Direction Grid $\begin{array}{c} + \text{ Convergence W} \\ - \text{ Convergence E} \end{array}$ = Direction True

Example
Heading Grid is 150°, Convergence 10°W, What is Heading True?

$$\begin{aligned} \text{Hdg(T)} &= \text{Hdg(G)} + \text{Convergence W} \\ &= 150 + 10 \\ &= 160° \text{ (see Fig. 9.3)} \end{aligned}$$

Fig. 9.3   Converting heading from grid to true

Problems

(1)   Hdg(T) is 258°, Convergence 20°E, What is Hdg(G)?

Answer: 278°.

(2)   Hdg(G) is 040°, Hdg(T) is 065°, What is the convergence?

Answer: 25°W.

Grivation and Isogrivs

We established the relationship between GN and TN in the preceding section. However, in mid-latitudes, aircraft still steer by magnetic compass and therefore it is necessary to establish the relationship between GN and MN as well. The angle between TN and MN is variation. The angle between GN and MN is called Grid Variation, abbreviated to *Grivation*. Its value for any particular place is obtained from the lines of equal grivation, called *Isogrivs*. Isogrivs might be printed on a gridded chart or they may be added to such chart by plotting co-ordinates from simple calculation. As regards grivation, the convention is:

If MN lies to East of Grid North, Grivation is East.
If MN lies to West of Grid North, Grivation is West.

From Fig. 9.4 we establish the relationship in the following formula:

$$\text{Grid Direction} = \text{Magnetic Direction} \begin{array}{l} + \text{ Grivation E} \\ - \text{ Grivation W} \end{array}$$

Thus, by measuring the Grid heading and applying local Grivation, magnetic heading to steer is obtained.

Grivation is the algebraic sum of convergence and variation
In Fig. 9.4(a),

$$\text{Grivation} = 20°E + 15°E$$
$$= 35°E$$

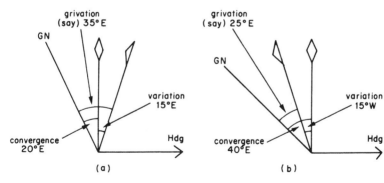

Fig. 9.4 Applying grivation

In Fig. 9.4(b),

$$\text{Grivation} = 40°\text{E} + 15°\text{W}$$
$$= 25°\text{E}$$

When converting one heading to another, from above diagram, we establish the following rule:

$$\text{Hdg(M)} \begin{matrix} + \text{E Var} \\ - \text{W Var} \end{matrix} = \text{Hdg(T)} \begin{matrix} + \text{E Convergence} \\ - \text{W Convergence} \end{matrix} = \text{Hdg(G)}$$

In Fig. 9.4(a), if the magnetic heading is 075°,

the grid heading = 075° + 15°E(Var) = 090° Hdg(T) + 20°E (Conv)
= 110° Hdg(G)

If you are converting in the opposite direction, that is from Hdg(G) to Hdg(M), reverse the sign. E throughout is minus, W is plus. In Fig. 9.4(b), given Hdg(G) = 130°, then

Hdg(M) = 130 − 40 (E conv) = 090° Hdg(T) + 15° (W Var)
= 105° Hdg(M)

Alternatively, Hdg(M) may be converted directly to Hdg(G) and vice versa by application of Grivation. In Fig. 9.4(a),

Hdg(M) = 075° + 35 (E Griv) = 110° Hdg(G)

In Fig. 9.4(b)

Hdg(G) = 130° − 25 (E Griv) = 105° Hdg(M)

Construction of grid on Lambert's

Two steps are involved in the construction of grid on a plain chart: construction of grid itself and plotting the isogrivs.

Construction of grid is quite simple. Simply choose a convenient meridian

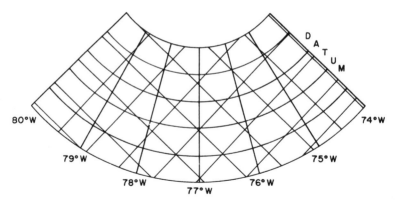

Fig. 9.5   Plotting a grid

as the datum meridian and draw up lines parallel to the datum at a convenient distance (usually 60 or 100 nm). It should be appreciated that only those charts could be gridded which are considered constant scale charts. Grid is completed by drawing up another set of parallel lines, same distance apart but at 90° to datum meridian if necessary for plotting purposes. The chart will then look like the one in Fig. 9.5.

Isogrivs contain two elements – variation and convergence. Variation lines (isogonals) are already on the chart. Therefore, in order to plot isogrivs, we will first need to draw up lines of convergence at 1° apart.

It will be remembered from the study of Lambert's that the convergence on this projection, (i.e. value of n) is always less than one. That is, one degree ch long on the earth will appear at a distance less than one degree on the chart. For gridding purposes, we must calculate the distance from datum where one degree convergence will occur. This will invariably occur beyond one degree ch long printed on the chart. The calculation is simply carried out by dividing 1° (that is 60 minutes) by the value of chart convergence, that is, n.

Say, chart convergence was given as n = 0.7488. Then, 1° convergence on the chart =

$$\frac{60}{0.7488} = 1°20.1'$$

Plot the first line of convergence on the chart at distance of 1°20.1' from the datum. For example, if the datum was Greenwich meridian, one degree convergence occurs at 01°20.1'W; two degree convergence at 02°40.2'W and so on. These lines are lightly drawn on the chart so that they can be removed when isogrivs are drawn.

Next step is to calculate the value of grivation individually at every point where the line of convergence intersects isogonals on the chart. Finally, points having the same value of grivation are joined up by a smooth curve to give isogrivs. (Fig. 9.6) The square grid is omitted for clarity.

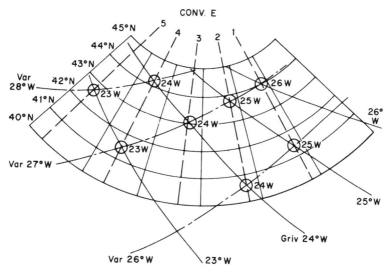

Fig. 9.6   Constructing isogrivs

Grid on polar charts

In polar regions, polar stereographic with a grid is generally used. A modified form of Lambert is also available and with its one standard parallel very near the pole it hardly differs from the other. Transverse Mercator may also be gridded in polar regions since meridians appear as straight lines radiating from the pole and curves of latitudes may be considered to be concentric. For all practical purposes near polar regions transverse Mercator may be considered to be a constant scale chart.

On these charts, convergence is 1; that is, one degree of ch long on the earth appears at 1° distance on the chart. This makes construction of the grid easy in that lines of convergence need not be first constructed. Thus, if the datum is Greenwich meridian, then parallels of grid lines will cut 30W at an angle of 30°, 60W at an angle of 60° and so on (see Fig. 9.7).

On a complete polar grid, the direction from NP along the Greenwich anti-meridian is generally the direction of Grid North. Therefore, at the North pole, instead of having all true directions south only, we have a complete compass rose with reference to grid direction. Study Fig. 9.8 to appreciate this.

As for the conversion of Grid value to True and reverse, since the value of n is 1 the conversion formula becomes

$$\text{Grid direction} = \text{True direction} \begin{array}{c} - \text{ Long E} \\ + \text{ Long W} \end{array}$$

and $$\text{True direction} = \text{Grid direction} \begin{array}{c} + \text{ Long E} \\ - \text{ Long W} \end{array}$$

For illustration, the Grid Heading of aircraft 2 in Fig. 9.8 is 225°

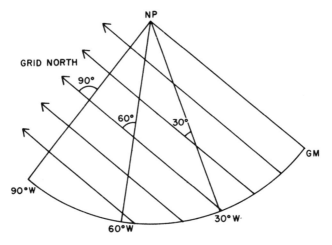

Fig. 9.7   Meridian relationship to grid north

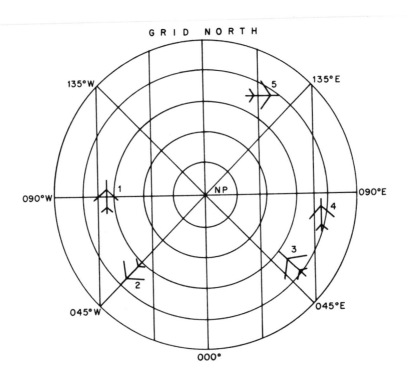

Grid Heading of aircraft	1 is 000
	2 is 225
	3 is 315
	4 is 000
	5 is 090

Fig. 9.8   Examples of grid headings

Its true heading   = 225 − 45 (Long W)
                    = 180°

True heading of aircraft 3 (heading along meridian to NP) is 360°. Therefore its Grid Heading   = 360 − 45 (Long E)
                              = 315°

These signs must be reversed in a South Polar Grid – See typical problem 3 below.

In the lower regions where the magnetic compass may still be used, isogrivs must be first constructed. These are again simpler since in this case the value of grivation is the value of ch long in whole degrees combined with the value of local variation.

Transverse Mercator outside polar regions

The task of gridding in such areas becomes difficult due to curving meridians. If it is necessary to grid such chart, convergence should be determined at numerous points all over the projection, before following up the normal steps.

Typical grid problems

(1) An aircraft in position 40°N 10°E has a magnetic heading of 150° and a grid heading of 170°. If variation is 10°W and n = 0.8, what is the datum meridian?

    (a)   Hdg(T) = 150 − 10°W (Variation)
                  = 140°

    (b)   Convergence = Hdg(G) − Hdg(T)
                         = 170 − 140
                         = 30°E (See Fig. 9.9)

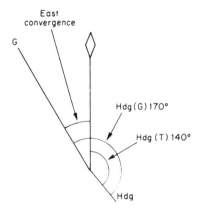

Fig. 9.9   Sketch for problem 1

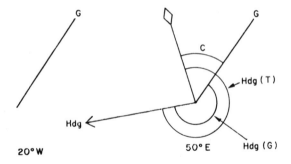

Fig. 9.10   Sketch for problem 2

(c)   Ch long from Datum = $\dfrac{\text{Convergence}}{n}$

$$= \frac{30}{0.8} = 37\tfrac{1}{2}°$$

(d)   Therefore Datum 10E + $37\tfrac{1}{2}$E

$$= 47\tfrac{1}{2}°E$$

(2)   Using Grid based on 20°W, what will be the magnetic heading of an aircraft in position 50°E, given variation 8W and n = 0.75. Grid heading of the aircraft is 224°.

(a)   Convergence = n × ch long

$$= 0.75 × 70$$
$$= 52\tfrac{1}{2}°\text{W (see Fig. 9.10)}$$

(b)   Hdg(T)   = Hdg(G) + Convergence W

$$= 224° + 52\tfrac{1}{2}°$$
$$= 276\tfrac{1}{2}°$$

(c)   Hdg(M)   = $276\tfrac{1}{2}°$ + 8°W (Variation)

$$= 284\tfrac{1}{2}°$$

(3)   An aircraft on south polar grid in position 75°S 20°W has a grid heading of 210°. What is its true heading?

Hdg(T) = Hdg(G) + Long W

$$= 210 + 20$$
$$= 230° \text{ (see Fig. 9.11)}$$

(4)   An aircraft on North polar grid is steering a true heading of 080°(T) and a grid heading of 140(G). What is its longitude?

$$\text{Hdg(G) = Hdg(T)} \begin{array}{l} - \text{E Long} \\ + \text{W Long} \end{array}$$

$$\therefore \text{Hdg(G)} - \text{Hdg(T)} = \begin{array}{l} - \text{Long E} \\ + \text{Long W} \end{array}$$

$$140 - 80$$
$$= +060$$
$$= 060W \text{ (see Fig. 9.12)}$$

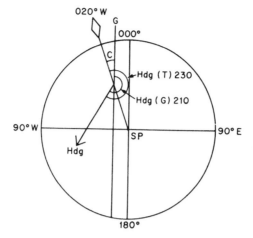

Fig. 9.11   Sketch for problem 3

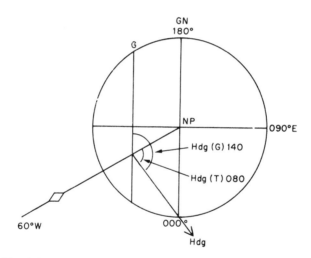

Fig. 9.12   Sketch for problem 4

Practice problems

(1)   Hdg(T) is 258°, Convergence 20°E; what is Hdg(G)?

Answer: 278°.

(2)   Hdg(G) is 040°, Hdg(T) 065°; what is the Convergence?

Answer: 25°W.

(3)   An aircraft on North Polar grid is steering a true heading of 080° and a grid heading of 140°. What is its longitude?

Answer: 60°W.

(4) An aircraft has a grid heading of 310° using a chart based on grid datum of 40°W. If the variation is 10°E, n = 0.8 and Hdg(M) 340°, what is the aircraft's longitude?

Answer: 10°E.

(5) Grid datum meridian is 50°W, n = 0.7, aircraft's position 50°N 20°W. If the grid heading is 257° what is the magnetic heading, given the variation is 8°W?

Answer: 286°.

Part 2
AIRCRAFT INSTRUMENTS

Chapter 10
AIRSPEED INDICATOR (ASI)

The principle of an Air Speed Indicator (ASI) is the measurement of two pressures called Static and Pitot pressures.

If you move an open ended tube through the air, pressure will be exerted at the closed end of the tube. This pressure is composed of two components. Firstly, that pressure which would be present at the closed end of the tube irrespective of whether the tube is stationary or moving. This is due to the atmospheric pressure and is called *static* pressure. The second component is the additional pressure entirely due to the tube's movement through the air. The faster the tube is moved, the greater the pressure that is exerted. This pressure is known as *dynamic* pressure. The sum total of the two components is known as *pitot* pressure. That *additional* or dynamic pressure mentioned above is the one representative of the air speed of the tube and the one we are interested in. But the pressure produced at the closed end of the tube is pitot pressure. Thus, to have an indication of the air speed it is merely a question of extracting dynamic from pitot pressure.

Pitot pressure, P, equals dynamic pressure, D, plus static pressure, S:

$$\text{or, } P = D + S$$
$$\therefore D = P - S$$

An ASI measures the dynamic pressure by solving the above formula, that is, by subtracting static pressure from pitot pressure continuously through the flight and presenting the information in terms of the aircraft's air speed.

Construction
The construction of an ASI is shown in Fig. 10.1 overleaf. In place of an open ended tube, the ASI uses an open ended capsule, fixed inside an airtight case. The open end of the capsule is connected to a tube installed in the aircraft's nose or on one of its wings, and facing the air flow. This tube is called a pitot tube or sometimes, pressure head. Thus, the pressure produced inside the capsule is the pitot pressure and the other face of the capsule will be displaced in response to the variations in this pressure. This pitot pressure is in fact passed through a short capillary before feeding into the capsule: this is to ensure a smooth supply of pressure, damping out any surges. Inside the case (but not inside the capsule) static pressure is fed. The result of the presence of this static surrounding the capsule is to check the expansion of the capsule

Fig. 10.1   ASI construction

since the face of the capsule expanding under pitot pressure must overcome the opposition due to this static. The resultant expansion will, therefore, be equal to the value of P − S which is dynamic pressure.

All that remains to be done now is to transmit this capsule face displacement to a pointer. This is done by means of a suitable mechanical linkage. We are not interested in the details of the interior mechanism except that somewhere in the mechanical linkage a bi-metallic strip is introduced to compensate for expansion/contraction of the linkage due to temperature variations, together with a compensator to provide a linear scale on the indicator despite the fact that the capsule displacement is in accordance with the square law given below.

Calibration

This is a problem, where, having constructed an ASI one asks oneself, 'Where, on the face of the dial, am I going to mark off 60 kt and 100 kt and the rest of the speed range?' The problem is not a simple one since here we are dealing with atmospheric pressures. You may, for example, take the ASI for calibration in a car. Run the car up to 60 kt, and where the pointer reaches at that speed, mark off 60 kt. But the question is, will the pointer reach the same position when the car is doing 60 kt the following day? Or, for that matter, the following hour? The answer would be 'no', for the pressures and air densities vary from hour to hour and day to day. It is, therefore, necessary first to adopt some standard in calibrating the ASI and then make allowance for known departure from that standard. The standard adopted is the International Standard Atmosphere (ISA) air density at sea level. This is that density which is produced when the pressure is 1013.2 mb and the temperature is +15°C. The calibration formula is:

$$P_D = \frac{1}{2}\rho\, V^2 \left(1 + \frac{V^2}{4C^2}\right)$$
where P_D = dynamic pressure
ρ = air density under ISA at msl
V = indicated air speed
C = speed of sound at msl

The style of presentation of IAS to the pilot on the ASI dial depends upon the particular instrument manufacturer and the operators' specifications but it is common to have, in addition to speed ranges being colour-coded, particular speeds marked with adjustable *bugs* or cursors so that pilots can readily see important speeds at a glance.

The precise specification at any time for colour-coding ASIs in aircraft registered in a JAA country is laid down in JARs 22 and 23. As speed is increased so the following colour codes apply. For the wing flap-operating range of speeds, there is a white arc upwards from the stalling speed, maximum weight, power-off, in the landing configuration, to the maximum speed for flight with flaps extended (V_{FE}). A green arc spans the normal operating speed range from 1.1 V_{S1}, gear and flaps up at maximum weight, to the rough air speed V_{RA} (the maximum structural cruising speed). For the upper caution speed range there is a yellow arc from the end of the green arc at V_{RA} to the never exceed speed, V_{NE}, which is itself marked by a radial red line. For piston-engined light twins there may be a blue radial line at V_Y, the best rate of climb speed for one engine out at msl and maximum weight, with another red radial at V_{MC}, minimum control speed at maximum weight.

Errors

An ASI suffers from the following four errors:

(1) *Instrument Error* This is due to small manufacturing imperfections and the fact that a very minute movement of the capsule is expanded to give a reasonable movement of the pointer. The extent of this error can be determined by comparing the readings at various air speeds against a standard ASI. The errors so found are recorded on a card. The reading you take from the Air Speed Indicator is known as *Indicated Air Speed* (IAS).

(2) *Pressure Error* This error is also known as *Position Error*. The pressures presented inside the capsule and inside the case must be correct pressures if correct speed is to be measured. As far as the pitot tube is concerned to a large extent it gives correct values. Static is the main source of the error since to be correct it must be entirely free from any air flow under pressure or from other disturbances caused by aerodynamic surfaces. If the static tube is combined with the pitot head, an arrangement shown in Fig. 10.2, it will be seen that the static tube will be surrounded by disturbed air flow and some dynamic pressure will enter it giving erroneous results. These errors can be minimised if the static source is completely divorced from the pitot head. Under this arrangement it takes the form of a *static vent* or *port* (as against static head). It consists of a small copper plate with a hole drilled radially through the centre. The air under static pressure enters a tube through this hole and is conveyed to the inside of the instrument case at the other end of the tube. An ideal position is found for installation of the static vent where the disturbance is minimum and to improve the results further the plate is fixed flush with the fuselage skin to avoid encouraging local disturbances. Approximately 95% of the pressure error is reduced by using this

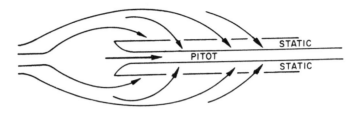

Fig. 10.2   Pressure head

arrangement. Many aircraft use two static vents, one on each side: this is to balance out any errors in static pressure caused by yawing or side slipping.

There are two distinct types of pressure errors.

Position Error   This is the error entirely due to the location of the pitot head and static vent, and the magnitude of the error depends on this. As we saw above, the static is the main source of the error and no matter how ideal a position for static vent is found there is bound to be some disturbance present around it. The magnitude of the error also depends on the aircraft speed, since, generally, the higher the speed the greater the disturbance. This error, like instrument error, is a known factor and can be determined throughout the ASI's speed range. In practice both instrument and position errors are combined together on a single card, called *Pressure Error (PE) Card*. PE is applied to the IAS to give Rectified Air Speed (RAS). This is also known as Calibrated Airspeed (CAS) but RAS is used throughout this volume.

Manoeuvre-Induced Error   This error occurs when the pressure head is not directly facing the air flow, for example, when an aircraft is in a climb or descent. The error also occurs when extraneous disturbance is caused by the pilot's actions such as lowering the undercarriage or manipulating flaps. The aircraft is then no longer aerodynamically 'clean' and the static will be affected. The situation is aggravated by the fact that short term pressure fluctuations are present during rapidly changing manoeuvres and that some time, however small, must elapse between arrival of the pressure at one end of the tube and its delivery at the instrument end of the tube. Thus you may have an indication which was true a few moments ago. These errors are random and therefore cannot be pre-determined for recording on a card.

To summarise, the magnitude of pressure errors depends on:

(a)   the position of the static vent;
(b)   aircraft speed;
(c)   angle of attack and type of manoeuvre;
(d)   aerodynamic state, e.g. whether flaps down etc.

(3)   *Density Error*   This error occurs due to the calibration of the ASI. An Air Speed Indicator reads correct air speed only when flying in an air mass of such density as would be produced if the prevailing pressure was 1013.2 mb and the temperature was +15°C. These data describe the ISA density at the sea level but the conditions may prevail above the surface in its near vicinity.

By *near vicinity* we mean a few hundred feet rather than a few thousand feet. At 5000 ft for example for this density to exist the temperature required is approximately −32°C and at 10 000 ft it is −73°C. Thus, it is most unlikely that an ASI would read correct air speed at 10 000 ft.

As for the nature of the error, as the height is gained the atmosphere becomes rarer and density decreases. Therefore, the dynamic pressure falls and the indicator gives a reading which is too low for a given air speed. The rectified air speed must therefore be corrected for density error to give the true indication of the speed and you will have noticed from above that in the majority of the cases it will be an additive correction. The correction is made on the computer by setting pressure altitude against temperature in the *air speed* window and reading off True Air Speed (TAS) on the outer scale against rectified air speed on the inside scale. To summarise:

$$\text{IAS} \pm \text{PE} \qquad = \text{RAS};$$
$$\text{RAS: Density Error} = \text{TAS}$$

TAS is the air speed the aircraft is actually doing through the air.

From the foregoing it will be appreciated that an aircraft flying straight and level from warmer air mass into colder air mass or vice versa will experience changes in the air speed indications. For example: an aircraft is flying at 10 000 ft and the temperature is −5°C, its RAS is 130 kt. The TAS for this pressure altitude, temperature and RAS is 150 kt. Later the same aircraft enters an air mass having temperature of, say, −15°C. This air mass is relatively colder and therefore denser, so the new dynamic pressure will be higher and the indications will change. On the computer, to maintain a TAS of 150 kt as before but under the new set of conditions, the RAS will show an increased reading of 133 kt – a higher indication. Alternatively if you are maintaining an RAS of 130 throughout the new TAS is reduced to 147 kt.

In absence of a computer, correction for density error may be estimated from the following formula:

$$\text{TAS} = \text{RAS} + (1.75\% \text{ of RAS per } 1000 \text{ ft of altitude})$$

For example, RAS is 130 and height 10 000 ft:

$$\text{TAS} = 130 + 1.75\% \text{ of } 130 \text{ per } 1000 \text{ ft} \times 10$$
$$= 130 + 17.5\% \text{ of } 130$$
$$= 130 + 22$$
$$\text{TAS} = 152 \text{ which compares with above illustration.}$$

(4) *Compressibility Error*   This error generally applies to high speed aircraft doing a TAS of 300 kt or over. At such speeds air compresses when brought to rest in front of the pitot head and consequently enters the tube under higher pressure, giving an overread of IAS. Thus, compressibility error is corrected as a subtractive factor. Air nearer the earth's surface is not easily compressed since it is already dense and the compressibility error near surface levels is negligible. The error increases with altitude. For a given altitude an increase in air speed increases the error. That portion of the

calibration formula given in the brackets is known as the Compressibility Factor. It confirms the above two statements. The correction for this error is made on the computer. Frequently graphs for a particular aircraft are available which correct for this as well as pressure error in one operation. RAS corrected for compressibility = equivalent air speed (EAS). EAS corrected for density = TAS.

Blockages

Blocked Pitot If the pitot tube gets blocked by ice or other obstruction before take-off there will be no reaction at all and the instrument will read zero. In level flight should the pitot get blocked the dial will hold the reading unless pressure leaks away in which case the pointer will return to zero. During a descent a blocked pitot will give an underread as the increasing static will put up increasing opposition to constant value pitot pressure trapped inside the tube.

If the pitot tube develops a leak the ASI underreads.

Blocked Static   Should the static become blocked during take-off the instrument will underread (high value static is trapped in). During level flight with a blockage the instrument continues to give the same reading. During a descent with a blockage it will overread and a dangerous situation can readily be envisaged when the aircraft could stall at an air speed indicated as being well above the stalling speed.

As a safeguard against serious errors occurring in the indicated airspeed due to blockage of the primary pitot/static source(s), an alternative source system may be installed in the aircraft. The normal changeover selector is readily available to the pilot, should emergency operation be required. However, because the alternate source (especially static) is not located in an ideal position for sampling the air around the aircraft, an increase in Position Error should be expected.

Serviceability checks

As far as the instrument itself is concerned there is nothing a pilot can check except that the pointer is not stuck on the dial. A pilot must check that the pitot head cover and the static vent pins are removed, that the pitot head is not bent, cracked, misaligned with the airflow or otherwise damaged in any way and that any drains are clear.

Because the greatest risk of blockage of a pitot head is by icing, pressure heads are provided with electrical heating elements. The serviceability of pitot head heaters is checked in the pre-flight checks.

Test questions
(1) In an Airspeed Indicator, a sample of static pressure enters
   (a)   both the capsule and the case
   (b)   the case only
   (c)   the capsule only.

(2) The capsule of an Airspeed Indicator is
 (a) partially evacuated of air
 (b) connected to a static vent
 (c) connected to a pitot tube.

(3) If, when correcting an RAS value of 150 kt, a TAS value of 146 kt is obtained
 (a) an error must have been made in the calculation
 (b) no allowance has been made for compressibility
 (c) the density of the atmosphere must be greater than the ISA mean sea level air density.

(4) Indicated airspeed is adjusted to rectified airspeed by the application of correction for
 (a) compressibility error
 (b) density error
 (c) pressure and instrument error.

(5) Rectified airspeed is corrected to True airspeed for
 (a) pressure error and density error
 (b) compressibility error only
 (c) density and compressibility errors.

(6) Equivalent Airspeed (EAS) is Indicated Airspeed (IAS) corrected for the errors
 (a) instrument, pressure, compressibility
 (b) instrument, pressure, density
 (c) instrument, temperature deviation, density.

(7) Compressibility error is most significant
 (a) in the lower speed range
 (b) at a TAS of 300 kt
 (c) at True Airspeeds in excess of 300 kt.

(8) Compressibility error always causes the RAS to be
 (a) under-indicated
 (b) over-indicated
 (c) correct at speeds over 300 kt.

(9) During descent a blockage of the static source will cause the ASI to
 (a) underread
 (b) overread
 (c) either underread or overread depending upon the rate of change of the static pressure.

(10) A leak in the pitot line will cause the ASI to
 (a) overread
 (b) continue reading correctly
 (c) underread.

Chapter 11
ALTIMETERS

Pressure altimeter

The atmosphere has weight and this weight exerts pressure. An ordinary household barometer measures this static pressure and indicates the weather. If we took this barometer to the top of a tall building it would be noticed that for the same weather conditions the pressure indication is less. This is because the atmosphere remaining above the barometer at height is less than at ground level. If we knew the rate of the fall of pressure with height, we could graduate that barometer to read in terms of height instead of reading the pressure. An aircraft altimeter is simply an aneroid barometer adapted for use in aircraft on the basis that 1 millibar of pressure change takes place for a change of height of approximately 27 feet. In the above illustration, if the barometer reads 1010 mb at ground level and 1008 mb at height, the top of the building is approximately 60 feet (30 ft to a millibar is a good figure to use unless the examination question gives a specific figure).

Construction and operation

Two or three capsules each having vacuum or partial vacuum in them are used to achieve sensitivity. They are stacked together with one face fastened down to the base permitting movement due to pressure changes at the other end. (Fig. 11.1)

To prevent the capsules from collapsing (because of the vacuum in them) a spring called the leaf spring is used to hold up the moveable face. The movement of the capsules in response to change in height is transmitted to the pointers, usually three pointers, through a suitable mechanical linkage. Somewhere in the linkage a bi-metallic bar or other similar device is inserted to compensate for temperature variations. The whole assembly is encased in a container, having an inlet for the static pressure but otherwise airtight.

As the aircraft gains height the value of static decreases and the capsule expands under the tension of the spring (Fig. 11.2).

Similarly, as the aircraft descends, static increases and the capsule contracts. These movements are magnified sufficiently to give reasonable pointer displacement, which move around a dial calibrated in feet.

Calibration

Like the ASI we are here dealing with constantly varying atmospheric pressures which show up so vividly on a household barometer. Therefore, a

Fig. 11.1   Altimeter construction

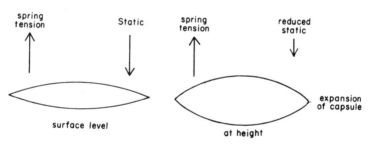

Fig. 11.2   Capsule expansion

standard for calibration must be adopted and this standard is the International Standard Atmosphere as follows:

(1)   The sea level pressure is presumed to be 1013.25 mb.
(2)   Sea level temperature +15°C.
(3)   The temperature falls with height at the rate of 1.98°C per thousand feet up to a height of 36 090 ft. Above this height the temperature remains almost constant at −56.5°C. Note that this item is not included in calibration of an ASI, and that this is not the complete definition of International Standard Atmosphere. (See *Ground Studies For Pilots, Volume 4, Meteorology.*)

Errors

The instrument suffers from five different errors as follows.

(1)   *Instrument Error*   This error is similar to that in an ASI except that one more factor must be considered. Some altimeters are calibrated on the

presumption that the rate of fall of pressure with change in height is a constant value. In ISA and in actual circumstances, as the atmosphere becomes rarer that rate of fall must decrease with height. (See Table on page 121) To this extent the altimeter becomes unreliable when flying at high altitudes.

(2) *Pressure Error*   This error occurs for reasons similar to an ASI and both its components, position and manoeuvre induced errors, are present. As regards the error due to the position of the static vent a PE card is available for correction to the readings taken from the instrument.

(3) *Barometric Error*   A household barometer again comes in handy to show that if it was calibrated to give 0 ft reading where the pointer stood one day, the next day the pointer would suggest that the house had gained or lost height. It is most important that the altimeter hands are set to read height above the ground or mean sea level before taking off, thus correcting for pressure difference from 1013.2 mb. This is done by setting the appropriate pressure on what is called the *millibar sub-scale*, the sub-scale being visible through a window on the instrument. A knob is provided on the instrument to set the desired pressure. When it is turned the whole mechanism inside the instrument turns, turning the pointers with it. Various pressure settings available are considered later in the chapter. When correct pressure is set the indication is correct (except for inaccuracies due to other errors) and the indication remains correct as long as the surface pressure remains unchanged. When that pressure changes, the indication is in error again: this topic is dealt with in detail later in this chapter (Pressure–altimeter relationship).

(4) *Temperature Error*   As mentioned earlier the instrument presumes the surface temperature to be +15°C, reducing at the rate of 1.98°C per thousand feet. This lapse rate prescribes an exact temperature for every flight level from the surface (SL) to the aircraft level. Therefore, if the flight level temperature is not the ISA temperature, and the temperatures in the column of air below the aircraft are not the ISA temperatures, an error in the indication will occur.

   The magnitude of this error is relatively small when at lower levels but at higher levels it does become significant. The corrections are carried out on the slide rule side of the navigation computer. Set pressure against the corrected outside air temperatures (COAT) in the window marked *altitude*. Then, against indicated altitude on the inside scale, read off the true altitude on the outside scale. For example, when at FL 5000 ft with COAT −12°C, the true altitude is 4700 ft. It must be pointed out that strictly speaking, not the outside temperatures but the mean temperature of the air column below the aircraft must be used to obtain correction. In the absence of this information the outside temperatures are used to give us an approximate value.

(5) *Time Lag Error*   This error occurs due to the time that the pressures take, however small, to travel from one end of the tube to the other.

(Pressures travel at approximately 1100 ft/sec and on a modern aircraft the distance to travel may quite easily be of the order of 50 ft.) This error is most noticeable during steep climbs or descents. During a climb, higher pressure is present at any given instant and the altimeter underreads. Similarly during a descent, time lag causes an altimeter to overread. Masked time lag errors are also present during other manoeuvres, in addition to the manoeuvre-induced errors mentioned under (2).

Blockage

Should the static vent become blocked through ice or other obstruction old static will remain trapped and height changes will not be indicated. On the other hand, should you break the glass of the face of the altimeter, the pressure which will act on the capsules will be that in the cockpit (and affected by any air conditioning or pressurisation system) and not the pressure derived from the static system.

Pressure settings

Due to the nature of calibration and various other factors an aircraft altimeter rarely reads correct height. With this limitation in mind we are ready to familiarise ourselves with various settings available. At the outset it must be emphasised that when a specific pressure is set on the sub-scale that pressure becomes the datum from which the difference in pressures between it and the actual pressure experienced at aircraft level is measured. It is this difference which positions the pointers.

Let us take an illustration. The datum set is 1000 mb and, say, the pressure acting upon the aircraft and its altimeter is 700 mb. The difference of 300 mb between the datum and actual pressures resolves into a pointer displacement of $300 \times 30 =$ approximately 9000 ft. If the datum set was 1020 in the same circumstances the difference would be 320 mb and the pointer displacement of $320 \times 30 =$ approx. 9600 ft. From the illustration we conclude that if pressure setting is increased, the height reading is increased, and vice versa.

Various settings available are given names in Q code. These are:

QFE

The barometric pressure at the level of the aerodrome. When set the altimeter indicates height of the aircraft above the highest point on the manoeuvring area on the aerodrome. This setting is generally used for take off, landing and particularly when carrying out radar approaches. When set, the correction for the barometric and temperature errors is duly made and if the aircraft is stationary on the ground, only the instrument error is present.

This setting is also used for checking the altimeter serviceability.

QFF

The barometric pressure at aerodrome level, reduced to mean sea level. This reduction is made using the values of actual pressure and temperature conditions prevailing at the time and not the ISA values. This setting is mostly used by meteorological offices for plotting synoptic charts.

QNH

The barometric pressure at aerodrome level, reduced to mean sea level using ISA formula. When set, an altimeter calibrated in ISA reads height of the altimeter above mean sea level. This height is called Altitude. Again, when set, it is corrected for the barometric and temperature errors, and when on the ground it will correctly indicate the altimeter's height above MSL. In flight, however, even if the pressure remains unchanged, a temperature deviation from ISA is likely to be present, introducing temperature error.

This setting is also used for checking altimeter serviceability. Two types of QNH values are available – spot QNH and Regional QNH. Spot QNH is only valid for the spot (aerodrome) where the pressure reading took place. This may be used when taking off or landing as an alternative to QFE. The law requires a pilot taking off in controlled airspace to have at least one altimeter set to aerodrome QNH value.

Regional pressure setting (i.e. QNH) in contrast to spot or aerodrome QNH is applicable throughout the region for which it is given. For the purpose of providing this service the UK is divided into 14 regions known as Altimeter Setting Regions (ASRs). Each region produces, on the hour, a forecast of the lowest values in the area, and such forecast QNH is valid for one hour. Being the lowest forecast value, the setting is used for the purpose of maintaining adequate terrain clearance. When a lower value is set, a lower indication results and maximum safety is assured. The indication may not be a correct indication of the altitude but the error is in favour of safety. It may not be correct, because, first of all, it is a forecast value, secondly, the value chosen is true for only a small area in the region where lowest values were recorded and thirdly, the chosen value is for an hour but may only prevail for part of that hour. Elsewhere in the region, higher pressures may be expected. Other reasons for an incorrect indication are instrument error, temperature error, and the pressure given being rounded off to a whole figure.

Standard setting

Strictly, this is the altimeter reading on the ground with 1013.2 mb set on the sub-scale, but is commonly taken to be 1013.2 mb setting, used for flight separation between aircraft flying under IFR. With this setting the altitude indicated is called pressure altitude and the level at which an aircraft flies is called flight level. For example, if 10 000 feet of pressure altitude is indicated, the aircraft's flight level is 100. It will be appreciated that the aircraft's altitude and pressure altitude will be the same only when the QNH value is also 1013.2 mb. At all other times the indication will be in error on a 1013.2 mb setting. However as between two aircraft flying close to each other and therefore in the same air mass, both will have similar error in indication. The separation can therefore be maintained accurately.

Pressure–altimeter relationship

From the above it will be apparent that once an aircraft departs from a place with correct setting, the indication will remain correct (disregarding limitations of QNH mentioned above) only as long as the datum pressure continues to prevail. When new pressures are encountered, the indication becomes erroneous. For the sense of the error, the rule is: when flying from an area of high pressure to an area of low pressure the altimeter overreads. The rule may more easily be remembered from the phrase – 'high – low – high'. The reverse is also true. This is illustrated in Fig. 11.3.

The pressure at position A is 1000 mb: and an aircraft is flying with this

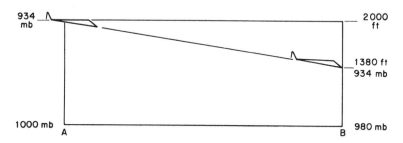

Fig. 11.3   High to low – altimeter over-reads

setting, its indication being 2000 ft. The pressure upon the altimeter

$$= \frac{2000}{30} = 66\,mb \text{ less than } 1000$$

$$= 934\,mb$$

In order to maintain an indication of 2000 ft the aircraft must fly in the airspace where the pressure on the altimeter is 934 mb. Let us assume that the pressure at B is 980 mb. At B, the height at which pressure of 934 will occur

$$= 980 - 934$$
$$= 46\,mb$$
$$= 1380\,ft$$

Thus, the aircraft will actually be at 1380 ft although the indication is 2000 ft. The aircraft flew from an area of high pressure to an area of low pressure and high – low – high rule applied.

Temperature–altimeter relationship

In Fig. 11.4 the area around A is warmer than the area around B which is on the same isobar. Therefore, at given level, the altimeter will experience higher pressure above it when over A than over B. Thus, flying from A to B without altering the datum will amount to flying from high pressure to low pressure: high–low–high: and the altimeter will overread. The reverse is also true.

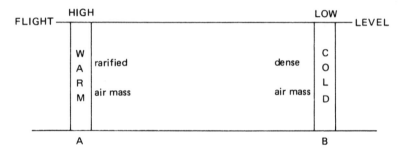

Fig. 11.4   Upper air mean temperature effect

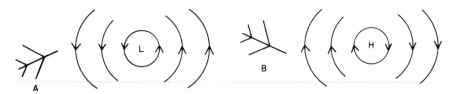

Fig. 11.5   Drift and altimeter error

Drift–altimeter relationship

From Fig. 11.5 it will be observed that if an aircraft (aircraft A in figure) experiences persistent starboard drift in the northern hemisphere, that aircraft is approaching a low pressure area and the pilot must anticipate that his altimeter will read too high. Aircraft B with port drift is approaching an area of high pressure and the altimeter will underread. Reverse results are obtained in southern hemisphere.

Density altitude

This is defined as the height in ISA at which prevailing density will occur. Density altitude is mainly used in ascertaining the performance data of aircraft. It is the same as pressure altitude when local temperature is ISA temperature. If the local temperature is lower than ISA the density altitude is lower than the pressure altitude, and vice versa. 1°C difference of temperature causes density altitude to separate from pressure altitude by approximately 119 ft. Generally, the term has been superseded in operational practice by the use of Temperature Deviation (from ISA) in conjunction with Pressure Altitude.

Indicator

There are various altimeter dial presentations, stemming mainly from efforts to eliminate risks of misreading instruments which may have contributed to the cause of aircraft accidents. The oldest indicators (which have sometimes been misread) have triple pointers (for 100, 1000, 10000 ft) but later models have combinations of pointer(s) digital counters or drum presentation (Fig. 11.6).

A few sample problems using the various settings and their implications may be useful. Use 1013.2 mb as the standard setting, and 1 mb = 30 feet. And remember that if you reduce the value of the sub-scale setting, the height indication decreases; and conversely, of course, an increase in the setting increases the height indication. A quick *situation sketch* is to be strongly recommended.

(1) When flying at FL 55, will there be a minimum of 1500 feet clearance over high ground, 3850 ft amsl when the QNH is 1007.2 mb?

Answer: No.

Solution

1013.2–QNH (1007.2) difference = 6 mb = 180 feet. When at FL 55, the true altitude is 5500 ft − 180 ft = 5320 feet. In order to maintain a 1500 feet clearance your true altitude should be at least 3850 feet + 1500 feet = 5350 feet.

(2) An aerodrome, 990 feet above mean sea level has QFE of 990 mb.
(a) What is the QNH?

(b) What clearance has an aircraft from a spot height in the vicinity of the aerodrome 3000 ft amsl, if the aircraft is at FL 40?

Answer: (a) 1023 mb; (b) 1294 ft.

Solution

(a) The altimeter reads 0 feet with 990 mb set. For QNH, wind it up until it reads the aerodrome's elevation that is, 990 feet. Thus, the number of millibars to add to 990 mb is

$$\frac{990}{30} = 33 \, \text{mb}$$

and   QNH = 990 + 33 = 1023 mb.

(b) QNH − 1013.2 difference = (1023 − 1013.2) mb
= 9.8 mb = 294 ft.
When 1013.2 set, the indication = 4000 ft
QNH − 1013.2 difference   = 294 ft (QNH greater)
Indication when QNH set   = 4294 ft
Elevation of the spot height   = 3000 ft
Clearance   = 1294 ft

(3) The en route spot height is 1600 metres amsl, and the regional QNH is 995 mb. Assuming 1 millibar = 29 feet, what is the actual clearance over this spot height when flying at FL 70?

Answer: 1224 ft.

Fig. 11.6 Altimeter dial

Solution

(a) 1600 metres = 1600 × 3.28 = 5248 ft.

(b) 1013.2 − QNH difference = (1013.2 − 995) mb
         = 18.2 mb = 528 ft.

(c) Indication when 1013.2 set = 7000 ft (QNH lower)
       1013.2 − QNH difference = 528 ft

       Indication when QNH set = 6472 ft
       Elev. of the spot height = 5248 ft

       Clearance   = 1224 ft

(4) An aircraft is flying at flight level 65. There is some high ground en route, the elevation of the highest point is 1350 metres. What actual terrain clearance will the aircraft have when passing over this high ground if the QNH is 1003.2 mb?

Answer: 1772 feet.

Solution

(a) 1350 metres = 1350 × 3.28 ft
          = 4428 ft.

(b) Difference between 1013.2 and QNH = (1013.2 − 1003.2) mb
                  = 10 mb = 300 ft (QNH lower)

(c) Indication when 1013.2 set = 6500 ft
                       −300 ft

       Indication when QNH set = 6200 ft
       Elevation of the high grd. = 4428 ft

       Clearance   = 1772 ft

(5)   An aircraft on a track of 089°(M) wishes to fly at the lowest flight level which will give it a clearance of 5000 feet amsl. If the regional QNH is 992 mb, calculate the flight level.

Answer: FL 70.

Solution
(a)   QNH − 1013.2 difference = (1013.2 − 992) mb = 21 mb.
                                       = 630 ft (QNH lower)
(b)   Indication on QNH   = 5000 ft minimum
       QNH − 1013.2 difference = +630 ft
       Indication on QNE   = 5630 ft minimum
(c)   Therefore, the lowest available flight level is FL 60 and the flight level appropriate for the track of 089°(M) is FL 70 (odd thousands).

Servo altimeters

These are second generation altimeters designed to overcome generally some of the serious limitations of the conventional altimeters and to improve overall performance.

Capsules are still retained – generally two of them and evacuated of air – which expand and contract with changes in pressure. The rest of the mechanical linkage is replaced by a servo-assisted transmission system. The altimeters operate as follows.

The mechanism consists of a two bar (called E and I bars because of their shape) induction pick-off, a servo and a cam. During a straight and level flight through a uniform air mass the system is in balance and the pointer remains steady.

When a pressure change is met the movement of the capsules is transmitted mechanically (this being the only unassisted mechanical link in the whole system) to one of the two bars of the pick-off, moving the bar in response (Fig. 11.7). This movement throws it out of balance and an error signal is raised in the pick-off. This signal is amplified and fed to the motor. As the motor turns it drives the cam which, in its turn, moves the other bar of the pick-off. When this bar has sufficiently moved to regain balance, the error signal disappears, movement of the motor, cam and the other bar stops and the system comes to rest.

As the motor turns, it also turns the height counters and the instrument's single pointer simultaneously with the cam. Thus, the transmission of information from capsules to counters can be said to be almost instantaneous.

Servo altimeters have the following advantages over conventional altimeters:

(1)   At high altitudes very little pressure change takes place for a given change of altitude with the result that the capsule movement is considerably less than for the same change of altitude at lower levels. This factor makes ordinary altimeters insensitive at higher levels whereas the

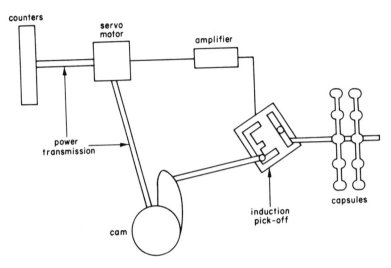

Fig. 11.7   Servo altimeter mechanism

Fig. 11.8   Servo altimeter dial

servo mechanism will pick up a capsule movement as little as 0.0002 inches per thousand feet (Table 11.1).

(2)   Power transmission gives better accuracy.

(3)   Virtually eliminates time lag between arrival of new pressure and placing of the counters.

(4)   Being an electrical system, correction for pressure error could be made and an Altitude Alerting device may be incorporated.

(5)   Although conventional altimeters now employ digital presentation, it is

Table 11.1 The pressure differences for 5000 ft in ISA at low and high levels.

ISA level (ft)	Pressure (mb)	Pressure difference in mb per 5000 ft
MSL	1013	
5000	843	170
10 000	697	146
15 000	572	125
20 000	466	106
⋮		
⋮		
35 000	238	
40 000	186	52
⋮		
⋮		
55 000	91	
60 000	72	19

Assuming a servo-altimeter accuracy of +/− 1 mb over the entire range, the accuracies would be of the order of:

At	2000 ft	+/− 30 ft
At	20 000 ft	+/− 50 ft
At	40 000 ft	+/− 100 ft

generally more common with the servo altimeters. These eliminate the possibility of misreading.

(6) A pointer is still available – a useful asset at low levels in assessing rate of change of height.

(7) It is capable of height encoding on Secondary Surveillance Radar.

The appearance of a typical indicator is shown in Fig. 11.8.

Test questions

(1) The pressure altimeter is calibrated in accordance with
   (a) the environmental lapse rate of temperature
   (b) the jet standard atmosphere
   (c) the International Standard Atmosphere.

(2) Pressure error causes an altimeter to
   (a) consistently overread
   (b) either underread or overread
   (c) consistently underread.

(3) An aircraft climbs away from the runway with static vents still sealed. If set to QFE, the altimeter will
   (a) continue to indicate zero feet
   (b) indicate correctly increasing altitude as the aircraft climbs
   (c) show a slower gain of altitude than correct.

(4)   When flying from HIGH pressure to a LOWER pressure area, the barometric error of a pressure altimeter will cause the instrument
   (a)   to read the true altitude
   (b)   to underread the true altitude
   (c)   to indicate higher than the true altitude.

(5)   During the latter stages of a rapid descent, a pressure altimeter set to QFE is likely to be
   (a)   under-indicating height
   (b)   over-indicating height
   (c)   reading correct height above the highest point on the airfield.

(6)   An altimeter is reading 1500 feet. If the sub-scale is changed from 999 mb to 1006 mb, the new altimeter reading will be
   (a)   1290 ft
   (b)   1710 ft
   (c)   1390 ft.

(7)   On a cockpit cross-check of pressure altimeters, the altimeter (A) when set to 1013 mb, when compared to the other altimeter (B) which is set to QNH 1029 mb, will indicate
   (a)   a lower altitude by approximately 480 ft
   (b)   a lower altitude by approximately 390 ft
   (c)   a higher altitude by approximately 390 ft.

(8)   An aircraft takes off from Southampton (Eastleigh) Airport (44 ft amsl) with the altimeter reading zero feet. On returning from a cross-country flight the pilot fails to re-set the altimeter sub-scale, leaving it set to Portland Regional QNH 993 mb. If the QFE at Southampton (Eastleigh) remains at 990 mb throughout the flight, on landing the altimeter will read
   (a)   90 ft
   (b)   134 ft
   (c)   44 ft.

(9)   An aircraft is cleared to descend to and maintain FL 40. If the Regional QNH is 990 mb, the aircraft will clear high ground of 2250 ft amsl by
   (a)   440 ft
   (b)   1750 ft
   (c)   1060 ft.

(10)   In an area with a constant QNH of 1012 mb, an aircraft is flying at FL 120. The aircraft's true altitude will depend upon
   (a)   the terrain below the aircraft
   (b)   the temperature of the air below the aircraft
   (c)   the correct setting of local QFE on the sub-scale.

(11)   In servo-assisted altimeters
   (a)   lag error is virtually eliminated
   (b)   lag error is unfortunately greater than in the pressure-sensitive altimeter, due to its extra components
   (c)   lag error affects them as much as in pressure altimeters.

(12) Compared to the pressure sensitive altimeter, the servo-assisted altimeter is
    (a) equally as accurate
    (b) less accurate
    (c) more accurate.

Chapter 12
VERTICAL SPEED
INDICATORS (VSI and IVSI)

Vertical Speed Indicator (VSI) is a pressure gauge which utilises the principle of differential pressure to indicate an aircraft's rate of climb or descent.

Construction and operation
In construction, the VSI consists of a capsule held in an airtight case and fed with outside static pressure. Capillary delivery to the capsule is employed for the same reason as in the ASI: the tube is longer than in the ASI, as the VSI's capsule is more sensitive. Outside static is also fed to the inside of the case (that is, outside the capsule) but in this case it has to pass through a carefully calibrated restrictive device called the metering unit. There are various types of metering unit, a common type being a system of capillaries and orifices, but in each case its function is to present static inside the case after a calibrated delay.

Thus, as the outside pressure alters, as it will when an aircraft commences to climb or descend, the capsule will be affected by the change almost immediately, whereas the change will reach inside the case only after a slight delay. This lag will occur every time the aircraft climbs or descends. Therefore as long as the aircraft maintains climb/descent attitude a differential will exist between the two (inside the case and inside the capsule). This differential will result in expansion or contraction of the face of the capsule depending on whether the pressure in the case is lower or higher than the pressure inside the capsule. For example, during a climb, denser pressure (appropriate to lower altitudes) will be present in the case and less dense (or current) pressure inside the capsule. The capsule will contract.

This expansion/contraction of the capsule is transmitted to the pointer system through a suitable mechanical link. The movement of the capsule being proportionate to the rate of change of pressure, the pointer indicates the rate of change of altitude. See Fig. 12.1.

In level flight both pressures will be equal and the pointer will indicate 0 position.

In order to ensure the correct rate of flow through the metering unit in varying density conditions, a mechanical temperature/pressure compensatory device is generally introduced in the metering unit. Thus, correct flow is maintained during climb and descent.

Fig. 12.1   Vertical speed indicator mechanism

Errors

(1) *Instrument Error* This is caused by constructional defects in the instrument and is kept within approved tolerances during regular maintenance checks. If after a period of service the pointer has moved from the 0 position, the zero adjustment screw is used to re-set the pointer to zero.

(2) *Time Lag Error* During sudden changes in pitch attitude, a certain time must elapse before the new pressures reach the instrument and the differential is established. The greater the differential (i.e. high rate of climb or descent), the greater is the error.

(3) *Pressure Error* Any error in the static pressure being supplied to the instrument and caused due to its positioning on the fuselage will not affect the indications in a prolonged steady climb or descent. This is because the instrument reads the differential pressure and not its magnitude. However, any disturbed airflow, caused by accelerations, decelerations, initiation of a climb or descent, lowering of the flaps, the undercarriage, will introduce an error.

(4) *Manoeuvre Induced Error* Errors induced by manoeuvres can cause any pressure instrument to misread for up to 3 seconds at low altitudes and up to 10 seconds at 30000 feet. The times for the VSI may even be longer than these. Thus, during any manoeuvres involving change of attitude or aerodynamic configuration, absolute reliance must not be placed on the VSI. Greatest error is caused by pitching motion of the aircraft.

(5) *Blockage Error* Blocked static would give a zero indication.

The indicator

Straight and level position is indicated by the pointer at 9 o'clock position. The pointer travels through the top portion of the indicator (Fig. 12.2) to indicate rate of climb up to 4000 ft per minute. Similarly, it travels through

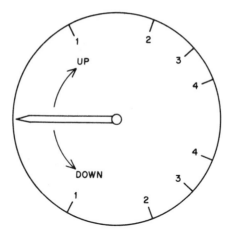

Fig. 12.2   VSI indicator

the bottom portion of the indicator to indicate rate of descent up to 4000 ft per minute. The maximum points are separated by an intervening space to prevent any chance of confusion as to which way the pointer movement took place. On most indicators the calibration is based on logarithmic scale (Fig. 12.2), the largest pointer movement occurring near the zero position. This enables small variations from straight and level flight to be shown up.

Instantaneous (or Inertial Lead) Vertical Speed Indicator (IVSI)

This instrument is designed, as the name implies, to give an immediate response to a vertical departure from a horizontal flight path. This is achieved by adding an accelerometer unit to the conventional VSI components. The accelerometer unit comprises an assembly of two dashpots, each of which contains an inertial mass in the form of a piston balanced by a spring, one spring being stronger than the other. The cylinders are fed with static pressure from the aircraft's static pressure system and connected by a tube to the inside of the pressure capsule. As soon as a change in vertical speed occurs, inertia causes the piston to be displaced so the accelerometer unit creates a pressure differential which produces an immediate response by the indicator pointer (Fig. 12.3).

After a few seconds, the effect of the accelerometer piston response dies away, but by this time the actual static pressure change becomes effective so that the instrument is then operated by the pressure differential produced by the metering unit in the normal way.

Errors

(1) *Instrument Error* As conventional VSI. Zero adjustment screw fitted.
(2) *Pressure Error* As conventional VSI.

Fig. 12.3   ISVI mechanism

(3)   *Lag Error* Virtually eliminated.
(4)   *Manoeuvre Induced Error* Also virtually eliminated.
(5)   *Turning Error* As the dashpots are not vertically stabilised, some error is produced during turns, and at bank attitudes in excess of 40°, the IVSI is unreliable.

Angle of Attack (AoA) Systems

Apart from the indications by the VSIs and IVSIs of vertical motion of the aircraft when in flight, precise reliable measurement and display of the aeroplane's longitudinal attitude, i.e. its angle of attack, can enhance aircraft performance and ensure operation at a safe margin above the stalling speed. Restating basic aerodynamic principles, Angle of Attack (AoA) is defined as the angle formed between the direction of the relative airflow and the wing chord line. As the angle of attack is increased so lift increases until a point is reached when the airflow over the wing starts to become disturbed, which the pilot feels as pre-stall buffeting. Stalling is the condition when the angle of attack is so increased that the lift generated will not support the aircraft's weight. The stalling angle is constant for a particular aircraft.

Angle of attack information may be integrated into other on-board equipments such as Air Data Computers and Flight Management Systems as described in chapter 20, Ground Proximity Warning Systems (GPWS) as described in Volume 1 or provided directly on to the flight deck to the pilot by an AoA Indicator, as depicted in Fig. 12.4.

The measuring element of an AoA system is a precision flow angle sensor in the form of a vane. The basic concept is for the sensor to be fitted on the fuselage but if a suitable fuselage location cannot be found, then the sensor is wing-mounted on a probe out from the leading edge where it is free from prop-wash or other flow disturbances (Fig. 12.5).

The sensor vane is free to rotate with its main shaft with the local airflow. It is designed to have a very low internal friction in its mounting and its motion is directly coupled to a rotary viscous damper and to potentiometers. Thus the sensor has a smooth output, excellent low speed accuracy and a fast

Fig. 12.4   Angle of attack indicator

fuselage mounted sensor   wing mounted sensor

Fig. 12.5   Angle of attack sensor

dynamic response to angle of attack changes. The potentiometer outputs can not only drive the angle of attack indicators but also stall warning systems, flight control systems and on those aircraft with HUD (Head-up displays – military aircraft) AoA Indexers, (which indicate fast, on-speed or slow approach). The vane is heated as necessary to keep it free of any icing through a self-regulating device which maintains the vane at a constant temperature.

The advantages to the pilot of angle of attack sensors in their use and application are:

(1) A clear, steady and unambiguous direct indication of the aircraft's attitude relative to the airflow over the wings;
(2) Easy to read and use;
(3) Sensitive at low airspeeds when angle of attack information is of especial importance;
(4) High reliability and weather-free;
(5) Provides a good reference measure for achieving optimum performance;
(6) Avoids loss of control and stalling due to over-rotation on take-off;
(7) Facilitates precise control of glide-slope on approach;
(8) During wind-shear recovery procedures the aircraft can be rotated directly to the optimum angle of attack, relieving the pilot from the

process of pitching up slowly in small increments while searching for stick-shaker;
(9) May be incorporated in EFIS and GPWS;
(10) Warning flag display when inoperative.

Test questions
(1) In the Vertical Speed Indicator, manoeuvre induced error
  (a) has an insignificant effect on the reliability of the reading
  (b) significantly affects the reliability of the readings
  (c) only significantly affects the readings when the aircraft rolls.
(2) When using the Vertical Speed Indicator, the pilot
  (a) can rely on its readings in all attitudes of flight
  (b) can only rely on the readings when changing to horizontal flight
  (c) cannot rely on its readings, especially when a change of pitch attitude is occurring.
(3) In the Inertial Lead (Instantaneous) VSI, lag error
  (a) is eliminated by feeding a sample of static pressure to the case and delaying it to the capsule
  (b) is virtually eliminated by using a special dashpot accelerometer assembly
  (c) is eliminated by the use of a logarithmic presentation.
(4) The purpose of the IVSI is to
  (a) automatically initiate climbs and descents through the automatic flight control system
  (b) give an instantaneous indication of the aircraft's vertical speed when a climb or descent has been initiated
  (c) indicate to the pilot instantaneously when an aircraft pitches in turn, especially steep turns.
(5) Using the IVSI, when initiating changes in the aircraft's pitch attitude
  (a) indications will only be reliable when the aircraft is established in an unchanging attitude
  (b) indications are unreliable at all times
  (c) indications are reliable at all times except in turns.

Chapter 13
MACHMETER

Mach number (MN)

A machmeter indicates an aircraft's mach number. A mach number is defined as the ratio of the aircraft's true airspeed to the local speed of sound, that is, the speed of sound in the airspace in which the aircraft is flying. Expressed in a formula this is:

$$MN = \frac{V}{C} \quad \text{where} \quad \begin{aligned} MN &= \text{mach number,} \\ V &= \text{the aircraft's TAS,} \\ C &= \text{local speed of sound.} \end{aligned}$$

Thus, a machmeter in fact gives the pilot a continuous indication of the ratio of his TAS to the local speed of sound.

It may be asked why this indication is necessary. Actually, this information is of vital importance to the pilot of high speed aircraft. As the flight approaches the speed of sound it is found that the behaviour of the aircraft changes. The physical principles involved at high speed flight are these.

As an aircraft travels through the atmosphere it creates vibratory pressure disturbances; these pressure waves travel ahead of the aircraft at the local speed of sound. They act to give an advance warning to the air ahead of the aircraft's approach which then diverges from the aircraft's path giving a streamlined flow past the aircraft. This is the normal operation. However, as the aircraft's speed increases this warning period gets shorter until the aircraft is flying at the speed of sound, at which time the air will give no warning at all.

Further, even at speeds well below the sonic speeds, say mach 0.75, the air over the thickest section of the wing could be travelling at sonic speeds. If this is so, then the physical conditions on the wing are the same as those which an aircraft flying at the speed of sound would have immediately on its front. These conditions give rise to a shock wave, and the pressure disturbances being created behind the wing will not be able to penetrate it.

The effect of this phenomenon is to increase the drag with possible loss of some lift. Violent impact with the air may cause buffeting and impose severe structural stresses on the airframe. An American test pilot described his sensations at this stage of the flight by comparing it with a motor cycle with iron wheels riding on a cobblestone road at full throttle.

As we noted, this condition does not just arise at the speed of sound: it

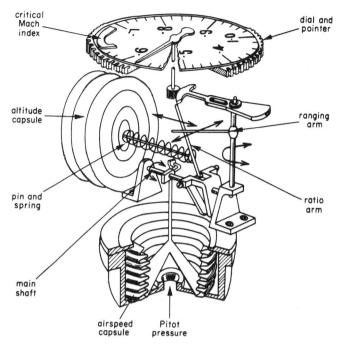

Fig. 13.1   Machmeter exploded view

arises well before this speed is reached. Also, the speed at which it occurs is not the aircraft's TAS, but how much notice it gives, by virtue of its speed, to the air ahead – this means, its speed in relation to the speed of sound. An aircraft which is designed for very high speeds generally employs very thin wing sections and the wings themselves are well swept back. These features delay the onset of the shock wave, and when it does occur, it is well in the rear.

That proportion of the speed of sound (i.e. mach number) which produces the first evidence of local sonic flow when the above described phenomenon occurs and a shock wave is formed for a given type of aircraft, is called *critical mach number* or M_{crit}. A pilot should not let his aircraft exceed this speed unless the aircraft is designed to fly beyond it. Thus, a knowledge of the mach number is of vital importance.

Principle of construction

We require the ratio of two elements – TAS and Local Speed of Sound. Now, TAS is the function of dynamic pressure, P − S, and the density. Speed of sound is the function of static pressure, S, and the density. Density being a factor to both sides of the fraction, the equation may be re-written as:

$$\text{Mach No} = \frac{P - S}{S}$$

Fig. 13.2   Machmeter dial

P — S suggests ASI, or more appropriately an airspeed capsule. Similarly, S suggests altimeter capsule. Therefore, if we had two capsules, one responsive to airspeed and the other to altitude, placed 90° apart to give a ratio, by interlinking their movement to the pointer we could read off mach number. That is precisely what is done in a machmeter (Fig. 13.1).

Operation
Expansion/contraction of the airspeed capsule is transmitted through main shaft to the ratio arm. Similarly, expansion/contraction of altitude capsule is transmitted to the ratio arm through a pin which is kept in position by tension of a spring.

The airspeed capsule causes movement of the ratio arm in one plane, whereas the altitude capsule causes movement of the ratio arm in another plane. The two planes of movement are 90° apart.

The movement of the ratio arm is transmitted through the ranging arm to the pointer. The movement of the various arms is linked to the pointer in such a way that for an increased altitude or airspeed, a higher mach number is indicated.

Mach numbers are printed on the face of the instrument (Fig. 13.2). An adjustable lubber mark is fitted over the dial as shown, to indicate critical mach number.

Errors
This instrument only suffers from Instrument, Pressure and Manoeuvre Induced errors, and these are similar to other pressure instruments.

Density Error   Machmeter does not suffer from this error since, as we saw above, density is a factor applicable to both sides of the equation and thus, its effect is eliminated.

Temperature Error   This again causes no error as it is eliminated with the density.

Compressibility Error   Since compressibility depends on $\dfrac{\text{dynamic}}{\text{static}}$ and the

instrument is calibrated for this ratio, there is no compressibility error.

Therefore, since instrument and pressure errors are relatively small in value as compared with the TAS of the aircraft we can say that indicated mach number equals true mach number. In practice, mach number is always spoken of as indicated mach number and no distinction is made between Indicated, Rectified and True Mach Numbers.

A blocked static will affect the indications in all circumstances when the outside static changes. Thus, for example, if the static line gets blocked while the aircraft is descending, the machmeter will overread. This is because the altimeter capsule will not contract any further (as it ought to with increasing pressure and density at the lower levels), holding the pointer at too high a reading. The ASI capsule also works to the same end, since the old static offers less opposition to the pitot pressure. The overall effect is to give an overread. This effect may also be seen in the formula $MN = V/C$. As you are descending, the value of C is progressively increasing. But since you are using the value of C appropriate to the higher level, you are dividing V by too small a number, giving too high a mach number.

TAS
(1)   In International Standard Atmosphere, RAS = TAS at mean sea level.
(2)   As the height increases, for a given RAS, TAS increases and vice versa.
(3)   RAS − TAS conversions may be made on the computer using the ISA rate of fall of temperature with height of 2C° per thousand feet.

Speed of sound
(1)   In the standard conditions the speed of sound is 661.7 kt at sea level and 573.8 kt at 36 090 ft and above.
(2)   The speed of sound normally decreases as altitude is gained. Although the speed varies with the ratio $T/T_{\text{msl ISA}}$, a reliable formula which can be resolved mentally is $(644 + 1.2t)$ kt, where t is the flight level OAT in °C, or speed may be calculated from formula $C = 39\sqrt{T}$ where T is Absolute temperature. It may also be directly read off the computer: set MN index against corrected air temperature, and read off speed of sound on outer scale against 1 on the inner scale, or it may be interpolated. As ISA temperatures decrease at very nearly 2C°/1000 ft, then $1.2t$ decrease = 2.4, i.e. approximately $2\frac{1}{2}$ kt per thousand feet.

The mach number, speed of sound, TAS and RAS are all interrelated, and we will now study the effect of change of any one of these factors on the remainder.

Aircraft in a climb/descent

Mach number constant
Let us say that an aircraft is climbing from sea level to 36 000 feet (tropopause) at a constant mach number of 0.72. In doing so, the aircraft passes through the regions in which the value of the speed of sound, C, falls from 662 kt to 574 kt.

$$MN = \frac{V}{C}, \quad \therefore TAS = MN \times C$$
$$SL\ TAS = 0.72 \times 662 = 476.64\ kt$$
$$36\,000\ ft\ TAS = 0.72 \times 574 = 413.28\ kt$$

RAS at SL = TAS = 476.64 kt;
RAS at 36 000 ft for ISA temp. of $-56.5°C$ = 231 kt (computer).

Thus, in a climb at a constant mach number, the TAS decreases. RAS also decreases, but at a greater rate.

In descent, the above set of figures reverses, that is, both RAS and TAS increase.

A similar conclusion may be drawn from the inspection of the mach number formula and without use of any mathematics. In this formula, if you are climbing, the value of C decreases and if the mach number is kept constant, the TAS must also reduce proportionally.

TAS constant
If the TAS is kept constant, the RAS must decrease with altitude. In a climb, therefore, the RAS decreases; in a descent, the RAS increases.

MN is the fraction TAS/C. As the aircraft climbs and the value of C decreases, the value of the fraction TAS/C increases and thus, the mach number increases. For similar reasons, in a descent the mach number decreases. Putting this in figures, a mach number of 0.75 at 36 000 feet gives a TAS of 430.5 kt. Descending with the same TAS, at sea level,

$$MN = \frac{430.5}{662} = 0.65, \text{ a decrease.}$$

RAS constant
Let us climb from sea level to 36 000 feet at a constant RAS of 240 kt.

At SL, RAS = 240 kt
TAS = 240 kt

$$MN = \frac{240}{662} = 0.36$$

At 36 000 ft, RAS = 240 kt
TAS = 420 kt   for ISA temp. of $-56.5°C$ (computer)

$$MN = \frac{420}{574} = 0.73$$

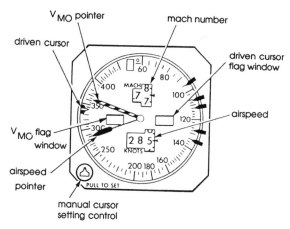

Fig. 13.3   Mach/Airspeed indicator

Thus, in a climb at constant RAS, both the TAS and the mach number increase. Examining the mach number formula, as the aircraft climbs at constant RAS, the TAS must increase and if the TAS increases then the value of the fraction TAS/C increases. This is the increase in the mach number indication. At the same time, as the aircraft climbs, the value of C decreases, increasing the value of the fraction and the mach number.

In a descent, the TAS decreases, and so does the mach number.

Aircraft in a level flight

Even when the RAS or mach number of the aircraft are unaltered on purpose, the mach number indication may change because of changes in the outside temperature. When flying from regions of high temperature to regions of low temperature, the speed of sound decreases. If the mach number is to be kept constant, the TAS must proportionally decrease. Similarly, when flying from cold air to warm air for constant mach number, the TAS must increase.

For the above reasoning, if two aircraft are flying at different levels but doing the same mach number, the one at the lower level has higher TAS.

Serviceability checks

On the ground: check that the pointer is not resting at any place other than at 0 position.

In flight: a rough check may be made by noting a reading of 0.5 mach against IAS of 330 kt near sea level.

Accuracy

±0.01 mach, except at limit of the range where it falls to ±0.02 M.

Mach/Airspeed Indicator (MASI)

This instrument combines the functions of both the airspeed indicator and the machmeter. A typical presentation of the instrument dial is illustrated in Fig. 13.3.

As already described, the machmeter has an airspeed capsule as has the airspeed indicator so there is no difficulty in presenting on the same dial both airspeed and mach number. It is not unusual for both the mach number and the airspeed to be shown digitally on the instrument face as well as by the pointers.

It is usual to provide a pointer for maximum operating speed (V_{MO}). This pointer is striped red and white and is set to the critical mach number. There is also a setting knob by which the pilot can position *bugs* or cursors for important reference speeds such as V_1, V_2, V_R etc. at appropriate locations on the dial. There may be external index pointers too for setting against particular reference speeds.

Because it uses the same source sensor units and the same principles for calibration, the MASI is subject to the same errors as the two individual instruments.

The Mach/Airspeed Indicator is normally linked into the autothrottle/flight management system (see chapter 20) while another use is for it to actuate visual or audio warning systems which are speed related such as indicating the reaching of say, the mach limiting speed or the maximum speed for lowering the landing gear.

Machmeter problems

(1)   The TAS of an aircraft flying in the atmosphere where the speed of sound is 600 nm per hour is 450 kt. What is its mach number?

$$MN = \frac{V}{C} = \frac{450}{600} = 0.75 \quad \text{Answer}$$

(2)   An aircraft is doing a mach number of 0.7 whereas its TAS is 430 kt. What is the speed of sound?

$$C = \frac{V}{MN} = \frac{430}{0.7} \text{kt} = 614.3 \text{kt} \quad \text{Answer}$$

(3)   An aircraft is doing mach 0.66 in an atmosphere where the speed of sound is 615 kt. What is its TAS?

$$V = MN \times C$$
$$= (0.66 \times 615) \text{kt}$$
$$= 405.9 \text{kt} \quad \text{Answer}$$

(4)   A computer may be used in this problem. The rectified airspeed of an aircraft at FL 350 is 230 kt. The corrected outside air temperature is $-60°C$. (a) What is the local speed of sound? (b) What is the aircraft's mach number?

(a) Set the mach number index in the airspeed window against $-60°C$ on the corrected air temperature scale. Read off the speed of sound on the outside scale against 1 on the inside scale. Answer: 568 kt.

(b) RAS converted to TAS is 392 kt (density and compressibility errors). Set the speed of sound against 1 on the inside scale and read off the mach number on the inside scale against TAS 392 kt on the outside scale. Answer: 0.69.

(Note: different computers read slightly different answers.)

(5) An aircraft is doing mach 0.82 in an atmosphere where the speed of sound is 1060 ft/s. What is its TAS?

First convert the speed of sound from feet per second to nm per hour.

$$\text{Speed in kt} = \frac{1060 \times 3600}{6080}$$
$$= 628\,\text{kt} \quad \text{(computer or calculator)}$$

(Note. Alternatively, the relationship 60 mph = 88 ft per second may be used but do not forget to convert mph to kt.)

$$TAS = MN \times C$$
$$= 0.82 \times 628$$
$$= 515\,\text{kt.}$$

(6) If mach 1 at sea level equals 740 mph, give the speed of sound in feet per second. In one hour, distance = 740 sm

$$= 740 \times 5280\,\text{ft}$$

and in one second, distance $= \dfrac{740 \times 5280}{3600}\,\text{ft}$

$$= 1085\,\text{ft} \quad \text{(computer or calculator)}$$

Speed of sound is 1085 ft/s.

(7) At FL 400 where the temperature deviation from jet standard atmosphere is $+10°C$, a TAS of 470 kt is obtained when operating at mach 0.82. What temperature deviation is required to obtain the same TAS for the same mach number when flying at FL 320?

Mach number/TAS relationship only depends on the local speed of sound and is independent of the flight level being flown. The speed of sound, in its turn, is dependent on the ambient temperature which means that for every temperature there is one speed of sound. Thus the problem involves first discovering the actual temperature at FL 400.

FL 400:

	Jet standard temp.	$= -65°C$
	Deviation	$= +10°C$
	Actual	$= -55°C$

What we have now established is that the speed of sound that results from an ambient temperature of $-55°C$ gives a TAS of 470 kt for mach 0.82.

FL 320:   Standard temp. $= -49°C$
               Temperature necessary $= -55°C$
               Deviation necessary $= -\ 6°C$ Answer

(8)   If the local speed of sound is 450 kt, what will be the increase in TAS if the mach number is increased by 0.06?

For a constant speed of sound, the TAS increase in direct proportion to the increase in mach number. Therefore

$$\text{increase in TAS} = (450 \times 0.06)\,\text{kt}$$
$$= 27\,\text{kt}\quad\text{Answer}$$

(9)   It is given that temperature in the jet standard atmosphere decreases at 2°/1000 ft from +15°C at sea level with no tropopause. The speed of sound is 660 kt at +15°C and varies as the square root of the absolute temperature.

Using these assumptions, give the temperature (°C) in the jet standard atmosphere where the TAS is 400 kt for a mach number of 0.735.

For a TAS of 400 kt at mach 0.735, the speed of sound is 544 kt (calculator). Therefore, the ratios are:

$$\frac{544}{660} = \frac{\sqrt{T}}{\sqrt{(288)}};\ \sqrt{T} = \frac{544\sqrt{(288)}}{660}\quad\text{and}\quad T = \frac{544^2 \times 288}{660^2}$$

$$= 195.7\ \text{(by calculator)}.$$

where T is the absolute temperature and $A = 273 +\ °C$
$\therefore\ 195.7 - 273 = -77.3°C.$

Alternatively, on the computer, set TAS on the outside scale against mach number on the inside scale. Against 1 on the inside scale, read off the local spedd of sound. Then solve the formula $C = 39\sqrt{T}$.

(10)   At FL 280 a decrease in mach 0.1 results in a decrease in TAS of 58 kt. What is the local speed of sound?

$$C = \frac{V}{MN} = \frac{58}{0.1}\,\text{kt} = 580\,\text{kt}\quad\text{Answer}$$

Test questions
(1)   A leak in the pitot source will
   (a)   have no effect on machmeter reading accuracy
   (b)   cause the machmeter to overread
   (c)   cause the machmeter to underread.
(2)   A machmeter is subject to
   (a)   instrument and pressure errors
   (b)   instrument and density errors
   (c)   instrument, pressure and density errors.
(3)   If the static vent becomes blocked with ice and the aircraft descends rapidly, the machmeter will

(a) not be subject to any error because of the dual capsule system

(b) overread

(c) underread.

(4) In presenting the indicated mach number whilst cruising at 30 000 ft, the machmeter is representing the aircraft's TAS as a decimal fraction of the speed of sound

(a) in ISA at msl

(b) in ISA at 30 000 ft

(c) locally at 30 000 ft.

(5) The local speed of sound in air at ambient temperature of −25°C is

(a) 674 kt

(b) 614 kt

(c) 644 kt.

(6) The machmeter mechanisms measure

(a) ambient speed of sound

(b) the ratio of dynamic pressure to static pressure

(c) the ratio of pitot pressure to static pressure.

(7) In the machmeter, pitot and static pressures are fed respectively to

(a) the case and one capsule

(b) one capsule and the case

(c) their own capsules.

(8) The formula for calculating mach number is

(a) $39\sqrt{T}$

(b) $644 + 1.2t$

(c) $TAS/39\sqrt{T}$.

Chapter 14
GYROSCOPE

Try balancing a stationary bicycle wheel and see how hard the task is. Now give it a gentle tap at the rear and make it roll. You will notice that while it is rolling at reasonable speed it does not fall down. The explanation is contained in the gyroscopic properties of the rolling wheel. A gyroscope may be described simply – any wheel that spins on its axis is a gyroscope. A spinning top, motor car wheels, aircraft propellers – these are just a few examples.

When a wheel spins on its axis it acquires two properties called Rigidity in Space and Precession.

Rigidity
This is the reluctance of a gyroscope to change the direction of its spin axis. This property is acquired in obedience to Newton's First Law of Motion which states that a body continues to remain in state of rest or uniform motion unless an external force is applied to change that state.

In Fig. 14.1 the gyro axis is in the horizontal plane and the wheel is spinning in the vertical plane. As the wheel spins, each particle of the wheel tends to continue in its instantaneous direction as shown in the figure. This is to be expected, according to Newton. The fact that the particles do not fly off the wheel due to the tensile strength of the metal does not in any way affect this directional characteristic acquired by the moving particles. Any attempt to change the direction of the spin axis in any plane will therefore be met with opposition. This is the property of rigidity: once spinning, the gyro axis will remain pointing in the same direction in space. For the bicycle wheel to fall down while rolling, the spin axis must change its direction by 90° and unless external force is applied, it will not do so as long as it has a reasonable speed. The magnitude of rigidity is directly proportional to the speed of the wheel. The faster it spins, the greater the rigidity it acquires. It is also proportional to the moment of inertia of the wheel. To improve moment of inertia, the gyro wheel is given as large a radius as the design factors would permit and the bulk of its weight is concentrated at the rim. If you think of the magnetic compass you will notice that this is just the opposite of what is done in that compass to achieve aperiodicity. Finally, rigidity is inversely proportional to the external force applied. To put this in mathematics,

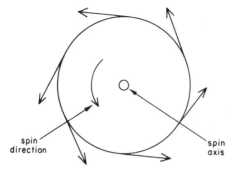

Fig. 14.1   Rigidity in space

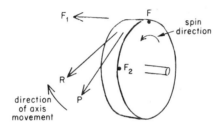

Fig. 14.2   Precession

$$R \propto \frac{SI}{F} \quad \text{where} \quad \begin{aligned} R &= \text{rigidity} \\ S &= \text{speed of the wheel} \\ I &= \text{moment of inertia and} \\ F &= \text{External Force} \end{aligned}$$

Precession

In Fig. 14.2, P is the instantaneous direction of travel of a moving particle in a wheel spinning with its axis horizontal. F is a force applied at top of the wheel, resulting in force vector, F_1. If the wheel was stationary the effect of F_1 would be to topple the gyro, since vector P is absent. In the case of a spinning wheel, however, the two vectors will resolve into a resultant direction, R, and the axis will move clockwise from P to R. This is like saying that force was applied at point F_2 on a stationary wheel. This is precession.

In Fig. 14.3(a) force F is applied so as to rotate the axis anti-clockwise in the horizontal plane, as viewed from above. (Force F is applied at the paper, coming out towards us.) That force will travel through 90° and act at point F_1 and the gyro will topple – Fig. 14.3(b). This is again precession. Precession can, therefore, be described as follows: when a force is applied to a spinning wheel, that force does not act at the point of application, but acts at a point which is 90° removed from it in the direction of the spin. Going back to the

Fig. 14.3 Precessed force

bicycle wheel, if you wish to turn the direction, you tap the appropriate side of the wheel at the top. A stationary wheel would have fallen down with this tap. In a moving wheel this force travels forward through 90° and acts. Thus, say the tap was from left to right. This left to right force acts at the forward-most point (90° removed in the direction of the spin) of the wheel and turns the wheel to the right.

In order to precess a gyro we must overcome its rigidity. The higher the speed, the greater the force required to precess it. Similarly, the larger the moment of inertia the greater the force required. Mathematically, therefore:

$$\text{Precession} \propto \frac{F}{SI}$$

These two expressions reveal that rigidity and precession are opposing terms, which is quite true. Rigidity is the reluctance to move; precession is the tendency to move.

Types of gyroscope
The basic classification of gyroscopes is as follows:

Space (or free) gyro
A gyroscope having freedom in all three planes is called a space gyro. The gyro is mounted in two concentrically pivoted rings, called the inner and outer gimbal rings. The three planes relate to the three axes of aircraft, i.e. fore-and-aft axis, athwartships axis and vertical axis. There is no means of any external control over a space gyro, a feature which distinguishes it from tied gyro and earth gyro.

Tied gyro
This is a space gyro which has a means of external control in one or more planes. Being basically a space gyro a tied gyro has freedom in all three planes. An uncontrolled space gyro would be of no practical use in an aircraft instrument where the gyro is required to be set up and maintained in a certain direction. We will learn the control systems with individual instruments later.

Fig. 14.4   Ring laser gyro

Earth gyro
This is a tied gyro but controlled by the gravity of the Earth.

Rate gyro
This is a gyro having two planes of freedom only, the planes of freedom being 90° removed from the plane of rotation. It is utilised to measure rate of turn in the plane of no freedom and we will learn more about it later.

Solid state gyro
A ring laser gyro (Fig. 14.4) is a rate sensor and has no rotor as in the conventional gyroscope. It consists basically of a solid block of thermally-stable glass within which there is a cavity, or laser path, filled with a lasing medium such as helium-neon. Ring laser gyro (RLG) accuracy is proportional to the area enclosed within the laser path, so a circular shape would provide the ideal ratio of minimum path length to maximum area enclosed. However laser beams travel in straight lines and although square RLGs have been tried, generally triangular RLGs with three mirrors to 'fold' the laser beams have been adopted. Two laser beams travel around the triangular path in opposite directions. When the gyro rotates about its axis, one beam takes slightly longer to complete its journey and the other takes slightly less. The beams are combined and the time difference measured by an optical sensor, delivering a digital readout proportional to the rate sensed. RLGs are not cheap, with the mirrors which determine the laser path accuracy being particularly expensive. Nevertheless they have distinct advantages of being operational within a second of being switched on, of a high degree of

reliability compared with conventional spinning-mass gyros, of being insensitive to *g* while being sensitive to low rates over a wide dynamic range.

Methods of driving gyro rotors

There are two main methods used to spin the rotors of aircraft gyroscopic instruments: electric and pneumatic. On a flight deck it may be found that while the main panel instruments use one method, the standby instruments use the alternative method. In each case, achieving a high rotor speed (rev/min) will give greater stability of instrument indications.

Electrically driven gyros generally use power derived from an inverter or engine-driven alternator. Pneumatically driven gyros are mounted in instrument cases connected to the aircraft's vacuum system, often produced by an engine-driven vacuum pump. The vacuum in the system is usually controlled by a relief valve to a value between 3.5 and 4.5 inches Hg. Another connection leads from the instrument case to the outside atmosphere. As the vacuum system draws air from the instrument case, surrounding air enters through jets. This higher pressure air from the jet(s) impinges on 'buckets' cut into the rim of the gyro rotor, so causing it to rotate at high speed. Disadvantages of the air driven system are that a filter to exclude dust in the air must be incorporated in the system, and at high altitudes there is a smaller pressure differential, so reducing rotor speed.

Gyro wander

Any deviation of the gyro axis from its set direction is termed as gyro wander. It is of two types.

Real wander

Any physical deviation of the gyro axis from a fixed direction in space is called real wander. A gyro axis ought not to wander away but various forces do effectively act on the gyro and cause it to precess. For example, some friction is always present at the spin axis. If this friction is symmetrical it merely slows down the rotor; if it is asymmetric, a force will arise which will have a precessing effect on the gyro. Similarly, friction in the gimbal rings (rings that hold the rotor and allow it movement in various planes) will precess the gyro. Another instance is the shift of the centre of gravity of the gyroscope from its dead centre position. This usually occurs as a result of wear on the gyro. When flying through turbulent air, turbulent vectors acting on the gyro will resolve in an ultimate direction and a precessing force will result. These errors are not constant; they vary with time and therefore no calibration cards are produced.

Apparent wander

As the term suggests the gyro axis in this case does not physically wander away and yet to an observer it appears to have changed its direction. The

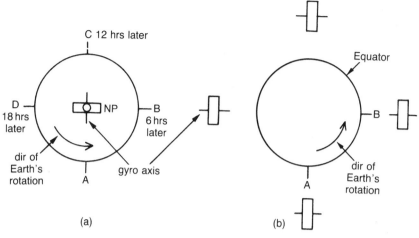

Fig. 14.5   Drift and topple of horizontal axis gyro

reason for this is quite simple: the gyro maintains its direction with reference to a fixed point in space whereas we, on the earth, rotate with or move over the rotating earth. Thus, since we ourselves do not maintain a fixed direction in space, the gyro must appear to us with the passage of time to have altered direction. We will study the effects due to the earth's rotation on a horizontal axis gyro and a vertical axis gyro separately.

Horizontal axis gyro

In Fig. 14.5(a) we have a horizontal axis gyro at the North Pole. An observer at A sets the gyro so that its axis is aligned with him, as shown in the figure. Six hours later the earth will have rotated through 90° and the observer will be viewing the same gyro from position B. To the observer who does not appreciate his own velocity, the gyro axis appears to have moved clockwise in the horizontal plane through 90°. Twelve hours later he will be observing the gyro along its axis but from the opposite end. Eighteen hours later he will be at position D and the axis will appear to have rotated through 270°. Finally, twenty-four hours later he will be again at Position A and view the axis just as he had initially set it.

This is an example of apparent wander. Apparent wander in the horizontal plane as we discussed above is known as *gyro drift*, and since at the Poles there is a drift of 360° in 24 hours, we can say that the drift experienced at the poles is the maximum possible value (that is, rate of drift is the same as the angular velocity of the earth). To be more precise the rate of drift is 15°.04 per hour.

In the above discussion, you would notice that with the horizontal axis gyro all the apparent movement occurs only in the horizontal plane. In other words, the gyro does not show up any movement in the vertical plane in terms of its axis rising or falling. Any movement of the gyro axis in the vertical plane is called *gyro topple (or tilt)*, and in this case there is no topple or tilt.

In Fig. 14.5(b) the gyro is a horizontal axis gyro and is placed at the equator. Here, its axis may be aligned in the north–south direction, that is along the observer's meridian or it may be aligned in the east–west direction, that is along the equator. At the equator all meridians are parallel to each other and a gyro axis aligned with a meridian will remain with that meridian throughout the period of 24 hours. This means that there will be no drift and no topple. If the axis is aligned with the equator as in the figure it will be noticed that six hours later the horizontal axis gyro will appear to be a vertical axis gyro (position B). This is an apparent change in the vertical plane and therefore, a topple. Further, the axis appeared to move through 90° in six hours, which means the rate of topple at the equator is the maximum possible (15°.04 per hour). The axis otherwise does not appear to move in the horizontal plane and thus there is no drift. To summarise:

Horizontal axis gyro: at Poles   : maximum drift; no topple;
at equator: no drift; maximum topple.

Vertical axis gyro

In Fig. 14.6(a) an observer at the North Pole sets up a gyro with its axis vertical. It will be apparent that the earth will rotate beneath the axis, and the gyro axis will neither appear to topple nor drift.

In Fig. 14.6(b) the observer is shown at the equator at position A with gyro axis vertical. The effect is similar to the horizontal gyro in Fig. 14.5(b). Six hours later when in position B the gyro axis will appear to have spun through 90° in the vertical plane to become apparently a horizontal axis gyro. To summarise:

Vertical axis gyro: at Poles   : no drift; no topple;
at equator: no drift; maximum topple.

Combining the two we may summarise that drift at the Poles is 15°.04 per hour and 0 at the equator. Topple is 0 at the Poles and 15°.04 per hour at the equator. From this, drift and topple at intermediate latitudes bear the following relationship:

Drift   = 15°.04 × sine of the latitude per hour, and
Topple = 15°.04 × cosine of the latitude per hour.

Let us take an example to clarify the discussion. Say we set up a horizontal axis gyro, the axis facing east–west direction at 30°N. We want to know what will be the attitude of the axis after four hours. Since it is a horizontal axis gyro at an intermediate latitude facing east–west, it will both drift and topple.

Drift = 4 × 15.04 sin 30
= 30°.08

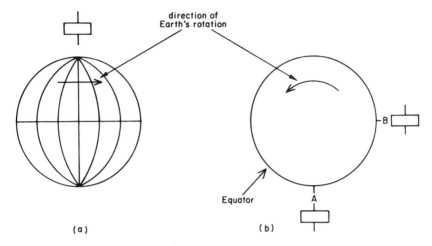

Fig. 14.6   Drift and topple of vertical axis gyro

From Fig. 14.5(a) we note that the gyro axis drifts clockwise in the northern hemisphere (and therefore anti-clockwise in the southern hemisphere). Thus, the axis is now aligned with 090 + 30.08 = 120°.08/ 300°.08 direction.

$$\text{Topple} = 4 \times 15.04 \cos 30$$
$$= 52°.1$$

As the earth travels from west to east and the axis remains pointing in the same direction in space, the eastern end of the axis will appear to have risen by 52°.1 and the western end to have been similarly depressed.

On modern aircraft, gyroscopes are remote from the instrument panel. There are usually two vertical reference and two horizontal reference gyros from which electrical signals are conveyed to the flight deck instrument panel.

Test questions
(1) Increasing the angular momentum of a gyro rotor will
   (a) have no substantial effect on gyroscopic rigidity
   (b) increase the gyroscopic rigidity
   (c) decrease the gyroscopic rigidity.
(2) The efficacy with which a spinning rotor will remain aligned with a given datum is dependent upon the rotor's mass being
   (a) concentrated at as great a radius as possible
   (b) concentrated at as close to the axis of spin as possible
   (c) uniformly distributed throughout the rotor.
(3) The degree of rigidity of a gyroscope depends upon
   (a) the weight of the rotor only
   (b) the speed of rotation of the rotor only
   (c) the distribution of the rotor weight and the speed of rotation.

(4) A force applied to the spinning axis of a rotor is precessed
    (a) through 90° in the direction of spin of the rotor
    (b) through 270° in the direction of spin of the rotor
    (c) through 90° in the direction of spin of the rotor in the Northern Hemispher, and 270° in the direction of spin in the Southern Hemisphere.

(5) Real wander of a gyroscope can be caused by
    (a) asymmetrical friction at the spinning axis
    (b) the earth's rotation beneath the gyroscope
    (c) the instrument being a tied gyro as opposed to a space gyro.

(6) Apparent wander in the horizontal plane caused by the earth's rotation varies
    (a) as sine latitude
    (b) as cosine latitude
    (c) in direct proportion to the angular velocity of the rotor.

(7) A space gyroscope with complete freedom of movement in all three planes is spinning at the equator with its spinning axis in the local vertical. After six hours, neglecting mechanical wander, the spinning axis will be
    (a) still in the local vertical
    (b) in the local horizontal
    (c) in the local vertical, having turned through 180°.

(8) A gyroscope which is constrained so as to have one plane of freedom only is known as
    (a) a tied gyroscope
    (b) an earth gyroscope
    (c) a rate gyroscope.

(9) On a ring laser gyro
    (a) there is one laser beam which circulates clockwise
    (b) there is one laser beam which circulates anti-clockwise
    (c) there are two laser beams circulating in opposite directions.

(10) A RLG
    (a) has a vertical gyro
    (b) is a rate sensor
    (c) has a horizontal gyro.

Chapter 15
DIRECTION INDICATOR (DI)

The Direction Indicator (DI) employs a horizontal axistied gyro and utilises the principle of rigidity to indicate aircraft's heading. A spinning rotor, as we saw in the previous chapter, has the property of rigidity in space. Thus once the DI rotor attains its full speed and its axis is manually aligned with a datum (true or magnetic north) it will continue to point in that direction in space during the rest of the flight. When the aircraft alters its heading it does so relative to the gyro axis, that is, the aircraft and the gyro case turn about the gyro axis. Changes in headings are thus indicated instantaneously.

It also utilises the property of precession for two purposes:

(a)   to provide gyro control and
(b)   to compensate for apparent wander.

Although the DI was the first gyroscopic instrument to appear on the flightdeck as a means of indicating heading, as newer aircraft have come into service it has been replaced by remote indicating compass systems (see Chapter 26) and Flight Director Systems.

Construction

The DI rotor is mounted in two rings called the inner gimbal and outer gimbal. Each gimbal has movement independent of the other. The rotor is mounted in the inner gimbal, the gimbal itself lies in the horizontal plane and the rotor which it holds spins in the vertical plane. The inner gimbal is mounted in the outer gimbal pivoted at two points on the inner gimbal which are 90° removed from the rotor axis. See Fig. 15.1. This allows the rotor to move about the horizontal axis. This movement, however, is restricted to 110°, that is, 55° either side of the rotor's vertical plane. This limits indications of the aircraft's manoeuvres in pitch and roll and if the limits are exceeded the inner gimbal will come in contact with a mechanical stop and the gyro will precess. The restriction is necessary in order to prevent the inner gimbal from coming in contact with the outer gimbal and damaging the instrument.

The outer gimbal is mounted in the case of the instrument and pivots about the vertical plane. This ring has freedom of 360° and carries the scale card. The rotor is driven by a jet of air from a nozzle, air entering the rotor case through a hole in the periphery of the case. Air impinges on small buckets carved out of the rim and spins the rotor at about 12 000 rpm.

Fig. 15.1   Direction indicator exploded view

The initial setting of the heading and subsequent resettings during the flight are carried out by use of the gyro caging control. The caging knob on the instrument is depressed and turned until the required heading appears in the window. When the knob is so depressed a bevel pinion engages a system of bevel gear, part of the outer gimbal. Thus, by turning the knob, the outer gimbal carrying the scale card is turned. The knob, when depressed, also locks the inner gimbal by means of a caging arm. This prevents the rotor from toppling while the force is being exerted on the outer gimbal. (Set the heading when the aircraft is flying straight and level as otherwise a small error may occur in the reading.)

The gyro should be caged during violent manoeuvres or manoeuvres likely to exceed the limits. The caging control is also used to erect the gyro should it inadvertently topple. This is because the caging arm rights the rotor before it locks it.

Finally it is important to remember that the gyro must be uncaged and resynchronised before the DI is used again.

Gyro control

When an aircraft alters its heading it turns about its vertical axis. Thus, the heading measurements will only be correct when measured with reference to that axis. This means that the rotor attitude must be controlled so that during banked turns it remains spinning in the aircraft's vertical plane (and not true vertical). This is achieved as follows. In Fig. 15.2(a) the aircraft is straight and level, the rotor is in the aircraft's vertical plane and the air jets driving force, X, is fully utilised to drive the rotor. In Fig. 15.2(b) the aircraft is in right bank. It will be seen that the driving force is not fully utilised to drive the buckets. Therefore, this force, X, must break down into two components, X_1 and X_2 at 90° to each other. X_1 acts along the rotor, now driving it at reduced speed. X_2 acts on the rim of the rotor. This component will precess through 90° in accordance with the precession rule in the direction of spin and

Fig. 15.2   DI gyro control

act at X_3 in the direction shown. The effect of this force is to precess the rotor until it is aligned once again with the air jets as illustrated in Fig. 15.2(a). The rotor is then in the aircraft's vertical axis.

Gyro drift

All horizontal axis gyroscopes are subject to drift as explained in the previous chapter, and the DI is no exception. The drift occurs due to both real and apparent wander and the DI should be reset at regular intervals during the flight. An air driven instrument in good condition should not precess more than 4° every 15 minutes.

The real wander occurs due to friction, static unbalance (e.g. shift of the centre of gravity) and air turbulence. There is no means of predicting these errors to enable us to allow for them since wear and tear alters the values. The apparent wander due to the earth's rotation occurs at the rate of approximately 15°.04 sin lat per hour. The effect of this on heading indications is discussed in the following paragraphs.

We will take the northern hemisphere for illustration and study the effect on the heading reading in four situations, that is, effect when aircraft is stationary, aircraft on easterly track, aircraft on westerly track and finally, aircraft on northerly–southerly track.

In Fig. 15.3(a) let us say that we lined up the DI with the local meridian at position A. The heading indicated is 090°. Consider the effect one hour later, the gyro remaining stationary. The local meridian will have changed its direction in space due to the earth's rotation and let us say that it arrives at position A_1. Now, the gyro rotor remains aligned with the local meridian direction one hour ago (assuming that there is no real drift) and this phenomenon must cause a discrepancy between the two gyro readings, that is the initial reading of 090° and the reading one hour later. The error occurs at the rate of 15°.04 sin lat/hr and the readings, as will be seen from the diagram, decrease.

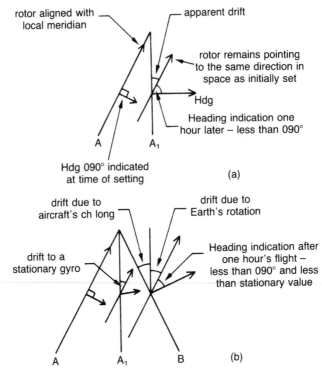

Fig. 15.3   (a) DI gyro drift – aircraft stationary, (b) DI gyro drift – aircraft heading east

Suppose the aircraft took off from A on an easterly track. One hour later, when the earth's meridian A has reached A_1, the aircraft will have travelled to a new meridian, B. At B the heading will be in error due to two causes: earth's rotation and the aircraft's change of longitude (again assuming no real wander) and the reading will be still less, Fig. 15.3(b).

In Fig. 15.4(a) the gyro is shown with its axis aligned with local meridian A and the aircraft is on a track of 270°. In one hour's time meridian A will have changed direction to A_1 and if the aircraft was stationary an error of 15°.04 sin lat would be recorded, the readings reducing. However, the aircraft flying on westerly track will arrive at longitude B in one hour's time. The reading at B will still be less than 270° but more than what would be indicated if it remained stationary. The aircraft in the illustration is presumed to have its speed less than the speed of the earth at the local parallel of latitude. It will be appreciated that if an aircraft is flying at the same speed as the speed of the earth but on a westerly track it would negate the earth's easterly velocity. In that case it would reach position A in the same time that original A displaced itself to A_1 and the gyro would give no error.

In Fig. 15.4(b) the aircraft having aligned its gyro to the local meridian sets off from A on a southerly track and arrives at A_1 after one hour. The aircraft

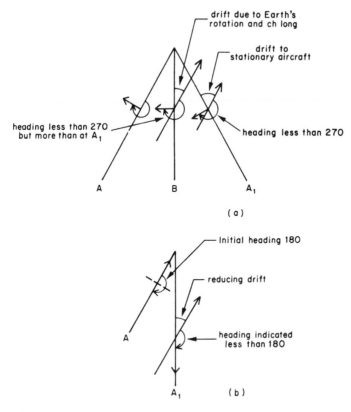

Fig. 15.4 (a) DI gyro drift – aircraft heading west, (b) DI gyro drift – aircraft heading south

is flying down the same meridian; the deviation to A_1 is due to the earth's rotation. The reading here is less than 180, and it should be noticed that the magnitude of the error is a continuously decreasing value as the aircraft travels southward (sine of equator is 0). Similarly on northerly track the readings decrease but the rate of decrease quickens as the flight progresses northward.

Southern Hemisphere

The results are opposite to NH in that the readings increase. One example is sufficient to show this. In Fig. 15.5 an aircraft on longitude A sets up its gyro with the local meridian and the reading is 090°. If the aircraft remains stationary, in one hour's time meridian A will change direction to A_1. The indicator reading as can be seen in the figure has increased, the rate of increment still being 15°.04 sin lat. If the aircraft was flying on an easterly track it will arrive at B in one hour and the heading indicated will have increased still further.

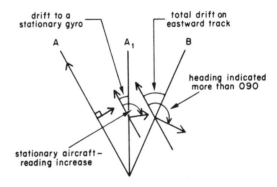

Fig. 15.5   DI gyro drift – southern hemisphere case

To summarise – unbalanced gyro
Aircraft speed less than that of the earth at that latitude.

Northern hemisphere
Aircraft travelling east   – the readings decrease.
Aircraft travelling west   – the readings decrease but at a lesser rate.
Aircraft travelling south – the readings decrease at a decreasing rate.
Aircraft travelling north – the readings decrease at an increasing rate.

Southern hemisphere
Aircraft travelling east   – the readings increase.
Aircraft travelling west   – the readings increase at a lesser rate.
Aircraft travelling south – the readings increase at an increasing rate.
Aircraft travelling north – the readings increase at a decreasing rate.

Compensation for apparent wander
Where an aircraft operates in the vicinity of a given latitude the gyroscope may be mechanically precessed equally and in the opposite direction to the drift experienced at that latitude, thus compensating for the apparent wander. The mechanism involved is a nut called the latitude nut which is screwed on the inner gimbal ring. A balance weight at the opposite end of the axis balances the weight of the nut when the nut is riding in the central position. The latitude nut is then screwed inward or outward as required to produce a force in the vertical plane which precesses the rotor in the horizontal plane. In Fig. 15.6 the nut is screwed outward to compensate for drift in the southern hemisphere. It should, however, be appreciated that it only compensates for that latitude for which it is corrected, as long as the gyro remains stationary. Errors will arise on all tracks, and in assessing these errors the effect of the compensating device will have to be considered. A latitude balanced gyro will give errors as follows:

Fig. 15.6   Latitude nut

N. hemisphere
(the correction is +15° sin lat per hour to compensate for a decrease)

Stationary   nil drift at the latitude of compensation

Fly east   readings *decrease* as aircraft speed adds to earth's rotation, so 15° sin lat per hour is too small a correction

Fly west   readings *increase* as aircraft speed subtracts from earth's rotation, so 15° sin lat per hour is too large a correction

Fly north   readings *decrease*: sin lat is getting larger, and 15° sin lat per hour is insufficient correction

Fly south   readings *increase*: sin lat is reducing in value, and a correction of 15° sin lat is too large

S. hemisphere
(the correction is −15° sin lat per hour)

Stationary   nil drift at the latitude of compensation

Fly east   readings *increase* as aircraft speed adds to speed of earth's rotation, so correction of 15° sin lat per hour is not enough

Fly west   readings *decrease* as aircraft speed subtracts from speed of earth's rotation, so correction of 15° sin lat per hour is too much

Fly north   readings *decrease* as sin lat decreases, so correction of 15° sin lat is too much

Fly south   reading *increase* as sin lat gets greater, and correction of 15° sin lat is not enough.

Finally on this important point, if a gyro is compensated for wander at 60°N, an amount of drift of +15° sin 60° has been put in. Taking that gyro to 30°N means that too much has been put in and the readings would be in error on this account only. Taking the same compensated gyro to 60°S would mean that +15° sin 60° has been put in to add still to the 15° sin 60° wander there anyway – in fact, doubling the drift.

Gimballing errors

These are minor errors which occur due to the geometry of the gimballing system. They occur when the aircraft is banked, in a climb or a descent. They disappear as soon as straight and level flight is resumed.

Type of gyro

The gyro used in DI is a tied gyro, having freedom in three planes. The axis of the gyroscope is aligned with the 000–180 indication. Being a horizontal axis gyro, the forces imposed on the axis during a turn result in the movement of the rotor in the vertical plane. Any such movement has no effect on the heading indication and therefore a DI does not suffer from conventional turn and acceleration errors.

Gyro problems

The gyro problems revolve about four basic conditions: the gyro is unbalanced; the gyro is balanced for a latitude; the gyro is stationary; the gyro is moving. All problems will have somewhere in them the application of the fundamental formula: drift = 15° sin lat. Repeating here, the readings decrease in the northern hemisphere; increase in the southern hemisphere. This is purely the effect of the earth's rotation and we are not concerned at this stage whether the gyro is balanced or unbalanced, stationary or mobile. When the gyro is mobile, the changing meridians modify the result in the formula 15° sin lat. When the aircraft is on an easterly track the amount of convergency (ch long × sin mean lat) is added; when on a westerly track it is subtracted from the result of 15° sin lat. And this rule applies to either hemisphere. We now propose that you adopt the following layout in working out your gyro problems.

(1) Apparent wander due to the earth's rotation (15° sin lat) _____
            (enter decrease if in the NH; increase if in the SH)
(2) Apparent wander due to convergency (ch long × sin lat) _____
            (+ if easterly Tr; − if westerly Tr)
(3) Sum of items 1 and 2 is the total wander _____ (inc or dec)
(4) Add the real wander (or lat nut)   _____ (inc or dec)
(5) The sum is the total drift   _____ (inc or dec)

Note that you may not need to use all the steps in the above layout, neither would you always start at the top and work downwards. You may start at the bottom and work upwards. The idea is to complete initially as much of your proforma as possible from the data in the question and work out the rest. You will also notice that when the question involves the aircraft's new meridian, or the distance travelled in an E/W direction (departure) or the aircraft's ground speed, the information in item 2 will yield the answer. All these factors are directly concerned with the convergency.

$$\text{Convergency} = \text{ch long} \times \text{sin mean lat.}$$

Ch long × sin mean lat is the figure that goes in item 2. If departure is given in the question you may convert it to convergency in two steps.
(a)   Ch long = departure × sec lat.
(b)   Convergency = ch long × sin mean lat.
These two steps may be cut down to a single simple operation as follows:

$$\text{ch long} = \frac{\text{dep}}{\text{cos lat}} \quad \text{and} \quad \text{convergency} = \text{ch long} \times \text{sin lat}$$

$$\therefore \text{convergency} = \frac{\text{dep}}{\text{cos lat}} \times \text{sin lat}$$

$$= \text{dep} \times \text{tan lat}$$

and since we want convergency in degrees, the departure in the above formula is also in degrees of longitude.

The same formula may be rewritten to find departure:

$$\text{departure} = \frac{\text{convergency}}{\text{tan lat}}$$

and since departure is in nautical miles rather than in degrees of longitude, the convergency in this formula is in minutes of longitude. All this should be crystal clear after you have done a few problems.
(1)   An unbalanced gyro free from real wander is set up at 60°N. What will be the effect on the gyro reading after one hour?

Solution

$$\text{Apparent wander} = 15° \sin 60°$$
$$= 15° \times 0.866$$
$$= 13° \text{ reading's decrease in one hour.}$$

(2)   A directional gyro is balanced at 45°S. If it is free from other real wander, what will be the effect on the reading if the gyro remains stationary at 45°S?

Answer: The gyro will continue to give correct readings.

(3)   A DI gyro is balanced so that the drift is zero when stationary at 45°S. What drift will it experience when stationary at 60°N assuming that there is no real wander apart from that due to the lat nut?

Solution
The first step is to ascertain how much correction has been applied at 45°S. This correction will be equal in magnitude and opposite in sign to the apparent wander at 45°S.

$$\text{Gyro drift at 45°S} = 15° \sin 45°$$
$$= 15° \times 0.7071$$
$$= 10.6°/\text{hr}$$

and since this is southern hemisphere, the readings increase. Therefore, the real wander due to compensatory measures is 10.6°/h decrease. Now we can work out the effect at 60°N.

$$\text{App. drift at } 60°N = 15° \sin 60° = 13°/h \text{ decrease}$$
$$\text{Real drift } = \underline{10.6°/h} \text{ decrease (lat nut)}$$
$$\text{Total } = \underline{23.6°/h} \text{ decrease}$$

(4) A perfect DI gyro has been balanced for 45°S. What drift will it experience when flying along the parallel of 45°S on a track of 090°(T), with ground speed 240 kt?

Solution

App. wander at 45°S = 15° sin 45°   = 10.6°/h increase

Convergency = dep tan lat = $\dfrac{240}{60}$ tan 45°   = +4.0°/h (easterly)

Total   = 14.6°/h increase

Real wander = 10.6°/h decrease

Total drift   = 4.0°/h increase

(5) A perfect gyro is balanced to give zero drift when stationary at 45°S. What drift will it experience when flying on a track of 270°(T) along 45°S at a ground speed of 240 kt?

Answer: 4°/h decrease.

Solution

App. wander 45°S   = 15° sin 45° = 10.6°/h inc
Conv.   = dep tan lat   = 4 tan 45°   = −4°/h (west)

Total   6.6°/h inc

Real (lat nut)   10.6°/h dec

Total   4.0°/h decrease

(6) A gyro is compensated for 45°N. What drift will be experienced when flying on 090°(T), at ground speed 240 kt in latitude 60°N?

Answer: 9.3°/h decrease.

Solution

Correction at 45°N = 10.6 inc.
App. wander at 60°N   = 15° sin 60°   = 13.0°/h dec
Conv. = dep tan lat   = 4 × 1.7321 = +6.9°/h (east)

Total   19.9°/h dec

Real wander (lat nut)   10.6°/h inc

Total   9.3°/h dec

(7)   A DI gyro is adjusted to give zero drift at 50°N. What drift will be experienced when flying at 60°N on a track of 270°(T) at a ground speed of 360 kt?

Answer: 8.9°/h increase.

Solution

App. wander at 50°N = 15° sin 50° = 11.5°/h dec

∴ Correction = 11.5°/h inc

App. wander lat 60°N = 15 sin 60°   =   13.0°/h dec

Conv. = dep tan 60° = 6 tan 60   −10.4°/h (west)

Total   2.6°/h dec

Real (lat nut)   11.5°/h inc

Total   8.9°/h inc

(8)   A stationary gyro on being tested at 58°N gives a drift of 9°/h, the readings decreasing. At which latitude would this gyro give zero drift?

Answer: 14°17′N.

Solution

The first thing we want to check is the apparent wander at 58°N to see if it is in fact 9°/h decrease. If it isn't then there is some real drift which we must calculate.

App. drift at 58°N = 15° sin 58° = 12.7°/h dec

Actual drift in the gyro   =   9.0°/h dec

∴ Real drift   =   3.7°/h inc

We know now there is real drift in the gyro which increases the reading at the rate of 3.7°/h. In order to reduce this drift to zero all we have to do is to take the gyro to a latitude where the apparent drift is the same in magnitude as the real drift, but opposite in sign. Thus, in the present problem the real drift is 3.7°/h, increase: the latitude we want is where the apparent wander is 3.7°/h, decrease. The hemisphere is immediately indicated by the term decrease: the latitude we are looking for is in the northern hemisphere. Now for the second part

app. drift = 15° sin lat, or

$$\text{sin lat} = \frac{\text{app drift}}{15°}$$

$$= \frac{3.7°}{15°} = 0.2467$$

$$= 14°17′N$$

(9)   With reference to problem 8 above, what drift would you expect at 30°S?

Answer: 11.2°/h increase.

Solution

$$\begin{aligned}
\text{App. wander at 30°S} = 15° \sin 30° = 7.5°/\text{h inc} \\
\text{Real drift} = \underline{3.7°/\text{h inc}} \\
\text{Total} \underline{11.2°/\text{h inc}}
\end{aligned}$$

(10)   A gyro on a ground test at 60°S is found to have a drift of 8°/h, the readings increasing. Where would this gyro give zero drift?

Answer: 19°28′S.

Solution

$$\begin{aligned}
\text{App. wander at 60°S} = 15° \sin 60° = 13°/\text{h inc} \\
\text{Actual drift} = \underline{8°/\text{h inc}} \\
\text{Real drift} = \underline{5°/\text{h dec}}
\end{aligned}$$

$$\sin \text{lat} = \frac{\text{drift}}{15°}$$

$$= \frac{5°}{15°} = 0.3333$$

$$= 19°28′\text{S}$$

(11)   On ground test a gyro is found to have a drift of 6°/h at 30°N, the readings decreasing. What drift would it experience when flying on a track of 270°(T) at 50°S if the aircraft's ground speed is 360 kt?

Answer: 5.8°/h increase.

Solution

$$\begin{aligned}
\text{App. wander at 30°N} = 15° \sin 30° = 7.5°/\text{h dec} \\
\text{Actual drift} = \underline{6.0°/\text{h dec}} \\
\text{Real drift} = 1.5°/\text{h inc} \\
\text{At 50°S app. wander} = 15° \sin 50° = 11.5°/\text{h inc} \\
\text{Conv.} = \text{dep tan lat} = 6 \tan 50° = -7.2°/\text{h (west)} \\
\text{Total} 4.3°/\text{h inc} \\
\text{Real drift} = \underline{1.5°/\text{h inc}} \\
\text{Total drift} = \underline{5.8°/\text{h inc}}
\end{aligned}$$

(12)   A DI tested at 50°S gives a drift of 6°/h, the readings increasing. In what direction and at what speed must this aircraft fly at 30°S for the gyro drift to be zero?

Answer: Direction west (270°T); GS 207.9 kt.

Solution

$$\begin{aligned}
\text{App. wander at 50°S} = 15° \sin 50° = 11.5°/\text{h inc} \\
\text{Actual drift} = \underline{6.0°/\text{h inc}} \\
\text{Real drift} = \underline{5.5°/\text{h dec}}
\end{aligned}$$

In our gyro problem lay out

    (1) App. wander 30°S = 15° sin 30° _____
    (2) Conv. = dep tan lat   _____
    (3) Total app. wander   _____
    (4) Real wander   _____
    (5) Total drift   _____

we know the last item, that is, the total drift which is zero.
Enter 0 in the above blank layout and work backward.

    App. wander at 50°S = 15° sin 50° =   = 11.5°/h inc
    Actual wander is   =   6.0°/h inc

    ∴ Real drift present   =   5.5°/h dec

Thus, real drift is 5.5°/h and this is now entered under item 4. Working next step back, we know that the total apparent wander must be equal in magnitude and opposite in sign to the real wander. Therefore, the entry under total apparent wander is 5.5°/h increase.

Complete the layout by inserting the apparent wander in 30°S (7.5°/h increase) and we have sufficient information to calculate convergency:

    (1) App. wander 30°S = 15° sin 30° = 7.5°/h inc
    (2) Convergency = dep tan lat   = _____ ?
    (3) Total app. wander   = 5.5°/h inc

This gives the convergency value of −2°/h. A minus sign indicates direction WEST or a track of 270°(T), one answer. Departure is the aircraft's ground speed.

$$\text{Conv.} = \text{dep tan lat} = 2° = 120\,\text{min long}$$
$$\therefore \text{dep} = \frac{120}{\tan 30°} = \frac{120}{0.5774}$$
$$= 207.8\,\text{kt}$$

(13) A DI gyro has a drift of 8°/h (dec) when at 52°30′N. On what true heading should the aircraft fly in latitude 30°N for the drift to be the greatest and what would be the drift rate if the TAS is 420 kt? Assume still air conditions.

Answer: Hdg 090(T); drift 7.6 decrease.

Solution
Maximum drift is always on the easterly track.

    App. wander 52°30′N = 15° sin 52°30′ = 11.9°/h dec
                      Actual drift =   8.0°/h dec

                      Real drift   =   3.9°/h inc
    App. wander at 30°N = 15° sin 30°   =   7.5°/h dec
    Conv. = dep tan 30° = 7 × 0.5774 = +4.0°/h (east)

    Total app. wander   = 11.5°/h dec
                      Real drift   3.9°/h inc
                      Total drift =   7.6°/h dec

(14)   An aircraft's DI gyro is ground tested at 50°N and is found to have a drift of 8°/h, the readings decreasing. A compass comparison during the pre take-off checks give the following readings: DI reading 300°, Hdg(T) 281°(T). The aircraft then flies a due south track for four hours at a ground speed of 180 kt. What is the DI reading at the end of this time if the true heading of the aircraft is 174°?

Answer: $165\frac{1}{2}°$.

Solution

First establish the real wander due to the lat nut.

At 50°N app. wander $= 15°\sin 50°$	$= 11.5°/h$ dec	
Actual wander	$= 8.0°/h$ dec	
∴ Real wander (lat nut)	$= 3.5°/h$ inc	

Next, establish the total wander per hour on mean lat basis.

$$GS = 180\,kt \equiv 3° \text{ of latitude};$$
$$∴ \text{ In 2 hours (half time) ch lat} = 6°$$

and mean lat $= 50° - 6° = 44°N$.

App. wander 44°N $= 15°\sin 44°$	$= 10.4°/h$ dec
Convergency	$= 0.0$
Total apparent wander	$= 10.4°/h$ dec
Real wander (lat nut)	$= 3.5°/h$ inc
Total wander	$= 6.9°/h$ dec

Lastly, establish the heading as follows:
On initial check immediately before take off

Gyro reading	$= 300°$
True heading	$= 281°$
Gyro reading is	19° too high
Total decrease	$= 27.6° \ (6.9° × 4)$
Gyro's present reading should be	8.6° too low

∴ When the true heading is 174°, the gyro heading is
174° − 8.6° = 165.4°.

Alternatively

Initially the gyro reading is 19° too high, that is, if the check was made on a true heading of 174°, the gyro reading would have been 174° + 19° = 193°. This reading has decreased by 27.6° due to the apparent and real wander. The reading now is 193° − 27.6° = 165.4°.

(15)   A direction indicator compensated at the equator gives zero drift while flying a rhumb line track of 270°(T) along the parallel of 54°23'N. What is the aircraft's ground speed?

Answer: 524.4 kt.

Solution

The aircraft is flying against the direction of the rotation of the earth. The change of longitude is such that it cancels out the effect of the earth's rotation. Therefore, the convergency due to the change of longitude is equal to the apparent wander due to the earth's rotation.

App. wander at 54°23'N = 15° sin 54°23' = 12.2°/h dec
Conv. = dep × tan 54°23' also   = 12.2°/h

Resultant drift   = 0
Conv. = 12.2° = 732' of longitude

$$dep = \frac{convergency}{tan\ lat}$$

$$= \frac{732'}{tan\ 54°23'}$$

$$= 524.4\ kt$$

Test questions

(1) The limitations of a typical air driven DI are
   (a) 55° in roll and pitch
   (b) 110° in roll and 60° in pitch
   (c) 60° in roll and 110° in pitch.

(2) Gimballing error of a DI is caused by
   (a) unbalance of the gimbal system
   (b) the geometry of the gimbal system
   (c) excessive gyroscopic precession.

(3) A typical air driven DI will
   (a) topple on any heading if the pitch and roll limits are exceeded
   (b) not topple on any of the cardinal headings even if the aircraft is looped through 360°
   (c) not topple on certain headings even when the aircraft is rolled through 360°.

(4) The latitude correction nut of a gyro stabilised DI is to
   (a) correct for wander in the horizontal plane
   (b) correct for wander in the vertical plane
   (c) correct for the increase in the force of gravity from the equator to the poles.

(5) In a typical DI the air jets are attached to
   (a) the instrument casing
   (b) the gimbal attached to the instrument casing
   (c) the gimbal holding the rotor.

Chapter 16
ARTIFICIAL HORIZON

Principle

An artificial horizon employs a vertical axis earth gyro having freedom in all three planes and indicates the aircraft's attitude in pitch and roll. The gyro axis is maintained vertical with reference to the centre of the earth so that a bar across and at 90° to the rotor axis indicates the horizon. The symbol representing the aircraft outline is either fixed to the instrument case or adjustable by the pilot up and down for his height of eye and the pitch trim setting. In flight an aircraft rolls and pitches about the gyro axis which remains rigid and the indications are instantaneous.

Construction

The rotor of the gyro is encased in a sealed case which acts as inner gimbal. Air is let into the case under pressure, the pressure either created by a pressure pump or by creating suction inside the case. The suction required is around 4″ of mercury. The rotor spins under air pressure at the rate of approximately 15 000 rpm in an anti-clockwise direction when viewed from above. Having spun the rotor, the air escapes from the case through four exhaust ports in a pendulous unit mounted at the base of the gyro. Artificial horizons with air driven gyros are mainly fitted to training and general aviation aircraft when a suitable electrical supply is not available. Second generation electrically driven artificial horizons are designed to meet the needs for highly accurate, topple-free instruments for use world-wide over a wide range of temperatures and altitudes in the latest types of aircraft. They differ mainly from air driven artificial horizons in constructional details. Most electrically driven gyros require a supply of 115 V 3 phase 400 cycles AC and produce a spin rate of approximately 22 500 rpm.

The inner gimbal is mounted in the outer gimbal with its axis athwartships. The outer gimbal is mounted in the case with pivot points in the fore and aft axis of the aircraft. The horizon bar which is mounted on the outer gimbal, conveys indication of roll. The inner gimbal having its movement about the athwartships axis controls the indications in pitch attitude. Air driven artificial horizons currently have freedom of movement of 60° either side of the central position. Electrically driven artificial horizons usually have a resilient stop mounted on the top of the rotor casing, limiting the pitch

Fig. 16.1   Artificial horizon exploded view

movement to ±85° in the latest models. The outer gimbal controls the indications in the rolling plane (bank) and has 110° freedom from its central position in air driven models. Later models with electrical gyros have complete freedom in roll and 85° in pitch.

Operation

Any movement relative to the inner gimbal is transmitted to the horizon bar arm through a guide pin on the inner gimbal. The guide pin engages the horizon bar arm through a curved slot in the outer gimbal – Fig. 16.1. During level flight the aircraft's vertical axis is parallel to the rotor axis and the guide pin is in the centre of the slot. Horizon bar arm is in the centre, and its extension across the face of the dial is in the centre of the dial behind the miniature aircraft. When the aircraft climbs or descends the rotor case (that is, the inner gimbal) remains rigid whereas the outer gimbal and the instrument case move with the aircraft. Due to the movement relative to the inner gimbal the guide pin gets displaced in the slot taking the horizon bar arm with it. Thus an indication of climb or descent results. Fig. 16.2(a) represents the relative positions of the miniature aircraft and the inner and outer gimbals in straight and level flight. Fig. 16.2(b) and (c) represent the relative positions in climb and descent respectively.

The bank indication is given by an index on the sky plate which is directly connected to the outer gimbal. The index reads against a scale printed on the glass face of the instrument. When an aircraft banks, the rotor, inner gimbal and outer gimbal, horizon and bar remain rigid in level position and the instrument case together with the printed scale and aircraft symbol moves with the aircraft. Thus, the position of the index on the sky plate indicates the bank angle against the scale.

Fig. 16.2   Indicating level, climb and descent

Gyro control

The erection mechanism of an air driven artificial horizon consists of a pendulous unit with its four exhaust ports, two in the fore-and-aft axis and two in the athwartships axis of the aircraft. Pivoted on top of the ports are four vanes, each covering half the port in straight and level flight. In this condition the air escapes equally from all four ports and the system is in equilibrium.

If the rotor axis departs from the vertical, the pivoted vanes will still remain in the true vertical with the result that one pair of ports will be out of balance (one port will be more than half open; its opposite port similarly closed). In Fig. 16.3(a) the rotor axis is shown as vertical, air escaping equally through all four ports. In Fig. 16.3(b) the rotor axis is shown tilted. The vane on one port has fully uncovered the port and the vane directly opposite to it has fully covered up the port. Unbalanced airflow will take place as a result, setting up reaction in the direction of the closed port. This reaction force will precess through 90° in the direction of the spin and erect the gyro. The resulting rate of precession is deliberately kept low so that the rotor will not precess when the vanes are being thrown about in turbulent flight conditions.

Electrically driven rotors are controlled and kept in the vertical by means of a pair of torque motors and level switches. The torque motor correcting in the roll axis is mounted on the starboard side between the inner and outer gimbals and the one correcting in the pitch axis at the rear of the instrument between the outer gimbal and the case. Two level switches contain mercury liquid as a contact agent and the switches are placed at the base of the inner gimbal. When the gyro is level, the mercury is held in the centre of the trough, no contact is made at either of the two electrodes at the sides of the trough and the torque motor is switched off. When the gyro is not level, mercury rolls down to the lower sides and completes the circuit at one of·the contacts. This energises the appropriate torque motor which applies a torque to the rotor in the correct direction and erects the gyro (Fig. 16.4). It is possible for artificial horizons to be served by remotely located vertical gyros to which the instruments are electrically connected.

Fig. 16.3   Gyro control

Fig. 16.4   Mercury switches

Errors

Unlike the DI an artificial horizon suffers from both acceleration and turning errors. In the following discussion the rotor of the artificial horizon is assumed to turn anti-clockwise as viewed from above.

Acceleration errors

These are also known as *take-off* errors since they are most noticeable during this phase of the flight. There are two elements which introduce the errors: the pendulous unit and the vanes.

The pendulous unit makes the rotor assembly bottom heavy to aid initial erection. Thus when an aircraft accelerates, a force due to the unit's inertia is felt at the bottom, acting towards the pilot. This force precesses through 90° in an anti-clockwise direction and lifts up the right hand side of the outer gimbal. The skyplate and bar attached to the outer gimbal rotates anti-clockwise, the bank index indicating a false starboard turn.

Also during acceleration both port and starboard side vanes are thrown back with the result that the starboard side port opens up fully and the port side closes down fully. The reaction occurs on the port side, precesses through 90°, and lifts up the base of the inner gimbal towards the pilot to indicate a false climb.

Turning errors

During a turn the fore and aft vanes will be displaced due to the centrifugal force in a direction away from the centre of the turn. Thus, one port will be open and its opposite one closed. The reaction will be set up in the fore and aft axis of the aircraft which will precess through 90° to lift up the outer gimbal at the port or starboard side. This results in indication of false bank. The sense of the indication depends on the direction of the turn. This particular error is also known as erection error.

Centrifugal force also acts on the pendulous unit, the force acting from starboard to port or vice versa, depending on the direction of the turn. This force affects the inner gimbal, giving a false indication of climb or descent. This error is also known as *pendulosity error*.

The combined effect of the two is to displace the gyro rotor in two planes (pitch and roll). If a turn is made through 360° the error reaches maximum at 180° and then starts reducing until the turn is complete when the error will have reduced to zero. In modern gyroscopes, the rotor axis is displaced from the true vertical to counteract these errors. But the correction is only valid for a given rate of turn and a given speed. For example, an air driven gyro, offset $2\frac{1}{2}°$ forward and $1\frac{3}{4}°$ to port corrects for a rate one turn at 190 kt. The tilt does not affect straight and level indications as the scales are similarly offset.

Operational limits

If the gyro limits are exceeded the gyro will topple. Therefore, where the facility is available, the gyro should be caged before entering severe manoeuvres. An electrically driven gyro with 85° freedom in pitch may be taken through a loop without affecting the rotor. As the loop angle progresses between 80° and 100°, the horizon bar smartly travels across the face of the instrument from the bottom to the top. The skyplate bank index will similarly appear at the top. To the pilot who is inverted the indications will look correct. A similar change in the opposite direction takes place when the loop is going through the 260°–280° zone.

Fig. 16.5   Attitude indications

Pre-flight check

(a)   Artificial horizons with air driven gyroscopes
With engine power on, gyro suction indicated and thus suction first applied to the gyro in the artificial horizon, the horizon bar may oscillate violently for about a minute before settling. After about five minutes, even though the rotor will not yet have reached full speed, the instrument should give satisfactory indications. The horizon bar should then stay steady in a laterally level position even though the aircraft will execute turns during taxying. With a tail wheel aircraft, of course, the horizon bar will indicate a climbing attitude.

(b)   Artificial horizons with electrically driven gyroscopes

As soon as power is switched on, any power-warning flag or indicator should disappear from the dial and the gyro rotor spin up to operating speed. If, for any reason, the 'OFF' flag does not disappear, it is essential to *switch off* the power supply *immediately*. The cause can then be investigated to avoid serious damage to the instrument. Electrically powered gyros normally take about 90 seconds to settle the horizon bar to its position. Usually the fast-erection switch cannot be used until 15 seconds after the power has been switched on. Failing to wait the 15 seconds will cause the horizon bar to oscillate violently and damage the instrument. The fast-erection button must be released immediately the horizon has erected or else arc-ing will occur across the erection switch and damage the instrument. After using the fast-erection button, further time must be allowed before reliable indications can be assured. Again, the horizon bar should take up and retain a laterally level position when the aircraft turns during taxying to the runway. Electrical gyro Artificial Horizons are less pendulous than those with air-driven gyros so there is less pendulosity error. Also electrical *cut-offs* reduce errors.

Test questions

(1)   The artificial horizon uses
    (a)   a horizontally controlled gyroscope
    (b)   a gravity controlled gyroscope
    (c)   a rate or restrained gyroscope.

(2)   In an artificial horizon, the horizon bar arm is moved by a guide pin fixed to
    (a)   the outer gimbal
    (b)   the sky plate
    (c)   the inner gimbal.

(3)   Using a compensated air driven artificial horizon, during a turn
    (a)   the indications will be correct for a selected speed and rate of turn
    (b)   there will be significant errors in indications in pitch but not in roll
    (c)   there will be significant errors simultaneously in both pitch and roll indications.

(4)   A reduction in the forward speed of the aircraft will cause a typical air driven artificial horizon to indicate
    (a)   a climbing turn to starboard
    (b)   a descending turn to port
    (c)   a pitch up.

(5)   When using an artificial horizon, the indications require
    (a)   interpretation for lag error
    (b)   interpretation relative to the aircraft attitude
    (c)   no interpretation, as its presentation is similar to that obtained with the natural horizon.

Chapter 17
TURN AND SLIP (BALANCE) INDICATOR

While the Direction Indicator (DI) was the first heading indicator to use a gyro, the Turn and Bank Indicator was the first instrument on the blind flying panel to use a gyro. Now generally known as the Turn and Slip (Balance) Indicator, these two instruments are generally combined, with two pointers giving two types of information read in conjunction with each other.

Turn indicator

This part of the instrument indicates the rate of turn and utilises the principle of gyro precession to do so.

Construction

The instrument employs a horizontal axis rate gyro, the rotor being mounted in a horizontal ring in the athwartships axis. This ring itself is mounted in the fore-and-aft axis of the aircraft in the instrument case. Thus, the gyro has freedom of movement about two planes, that is the spinning plane and about the fore-and-aft axis, i.e. it is a rate gyro. The rotor is either operated electrically from the aircraft's DC system (with a power failure warning flag which will show *OFF* until the rotor is at full operating speed), or driven by an air jet which impinges upon the buckets on the rotor rim and spins it at an approximate rate of 9000 rpm and in some models only 4000–5000 rpm. This speed is considerably lower than DI or Artificial Horizon speed, for the reason that the Turn indicator utilises the principle of precession for its operation, and does not have a heavy gyro assembly to stabilise. The instrument incorporates a spring which holds the gyro axis horizontal in level flight. The rotor top normally spins away from the pilot.

Operation

During straight and level flight the spring holds the gyro axis horizontal preventing unwanted precession, and the pointer attached to the vertical rotor indicates central or zero position on the instrument against the printed scale (Fig. 17.1).

As the aircraft enters into a turn, say a turn to the left, the gyro axis being rigid, opposes the turn and a force is experienced on the axis, as shown in Fig. 17.2(a). On the left hand axis the force is coming out of the paper. Let

Fig. 17.1   Straight and level

Fig. 17.2   Turn to left

us call this force 1. This force will precess through 90° and act at the top of the rotor, force 2, causing the rotor to tilt. This tilt is called primary precession. If no spring were attached to the rotor axis, the rotor would continue to tilt until it is spinning in the horizontal plane, with its axis vertical. This attitude would give no indication of the rate of the turn. However, having the spring, as the rotor starts to tilt, the spring stretches to balance the turning force. In a left hand turn, as shown in Fig. 17.2(b) the left hand spring is stretched. This produces a pulling down force on the left hand axis or a pushing up force on the right hand axis – force 3. This vertical force on the axis will precess the rotor in the horizontal plane in the direction shown – force 4. This is called secondary precession. If you notice, force 4 acts in the same direction as the direction of the turn. As the rate of turn is established, force 1 becomes a constant value. When force 4 reaches the value of force 1, we have a situation where two forces of equal value are acting for opposite purposes (force 1 is due to rigidity of the axis; force 4 is precession force). At this stage, the gyro cannot tilt any further. Whatever tilt has duly occurred is entirely due to force 1, which in its turn, is due to the rate of turn. Therefore, the gyro tilt together with the pointer displacement represents the rate of turn. The rate of turn pointer moves over a scale calibrated 1, 2, 3, 4, corresponding to turn rates of 180°, 360°, 540° and 720° per minute respectively and is calibrated for a certain TAS.

If the instrument case is not airtight, air will be drawn in from leaking points due to suction inside the case and loss of efficiency will result. If the rotor speed is less than the rated speed, the primary and secondary precession will be less and the pointer will indicate a lesser rate of turn; similarly, if the speed is too high, it will indicate a higher rate of turn. Constant rotor speed is therefore critical.

The spring tension is adjusted for a given rate of turn, usually rate one, and the spring is designed to be linear but in practice at all other rates the indication will be progressively in error.

Movement in the looping plane theoretically will have no effect on the gyro provided that the aircraft is not in a turn or subject to slip or yaw, since the aircraft loops about the gyro axis and not against it as it does when it enters into a turn. Being a rate gyroscope, there is no need for any erecting mechanism nor correction for random precession, as the control spring system maintains the gyro axis horizontal in straight and level flight and it has no freedom in azimuth.

Slip indicator

This part of the instrument is entirely mechanical and uses one of two methods to indicate that the aircraft is correctly banked for the rate of turn being made. In the first method, the pointer depends on the forces acting on a pendulous weight for its indications. In straight and level flight the pendulous weight is acted upon by the force of gravity which keeps it in the true vertical. The pointer attached to the system indicates the central position, that is, no slip or skid.

During a turn the weight is acted upon by two forces: gravitational force acting downwards and centrifugal force acting away from the centre of the turn. The pendulum takes up the position which is the resultant of the two.

If the turn is a balanced turn, the two vectors must be of such dimensions as to shift the weight from the true vertical to the aircraft's vertical. This is so, because in a balanced turn weight opposes lift, and the lift acts at 90° to the wings, that is, in the aircraft's vertical axis. Therefore, the resultant must lie in the vertical axis (Fig. 17.3).

In Fig. 17.4, aircraft is shown in an RH turn with insufficient bank. The aircraft skids outwards from the centre of the turn. The pointer is displaced in the opposite direction to the direction of the turn.

In Fig. 17.5, aircraft is in an RH turn, having an excessive bank. The aircraft slips inwards, the pointer is displaced to the right of the zero, that is, in the same direction as the direction of the turn.

Most models employ a ball in a curved liquid-filled glass tube arrangement in place of a pendulum. The liquid used is usually white spirit. The ball itself has weight (it is not a bubble) and thus, it is affected by the aircraft's relevant manoeuvres in exactly the same way as the pendulum weight and the resulting

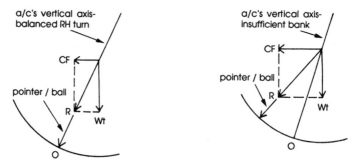

Fig. 17.3   Correctly banked right hand
turn

Fig. 17.4   Under-banked right hand turn

Fig. 17.5   Over-banked right hand turn

indications are alike, except that the ball itself indicates slip or skid instead of a pointer.

From the above, the rule of interpretation is that if the rate of turn pointer and slip pointer (or the ball) are displaced in the same direction, the aircraft is slipping inwards towards the centre of the turn. If the two are displaced in the opposite direction, the aircraft is skidding outward. If the turn is indicated but the slip pointer is at zero position, it is a balanced turn.

Serviceability check
While standing on level ground both pointers should indicate zero position. While taxying, check indications by a slight turn. The turn should be indicated in the correct direction and slip pointer or ball should indicate a skid (insufficient bank!).

Turn Co-ordinator
This is a variation from the instrument so far described, found in some general aviation light aircraft, designed to make the presentation and handling in a turn even simpler for the pilot. In the Turn and Balance Indicator,

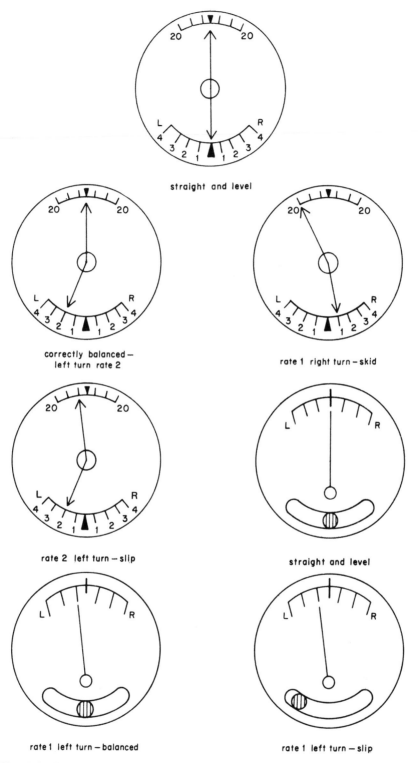

Fig. 17.6   Turn and balance indications

Fig. 17.7   Turn co-ordinator

the gyro (Fig. 17.1) has its spinning plane in the fore and aft axis of the aeroplane. In the Turn Co-ordinator, the spring-restrained gyro is mounted at some 30° to the fore and aft axis so making it respond to banking the aeroplane as well as to its turning.

When the pilot starts a turn by applying bank, this will cause the gyro to precess. The effect of this precession is displayed by moving the model aircraft symbol on the instrument to indicate the direction of the bank, and the pilot controls the turn to the required rate by aligning the model aircraft symbol with the graduations on the outer scale. The turn is co-ordinated by keeping the ball centred in the tube as in the Turn and Balance Indicator (Fig. 17.7).

Because of the similarity of the instrument presentation to that of a gyro horizon, the Turn Co-ordinator dial is annotated NO PITCH INFORMATION.

Electrical and pressure driven gyros

Electrically driven gyros have some distinct advantages over air driven gyros, the main advantage being that it is possible to run electrical rotors at higher and constant speeds. As we saw earlier, higher speeds impart greater rigidity and therefore greater accuracy where rigidity is utilised as the operating principle of the instrument. From the designing angle, electrical gyros yield neater designs since air passage tubing and filtration devices are no longer required. This permits gimbal designs giving greater operational limits. Further, since air no longer enters the rotor unit, there is freedom from filtration troubles and moisture corrosion. Electrical rotors are not affected by rarer atmosphere at high altitudes. Other advantages of electrically-driven instruments are that they are capable of variable erection rates and faster initial erection as well as having malfunction warning flags.

Test questions

(1) The principle of a rate of turn indicator is that
  (a) the precessional force on a gyroscope is balanced by a spring
  (b) variable gyroscopic rigidity is balanced by the rate of turn
  (c) the rate of turn is indicated by the angle between the case and a gyroscope tied in the vertical plane.

(2) If the rotor speed in a Turn and Balance Indicator is greater than the rated speed, the indicated rate of turn will
  (a) nevertheless be correct
  (b) be an overreading
  (c) be an underreading.

(3) If the case of a Turn and Slip Indicator develops a leak and the gyro is air driven, the indicated rate of turn will
  (a) still be correct
  (b) be an overreading
  (c) be an underreading.

(4) A suspect rate of turn indicator in a general aviation aircraft may be checked in the air by
  (a) exerting sideways pressure on the instrument panel holding the indicator
  (b) slipping the aircraft to the right or left
  (c) timing a rate one turn.

(5) On an instrument check while taxying, when carrying out a turn the slip pointer of a Turn and Slip (Balance) Indicator should indicate
  (a) a slip into the turn
  (b) a skid out of the turn
  (c) no slip or skid.

(6) When turning right onto the runway prior to take-off, the ball in a balance indicator will
  (a) move to the left
  (b) move to the right
  (c) stay central in its tube.

Chapter 18
AIR TEMPERATURE MEASUREMENT IN FLIGHT

Knowledge of the temperature of the air through which the aricraft is flying is important for a variety of reasons. These range from whether the aircraft is going into hazardous icing conditions to the fact that calibration of aircraft instruments and the assessment of aircraft performance is made on the assumption that the standard atmospheric conditions (ISA) prevail. As explained in *Ground Studies for Pilots, volume 4, Meteorology*, the deviation of ambient air temperatures from ISA is quite wide-ranging and may well be different over different phases of flight. Hence the need for aircraft thermometers to convey the outside air temperature to pilots.

The various principles on which temperatures involving an aircraft can be measured comprise:

(1) The expansion of a solid as its temperature increases, so a measure of its increase in length can be used to indicate its temperature rise. It is most likely that in fact it will involve the differing coefficients of expansion of two dissimilar metals where a helical bi-metallic strip coils and uncoils as the air temperature changes.

(2) The expansion of a liquid as its temperature increases so again measuring its expansion, say along a tube, can be used to indicate the temperature rise.

(3) The electrical resistance of a substance changes with variation of its temperature, so measuring changes of resistance can be used to indicate temperature change. Usually the element used is a platinum resistance wire.

(4) Dissimilar metals when joined at their ends (a thermocouple) produce an electro-magnetic force (emf). This thermo-emf depends upon the temperature difference between the junctions so measuring the emf gives a measure of the junction temperature.

(5) Many liquids change their state from liquid to vapour as the temperature rises. Rise in temperature can be indicated by measuring the rise in vapour pressure transmitted along a Bourdon tube. A Bourdon tube is a pressure-measuring device consisting basically of a spiral or C–shaped metal tube having an oval cross-section (Fig. 18.1). One end, into which the vapour under pressure is fed, is fixed while the other end is free to move and connected to the display system. As pressure increases in the tube because the temperature has risen, the tube's cross-

Fig. 18.1   Bourdon tube

Fig. 18.2   Types of air temperature indicators

section tends to become more circular and the tube to straighten. The tube movement is then linked mechanically to drive a pointer or a digital display.

(6)   The radiation emitted by a body is determined by its temperature. If the emitted radiation is measured this enables the body's temperature to be found.

From these basic principles, have been developed:

(a)   expansion-type thermometers – solid and liquid elements
(b)   electrical-type thermometers – resistance or thermo-electric
(c)   vapour-pressure type thermometers
(d)   radiation-type thermometers.

Of these types, in aircraft the radiation pyrometry system may be used in turbo-jet engines but for air temperature measurement, mainly one of the type (b) is used.

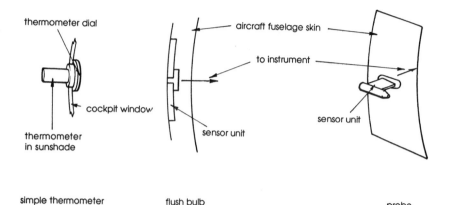

simple thermometer   flush bulb   probe

Fig. 18.3   Sensors

Thermometer sensor

In order to get the best measure of the ambient air temperature, often referred to as the Static Air Temperature (SAT) for instrument purposes, a position has to be selected for the temperature-sensing probe which as far as possible avoids air subject to compressibility (see pp 107–108). Nevertheless, the usual compromise between an ideal location and physically the most practical location will result in a chosen position subject to some error in the indicated temperature.

In some light aircraft, the thermometer sensor protrudes through the side window of the cockpit and is directly connected mechanically to the instrument's dial on the inside of the window. Most aircraft however have electrical resistance sensors remotely located. Either they are mounted flush with the fuselage skin – flush bulbs – or in specially designed probes, shielded from solar radiation Fig. 18.3.

Ram air temperature (RAT)

Where air is brought completely to rest at the stagnation points on leading edges, the relationship between the ambient or static air temperature and the ram air temperature, sometimes called the Total Air Temperature (TAT) is given by the formula:

$$T_A = T_R - \left(\frac{V}{100}\right)^2$$

where T_A = ambient temperature (SAT) in degrees Celsius
$\quad\ \ T_R$ = ram temperature (RAT) in degrees Celsius
$\quad\ \ V$ = true airspeed in knots

The difference between the two temperatures is often known as the RAM rise as although the friction of high speed airflow across an aircraft surface will cause a temperature increase, the great bulk of the RAM rise is due to adiabatic compression.

Corrected outside air temperature (COAT)

When the indicated outside air temperature as given on the aircraft's thermometer dial on the flight deck is corrected, either mentally by the pilot or automatically within the electronic systems for known errors, it is the best determinable value of the temperature of the air through which the aircraft is flying and for navigational purposes is called the Corrected Outside Air Temperature or COAT for short.

Errors

Instrument error
Small errors due to manufacturing imperfections. The errors can be determined and their correction is combined with that for position error.

Position error
As already described the best arbitrary position is determined at the aircraft's design stage and the error computed. Corrections are made available through tables, graphs or are built in electrically into the aircraft's computer.

Lag error
Although very minimal on large modern airliners, it should be guarded against by pilots of light aircraft with less sophisticated thermometers.

Test questions
(1) Converted into degrees Celsius, −40°F is
  (a) −56.5°C
  (b) −40°C
  (c) −20°C.
(2) In an aircraft thermometer with an electrical resistance sensor to measure the air temperature, the resistance wire element is probably
  (a) plutonium
  (b) platinum
  (c) potassium.
(3) Flying at high speed at high altitude, the difference between ram air temperature and static air temperature is
  (a) likely to be less than when flying low and slow
  (b) due to adiabatic cooling
  (c) due to adiabatic warming.

(4) Aircraft air temperature thermometers are shielded to protect them from
  (a) radiation
  (b) accidental physical damage on the ground or hailstones in flight
  (c) airframe icing.
(5) At a true air speed of 500 knots, a ram rise of air temperature can be expected of
  (a) 50 degrees Celsius
  (b) 25 degrees Celsius
  (c) 5 degrees Celsius.

Chapter 19
INERTIAL NAVIGATION

This is a technique for determining an aircraft's velocity and position by measuring its acceleration with respect to a known set of axes, and processing that acceleration in a computer. It has no need for external references, has nothing to do with magnetism, no plotting is required, it is unaffected by weather, all corrections for movement over the earth's surface and the movement of the earth itself are integral, and position in latitude and longitude, distance flown and other navigational information are presented on the flight-deck. Provided that the vital preflight setting-up is correctly done, there is no possibility of human error.

The term *acceleration* means rather more than just increasing speed as it is considered in the loose phraseology of daily life; it is changes in velocity, and velocity is speed measured in a definite direction along a straight line; and acceleration of a body is directly proportional to the sum of the forces acting on it. *Inertia* is the property of matter by which it continues in its existing state of rest or uniform motion in a straight line unless that state is changed by external force. An *accelerometer* is the device that measures the force required to accelerate a mass, i.e. it measures the acceleration of the vehicle containing the accelerometer. The motion of an aircraft in space can be determined therefore from information contained within the aircraft itself by measuring the accelerations in the north/south and east/west directions, producing velocities and displacements which can then be processed to give position and ground speed, to name but a few.

An accelerometer is fundamentally a torque-restrained pendulum of known mass which is moved from its datum position when the aircraft accelerates: the amount of movement from the state of rest can be measured, amplified, and current from the amplifier is returned via a torquer to bring the mass back to its datum position. The amount of current required is a primary indication of the acceleration experienced.

The signal also goes to an integrator, where it is multiplied by time: in other words, the acceleration is measured in feet per second squared, and the integrator turns it into feet per second: it is simple to transfer this via a second integrator into miles for the time flown (Fig. 19.1). Thus a single accelerometer has found how far the aircraft has gone in a definite direction for a definite time. If two accelerometers are used, one in the north/south axis, the other in the east/west, then from a definite start point in latitude and longitude, the new position of the aircraft can be shown.

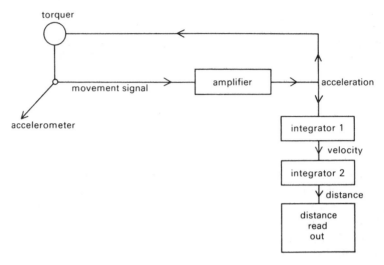

Fig. 19.1   INS principle

In its simplest terms, the system has two accelerometers in an aircraft, each held irrevocably in its chosen reference axis, north/south and east/west, each measures the acceleration along its axis, and the integration of this acceleration with respect to time will provide the velocity along this axis, though initial conditions must be known. A computer converts the time integrals along each axis into terms of distance travelled, and still further into latitude and longitude.

The system

The platform consists of a gyro-stabilised cluster of accelerometers whose outputs are fed to a computer. The platform isolates the accelerometers from angular rotations of the aircraft, and maintains them in a fixed orientation relative to the earth, usually with two of the input axes being locally level. Because the method used to stabilise the platform is based upon that devised by German engineer Maximillian Schuler to solve the problem of oscillating shipboard gyro compasses in the early 1900s, the platform is often referred to as *Schuler-tuned*. The structure, gimbal-mounted, on which the gyros (three of two-degrees-of-freedom) and two accelerometers are mounted, is called the *stable element*: the gimbals allow the aircraft to rotate without disturbing the stable element by detecting any movement from the level, and amplifying the signal to a gimbal drive motor which restores the gimbal assembly, i.e. the platform, level. Keeping the accelerometers exactly in the chosen reference axes, with an immediate reaction to the smallest deviation therefrom, is not regarded as much of a problem, using accurate gyros and high-performance servo mechanisms. The gyros act as error detectors to sense inadvertent rotations of the stable element, and apply corrections to gyro torque motors to cause the appropriate precession.

The computer calculates the aircraft's position and velocity from the outputs of the two horizontal accelerometers; it also calculates the gyro-precession signals which maintain the stable element in the desired orientation relative to the earth, since the earth itself is rotating and the aircraft is rotating about the earth, so the platform must rotate at these combined rates to stay aligned with the chosen earth's axes; it also calculates accelerations other than those caused by changes in the aircraft's motion relative to the earth.

In each case, the computer initiates the required compensation. When the computer is turned on, it must be set up so that it knows the initial position of the aircraft; the stable platform must have the correct initial orientation relative to the earth; the platform is typically aligned in such a way that its accelerometer input axes are horizontal, often with one of them pointing north. A vertical accelerometer is sometimes added to speed up the indication of altitude on the dial as measured by the barometric altimeter or air-data computer.

The calculation of velocity from the outputs of the horizontal accelerometers

It is necessary to derive the velocity of the aircraft relative to the ground, a ground which is part of a rotating earth. The first co-ordinate frame is centred at the earth's centre, projecting through the essential reference points of the equator, Greenwich and the pole, and considered to be motionless with regard to the stars. The second co-ordinate frame is similarly centred, but fixed to the earth. The axes of both will be aligned only at the instant of alignment, for the equatorial axis of the latter will move at 15°.04 per hour relative to the former, and only the polar axis will remain near-enough coincident. The third set is the actual co-ordinates of the aircraft itself at a given moment, one axis east/west, another north/south, another vertical, all radiating as it were from the aircraft itself.

Furthermore, the platform has its three co-ordinates with respect to the input axes of the accelerometers, at right angles to each other, set north-pointing or in the aircraft's axes lines. Thence, with the time factor since alignment of the system, the output of the accelerometers is solved in the computer to give a speed over the ground from a complex working of:

(a) the initial angular velocity of the platform
(b) the components of the platform axes proportional to the accelerometer outputs
(c) the angular velocity of the earth in inertial space
(d) the elimination of unwanted accelerations of gravity (not constant), of coriolis and centifrugal forces (the tendency to move outwards due to following a curved path in space in order to maintain a great circle path on a turning earth): these will be picked up by the accelerometers, which cannot differentiate, but are processed and rejected by the computer.

Fig. 19.2   Gyro-processing

A plan diagram (Fig. 19.2) will show the gyro-processing scheme to keep the platform level with the earth's surface as the aircraft moves over the rotating earth. Briefly, the sum of the two compensations reaches the gyro torquer and the amount of tilt thus caused is measured and amplified: this current, which is in proportion to the amount of tilt, is used to drive the gimbal motor which causes the gimbal to tilt and regain the correct horizontal at the aircraft's new position on the earth's surface. A further torquer is placed between the integrators to correct for coriolis, ellipticity of the earth and other sundry compensations consequent of flying over an imperfect rotating sphere.

In providing information about altitude, the vertical accelerometer does not perform its function with quite the facility of the horizontals. A small error in the early stage, whether of initial altitude, of altitude rate, or of the mechanisation of the vertical gravity component, will increase considerably with time, rendering the indications useless even after a few minutes. A baro-inertial altimeter is used therefore, a combination of the two, which utilises the basic stability of the barometric altimeter, but avoids the time-lag from measuring altitude to its dial appearance, utilising the accelerometer to do this.

The calculation of position from the velocities

From the sets of co-ordinates already mentioned and the measurement of ground speed, it becomes a simple matter for the computer to solve the position of the aircraft in terms of latitude and longitude continuously in flight. The resolved components of velocity provide the essential ingredients of position finding, since they are speeds in a given direction, and the direction as a northing or easting element is as intrinsic as the speed, all of which are instantly readable in the normal accepted figures.

Alignment

It is vital that the platform is accurately levelled and aligned in azimuth before takeoff and so maintained during flight.

Platform orientation co-ordinates

(a) Levelling until the output from the accelerometer is zero: the short-cut electronics involved eventually move the gimbals to move the accelerometer pendulum to zero, computed therefore to zero velocity.

(b) Lining the system up to true north, known as *gyro-compassing*. Again, with automatic compensation, this cannot be hurried. Compensation for the earth's rotation at that latitude is fed *in full* to the east/west gyro, the computer as it were assuming the north/south is accurately aligned: if there is a misalignment, however, the gyros are receiving a wrong compensation and the platform will tilt as the earth rotates: this tilt is automatically corrected, the platform points to true north, the gyros will receive the correct compensation, keeping the correct alignment in flight. Gyro-compassing need not always refer to true north. The north system is useless in high latitudes and over the pole, so an arbitrary angle can be set. The alignment procedure is much the same; the angle is primarily assumed to be zero, all the earth rotation compensation is picked up by the east/west gyro, and of course the platform will tilt, as the assumption is incorrect. This time the accelerometers actuate a torque which is split between the two gyros, eventually to determine the right combination to compensate for the earth's rotation for the particular angle required: the ratio to the gyros is then applied to compute the initial angle. This offset is coupled with the accelerations sensed in flight, and the computer knows the amount of offset.

Pre-departure

In a typical system, the procedure follows the sequence:

(1) Align – this in fact continues while pre-departure procedures are being carried out. The aircraft must not be moved during this stage of the procedure, although the system is not affected by vibration such as that caused by gusty winds, loading cargo and passengers, refuelling, etc.

(2) Set STBY, stand by.
The selector has the following positions:

TEST	
DSR TK STS	desired track angle.
WIND	
DIS/TIME	distance to go/time to go.
WPT	waypoint in lat/long.
POS	aircraft's position in lat and long.
XTK/TKE	cross track distance from that required/difference between actual and desired track angle.
HDG/DA	aircraft heading/angular difference between HDG and TMG.
TK/GS	TMG/GS.

(3) Test the CDU (control display unit) to ensure all points on it light up.

(4) Enter the present latitude and longitude.

(5)   Insert waypoint latitudes/longitudes; this is best done while:

(6)   Setting mode selector to 'align' to check alignment progress: and the display selector to DSR/TK/STS. On the right display, the number will have decreased from 90 (it's started) down to 02 (all finished, all well), and the READY NAV light will come on. Switch to NAV; and ready to go.

Of course, there are a number of refinements, and a number of differences with various types of presentation: the substance is scarcely variable, though. The only input required is the start latitude/longitude, nothing else: should this be entered sizeably in error, the compensations for earth's rotation and aircraft movement on a great circle track, to name but a few, will be incorrect. You can't get a correct updated position from an incorrectly inserted initial position on which the gyro-torquing was based.

Waypoints

These are positions along the route which can be inserted (in lat/long) pre-departure; up to 9 of them, and stored in the computer. WPT is selected, and the number of the waypoint corresponds to that shown on the display unit. Once NAV has been selected, the track and distance can be displayed between any two waypoints by switching to RMT (remote) and thus providing a check against the flight plan of correct insertion of waypoint co-ordinates.

To sum up

(1)   The inertial system measures and integrates the accelerations experienced in flight by two accelerometers at right angles to each other.

(2)   These accelerations are computed from velocity and time to latitude and longitude of the aircraft's position, starting from the aircraft's start position.

(3)   The accelerometers are kept level on a stable platform by three rate gyros and a system of gimbals and gimbal torques: thus only motions tangential to the earth's surface are measured.

(4)   Correction for the rotating earth, the aircraft's movement over a spherical surface, the earth not being a perfect sphere, coriolis, centrifugal and centripetal acceleration are compensated for automatically via a computer.

(5)   All track, and return to track, requirements can be computed, displayed or fed to the autopilot.

Errors

In-built errors of the inertial system are very few, and 1 nm/h is quoted by manufacturers as a never-exceeded error with some confidence. There is, though, a slight increase on this as a trip stretches out. An error is expressed as contained within the radius of a circle centred on the ramp position; more specifically, it is called the *radial* error. To calculate this in terms of nautical miles per hour from the lat and long of the destination ramp position vis-à-vis the INS position display is simply the solution of a right-angled triangle: distance on the latitude scale and the departure formula at mean latitude to bring ch long to distance. This is then divided by the flight time in hours in the navigational mode.

Inertial reference systems (IRS) with ring laser gyros

Because of its high degree of reliability there are attractions in using a ring laser gyro in a *strap-down* system rather than a gimballed platform with conventional spinning-mass gyros. In such RLG systems, the inertial platform rotates with the aircraft. Three accelerometers on the platform have input axes fixed in the longitudinal, lateral and vertical axes of the aircraft. The three laser ring gyros on the platform sense movement around these axes in roll, pitch and yaw relative to the surface of the earth. Their outputs maintain the platform stable relative to earth *mathematically* rather than mechanically. Thus the accelerometer outputs can be related navigationally to earth, i.e. North/South, East/West and in altitude. Among the advantages of ring laser gyros is the fact that they have no spin-up time as with the conventional gyro and are operational within a second so allowing a shorter INS alignment time. They are also insensitive to *g* so suiting high performance aircraft.

Advantages of the inertial system
  (1) Indications of position and velocity are instantaneous and continuous.
  (2) Utterly self-contained, with no need of ground stations or whatever.
  (3) Navigation information is obtainable at all latitudes and in all weathers.
  (4) Navigation information is substantially independent of aircraft manoeuvres.
  (5) If TAS is input, the W/V can be displayed on the CDU.
  (6) Any inaccuracies may be considered minor as far as civil air transport is concerned.
  (7) Apart from the overriding necessity for accuracy in pre-flight requirements, there is no possibility of human error.
  (8) Inertial Reference Systems (IRS) take attitude information to EFIS.

Disadvantages
  (1) Position and velocity information does degrade with time: and again, this is true stationary or airborne.
  (2) Equipment is far from cheap, and is difficult to maintain and service.
  (3) Initial alignment is simple enough in moderate latitudes when stationary, but difficult above 75° lat and in flight.

Checking Inertial Presentation

Using a basic knowledge of Form of the Earth, certain approximate checks can be made on the Inertial Navigation presentations of information. This

Fig. 19.3   Example 1

is best illustrated by practical examples. The methods used will only give approximate answers, the accuracy of which can be judged by the exact answers given in brackets which have been worked out for a spherical earth.

Example 1
Way point 3   55°15′ N 10°00′ W
Way point 4   55°15′ N 20°00′ W

(a)   What would be the DSR TK indicated on leaving WPT 3?

Solution
It is easiest to *think* Mercator (i.e. Rhumb lines) and then to make adjustments to allow for the fact that INS is a GC navigator.

RL track 270°
CA WPT3 to WPT4 = 0.5 × 10 × sin 55°15′ = 4°
Initial GC TK = 274°
(GC calculated 274°.1)

(b)   What is the approximate distance to go at WPT 3?

Solution
Departure (RL distance) = 10 × 60 × cos 55°15′ = 342 nm
                (GC distance calculated = 341.7 nm)

(c)   If the INS is showing 0 TKE when at 15°W, what latitude should the INS indicate?

Solution
CA from WPT 3 to the mid-point M will be 0.5 × 4 = 2°
Approximate distance will be 0.5 × 342   = 171 nm
Using '1 in 60' rule, M will be north of the RL by 171 ÷ 60 × 2 = 6 nm
Latitude of M = 55°15′ N + 6′ = 55°21′ N (Spherical calculation = 55°21′.8 N)

(d)   On reaching 20° W, what TMG should be indicated?

Solution
This requires the GC direction at WPT 4.
Using CA 4° again, final GC direction will be 266°. (GC calculation 265°.9)

Fig. 19.4   Example 2

Example 2

At the end of a 6 h 24 m flight, the INS shows a position when on the stand at Amsterdam of 52°20'.7 N 4°40'.3 E. Reference to the Airways Manual gives the actual stand position as 52°18'.5 N 4°45'.9 E. Give the INS error as a rate per hour of flight.

Solution

Stand	52°18.5' N 4°45.9' E
INS	52°20.7' N 4°40.3' E
Error	2.2' N 5.6' W (mins of long)

Mean lat 52°19.6' N   5.6 × cos lat = 3.42 nm
Solving triangle (Fig. 19.4): tan A = 3.42 ÷ 2.2   A = 57°16'
Distance INS to Stand = 2.2 ÷ cos 57°16' = 4.07 nm
Error is N57° W = 303° at a rate of 4.07 ÷ 6.4 h = 0.64 nm/h.

Test questions

(1) *Radial error* of an Inertial Navigation System is

   (a) $\dfrac{\text{Distance of ramp position from INS indicated position}}{\text{Elapsed time in navigation mode, in hours}}$

   (b)   bearing and distance of INS indicated position to destination position

   (c)   bearing and distance of waypoint fixed by independent means from the INS indicated position.

(2) The function of the INS stable platform is to

   (a)   ensure the accelerometers remain horizontal and correctly orientated

   (b)   provide a permanently horizontal basis for the system's gyroscopes

   (c)   provide a datum to integrate with the airborne computer.

(3) The function of the accelerometers in INS is to

   (a)   determine velocities and hence displacement and new position

   (b)   provide power to the torquers to maintain the stable platform's horizontality

   (c)   maintain the angular velocity of the stable platform.

(4) During the alignment procedure of the INS, the aircraft

   (a)   must not be moved

    (b)   may be taxied slowly but not subjected to accelerations of the magnitude used for take-off

    (c)   may taxi but not get airborne, as this involves vertical accelerations.

(5)   A TAS input is required in an INS in order to

    (a)   display wind information

    (b)   ensure the system starts to indicate change of position as it moves away from the loading ramp

    (c)   provide a datum against which the accelerometers can operate.

(6)   WPT 3 on an INS CDU is shown as 00°00′ N 178°25′ W. The desired track to the next WPT, (4), is 270° and the distance to go is 455 nm. The co-ordinates of WPT–4 will be shown as

    (a)   00°00′ N 170°50′ W

    (b)   00°00′ N 174°00′ E

    (c)   00°00′ N 186°00′ W

    (d)   00°00′ N 164°00′ E.

(7)   WPT 5 is 65°25′ N 048°36′ W, WPT 6 is 65°25′ N 131°24′ E. The desired track and distance between the waypoints will be

    (a)   000°   2950 nm

    (b)   090°   4493 nm

    (c)   270°   4493 nm

    (d)   either (b) or (c).

(8)   WPT 7 is 52°27′ S 017°45′ W and WPT 8 is 52°27′ S 004°15′ E. With WPTs 7 to 8 displayed, the desired track indicated will be

    (a)   081°

    (b)   099°

    (c)   095°

    (d)   085°.

(9)   The distance to go between WPTs 7 and 8 of question 8 would be shown as

    (a)   494 nm

    (b)   a little less than 494 nm

    (c)   804 nm

    (d)   a little less than 804 nm.

(10)   The initial heading (T) on leaving WPT 7 for WPT 8 of question 8, was 080°. Assuming constant drift, the heading (T) on reaching WPT 8 would be

    (a)   070°

    (b)   090°

    (c)   062°

    (d)   098°.

(11)   The following WPTs are correctly entered in an INS linked to the autopilot: WPT1 35°00′ N 17°30′ E; WPT2 40°00′ N 17°30′ E; WPT3 40°00′ N 14°14′ E. From WPT1 to WPT2, the desired track and distance would be shown as

    (a)   180° T   300 nm

    (b) 000° T   238 nm

    (c) 180° T   238 nm

    (d) 000° T   300 nm.

(12) Exactly half-way between WPT1 and WPT2 of question 11, the pilot selects WPT0 to WPT3 as the required track. The desired track now shown will be

    (a) approximately 045°

    (b) approximately 315°

    (c) much greater than 045°

    (d) much less than 315°.

(13) If the drift between WPT0 and WPT3 of question 11 remains constant, the change of true heading required will change by

    (a) 2° left

    (b) 2° right

    (c) 1° left

    (d) 1° right.

(14) The automatic flight control system in an aeroplane is coupled to the outputs of an INS in which the following waypoints have been correctly set. WPT 12–68°00′ N 175°00′ E WPT 13–68°00′ N 159°00′ W. For this stage, the desired track which will be shown would be

    (a) 078°

    (b) 102°

    (c) 066°

    (d) 114°.

(15) Flying between WPTs 12 and 13 of question 14, on crossing the meridian 172° W the approximate latitude indicated for the aircraft position would be

    (a) 67°30′ N

    (b) 67°45′ N

    (c) 68°30′ N

    (d) 68°15′ N.

Chapter 20
ELECTRONIC DISPLAYS AND SYSTEMS

In the same way as the present generation has seen the proliferation in homes, schools and offices of computers and colour televisions, so too the aviation industry has been able to take advantage of the rapid advances in this field. The *office* of the modern airliner has also moved away from mechanically-operated flight deck instruments to what have been called the *glass cockpits* of the 1990s. The electronic systems may vary in detail between aircraft and airlines, with the instrument manufacturers tailoring their equipment to meet the customers' wishes. The colours used on the various CTVs may not be uniform across different aircraft types and each operator has its own drills for its pilots to follow. Nevertheless the underlying principles are common, with new refinements continually being introduced.

Air Data Computer (ADC)

Although pilots have been provided with information on the instrument panel on the aircraft's speed, altitude, engine performance, etc. by individual instrument dials since the earliest days of flying, from World War Two onwards the outputs of the sensors for these instruments (e.g. the pitot head) have also been tapped for other purposes associated with the conduct of the flight.

The Air Data Computer (ADC) is a dedicated item of equipment used specifically to collect and distribute such in-flight measurements. The analogue Air Data Computers introduced into civil aircraft over thirty years ago are now being phased out to be replaced by digital ADCs. The block schematic diagram, Fig. 20.1, shows the general input to and output from an ADC.

The ADC receives inputs from the aircraft's pitot and static air pressure systems. The computer converts the sensed air pressures into electrical signals. Similarly there are inputs from the ambient air temperature probe. There is also a facility for a *configuration module* to be plugged into the circuit to provide information on the specific aircraft type such as V_{MO}, etc. and a switch interlock to isolate control of the ADC's self-test feature (see BIT below) unless the aircraft is on the ground. The outputs are to flight deck displays as described later in Electronic Flight Instrument Systems (EFIS), Flight Management Systems (FMS) etc.

Primarily, the equipment is installed in the aircraft's electronic bay where it is cooled by natural convection, but the Built-in-Test (BIT) facility can be

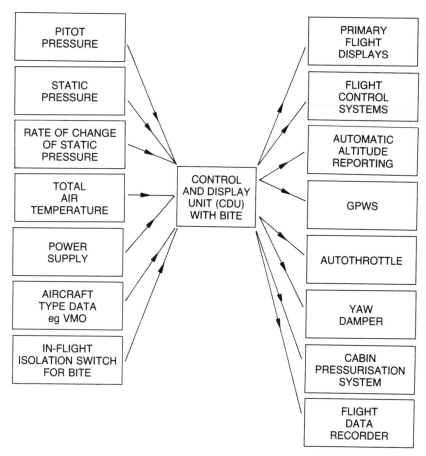

Fig. 20.1   Inputs and outputs of Air Data Computer

operated from a switch on the flight deck when the aircraft is on the ground (sometimes effectively at below a set airspeed) usually protected by a *strut switch*. Although Air Data Computers have a high degree of reliability, the function of the BIT facility is to check for the correct performance of the equipment both before and during flight.

There are three stages of BIT:

Power up BIT;
Continuous BIT;
Maintenance BIT.

Power-up BIT
When power is re-applied to the unit after an interval, this test makes a comprehensive check of the microprocessor, its memory store and the air data functions.

Fig. 20.2   Air data computer

Continuous BIT

This check is carried out automatically, without interfering with the operation of the ADC, and it does so at very short intervals (e.g. once every second) for all stages of the process, from input to output.

Maintenance BIT

The same BIT facility enables a maintenance check to be made when the aircraft is on the ground by the selection on the equipment of a *TEST* or a *TEST/HISTORY* switch, to show both current failures and any which may have occurred on the preceding flight(s).

Apart from the BIT facility, used by the maintenance crew on the ground, an Air Data Computer has no user controls or adjustments (Fig. 20.2). It may have a remote flight deck *ADC WARN* lamp to alert pilots to the appearance of a malfunction *flag* on the instrument panel.

Electronic Flight Instrument System (EFIS)

The natural process of evolution has now brought both civil and military flight decks to the Electronic Flight Instrument System (EFIS) or the so-called *Glass Cockpit* with its coloured cathode ray tubes (CRTs) presenting information previously shown by mechanically operated instruments. In the civil airliner, the necessary technical advances have been harnessed to the concepts of the forward facing crew cockpit and the 'dark–quiet' environment in which no lights or sounds appear when all of the aircraft systems are operating as they should. If any *alert* or *warning* sounds or flashes in this environment, it should then be immediately apparent to the crew.

The electronically-displayed information includes a primary flight display (PFD) usually embodying the basic *T* (airspeed, altitude, attitude, azimuth), and a navigational display (ND). There is also a multi-function display (MFD) which may embody or supplement the weather radar display. Other displays can include aircraft systems status and engine performance monitors, an electronic centralised aircraft monitor (ECAM), crew alerting system (CAS), or an electronic library (EL). The range of colours used usually leaves white for the various CRT code markings. The degree of brightness of the weather radar can usually be adjusted separately from the rest of the EFIS and the whole flight information is automatically kept at a readily readable level of illumination, as there are ambient light sensors on the instrument panel. There are manual brightness controls for the pilots. (Manufacturers warn pilots that operating the EFIS at maximum brightness for extended periods of time may eventually result in a condition known as *imprinting* on the CRT. This means that the image remains after the CRT is turned off. This may inhibit the use of the CRT if it is changed to another function.)

There may well be more than one control panel available to the crew.

Input

The input to, and the basic components for, a typical EFIS are shown in Fig. 20.3 overleaf.

Systems allow in the event of the failure of say the symbol generator on one side for the symbol generator on the other side to be brought in. If any of the CRTs has a *gun* fault, then the display reverts to monochrome but there is no loss of information being presented.

Cockpit display

Depending upon the demands of the aircraft operators and the flight-deck layouts offered by the aircraft manufacturers, so aircraft instrument manu-facturers have evolved various presentations for the glass cockpit, the control panel shown in Fig. 20.4 being an example.

With the increasing appreciation of the human factor, the actual format of the EFIS presentation is still evolving, although unfortunately not with international uniformity. However one essential element that has to be satisfied is that the captain and the co-pilot must have a good situational awareness at all times. Some EFIS favour displaying trends digitally while others use a deviation scale. On some EFIS there is automatic selection of the information displayed for that particular phase of flight. There may be linear or tape scales instead of dials for airspeed, altitude and engine performance. On the navigation display an arc may be preferred for the direction information rather than the traditional compass rose. One of the advantages of EFIS is that not only can the same information be displayed as

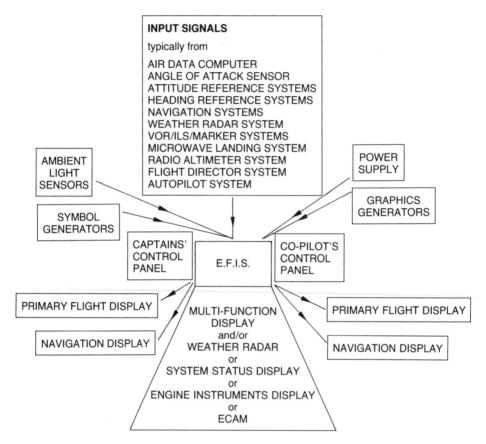

Fig. 20.3   Basic EFIS input

Fig. 20.4   Cockpit display control panel

on the *traditional* mechanically operated instruments but it is also possible to display additional information at the same time on the same CRT. Pilot efficiency can thus be improved by reducing eye movement to acquire vital information. The same CRT flexibility also allows for the complete removal from the display of a parameter which is not needed in a particular flight phase so reducing distraction to the pilot and reducing his scanning workload. Whether or not linear or tape scales for showing airspeed, altitude etc., are preferable to dials is however still a matter of debate amongst pilots.

Control panel/data unit

On the basic EFIS control panel there are usually two control units, one for the PFD and the other for the ND. The first control unit for the PFD, which is an Electronic Attitude Director Indicator (EADI), comprises a manually operated brightness control and a selector for Decision Height (DH). The selected decision height appears on the control panel via a three-digit lighted Liquid Crystal Display (LCD). The second control unit is for the ND – an Electronic Horizontal Situation Indicator (EHSI). This too has a manual brightness control, together with a display mode selector, weather radar ON/OFF, range control and a map data display selector.

Interpretation and use

The display mode selector typically allows selection to be made of:

MAP

The aircraft position is depicted at the bottom of the display with the track upwards to a compass rose or arc. Via push buttons on the control panel, the display also can show:

weather radar (WXR)
navigation reference or waypoints (WPT)
navigation aids such as VOR, ADF etc. (NAV AID)
airports (other than origin, destination) (ARPT)
ETA/alt at flight planned WPTs (RTE DATA)
bearing information of tuned navaids (VOR/ADF)

together with heading instead of track, holding patterns and procedure turns, selected reference points (SRP) with SRP radials and SRP distance circles.

CENTRE MAP

The aircraft symbol is shown in the middle of the display with either a compass rose or an arc. This mode enables the map information located behind the aircraft to be presented to the pilot.

PLAN

This displays the flight plan from the Flight Management Computer.

NAV

Navigation information. Selecting expanded NAV mode puts the aircraft symbol at the bottom of the display so enabling the simultaneous display of the weather radar.

VOR/ILS
When selected, the VHF frequency already tuned determines whether VOR or ILS is displayed. Again selecting the expanded mode puts the aircraft at the bottom of the display and enables the simultaneous display of weather radar and range.

Colour coding
With the EFIS currently coming into use operating with 16-colour cathode ray tubes, the colour presentation on EHSIs is generally:

Red – indicating Warning
Amber – indicating cautionary information, faults, flags
Green – indicating engaged flight mode displays, dynamic conditions, such as North pointer, source of nav data e.g. VOR/ILS
White – indicating present status situation, scales, armed flight mode displays, such as the full compass rose and the aeroplane symbol
Magenta – indicating command information, pointers, fly-to condition, such
(or pink) as holding patterns
Cyan – indicating non-active or background information
(or blue)
Black – indicating blank areas, off-condition states

Flight Management Systems (FMS)
In a light aircraft on an early solo cross-country flight exercise, flight management means much careful preliminary studying of maps of the route, the facilities available, the weather forecast, ATC limitations and the aircraft's performance before the pilot compiles the flight plan and seeks clearance. On the modern airliner, operating on a scheduled or a non-scheduled flight, to a strict timetable and often in marginal weather conditions, the airmanship decisions required for a safe, comfortable and efficiently-conducted flight have been significantly eased for far more complex conditions by Electronic Flight Management Systems (FMS). Such FMS embrace all the parameters that concern the solo student together with the greater sophistication of a modern large passenger transport aircraft. FMS has been described as

'pilot-interactive navigational computing and display systems designed to assist in flying an aircraft with maximum economy and safety to a previously planned route defined both laterally and vertically.'

The increased use in airborne applications of compact, high-speed computers enables FMS to provide fuel-efficient aircraft operation together with navigational guidance reducing flight-crew workloads especially in terminal airport areas.

Flight Management Systems basically consist of two units – the flight management computer unit (FMC) and the control/display unit (CDU). The computer unit is the store for the navigational data base and performs the functions of:

flight planning
optimum performance computation
navigation and position determination
air data and navigation sensor selection
guidance and steering, laterally and vertically
self-testing

The data base of an FMC is very comprehensive, typically including information relating mainly to the navigational features in the aircraft's field of operations, tailored to the particular operator's company procedures. The operator usually updates the information every 28 days by means of a cassette loader. The data base for example would include:

Airports   (identified by their ICAO 4-letter codes):
latitude and longitude, runways, approach aid frequencies and idents, decision heights, SIDs and STARs;

Waypoints   (identified by name):
latitude and longitude, magnetic variation, associated holding procedures;

Navaids   (identified by name):
type, latitude and longitude, frequency, elevation, associated holding procedures;

Airways   (identified by name);

Routes;

MORA   (minimum off-route altitudes);

Performance
aircraft type data including lift, drag, engine fuel flows, engine thrusts, performance factors.

In large airliners, twin flight management systems are fitted. They will accept and compare information such that data entered into No. 1 FMS will be passed to the No. 2 FMS and data entered into the No. 2 FMS will be passed to the No. 1 FMS.

Control/Display Unit (CDU)
A typical CDU is shown in Fig. 20.5 with the cathode ray tube presenting the information above the keyboard.

For simplicity, apart from its control outputs, the FMS computer may be looked upon as a book. The chapters and pages of the book are selected by the keys on the CDU and the contents displayed on the CRT. In most cases, the displayed information can be changed by the pilots in terms of modifying existing data or inserting new data.

Fig. 20.5   CDU

Above the CRT are light sensors controlling an automatic brilliance circuit which maintains the brightness of the display relative to the ambient light. (The keyboard also has a manual brightness control. This control has another function too in that when it is switched to 'OFF', all of the keys are inhibited.) The Flight Management System itself has no ON/OFF switch becoming *live* as soon as power is applied to the bus bar serving it. Typically, this part of the CDU has the annunciators for the main flight phases: climb (CLB), cruise (CRZ), descent (DES) and approach (APP) while below the CRT there are annunciators giving additional system status information.

The FMS is operated through three groups of keys comprising:

(a) Function keys   – used to select the display;
(b) Alphanumeric keys – used for data entry by the crew;
(c) Line keys   – used for crew interaction with the displays.

Each 'page' when displayed on the FMS consists of:

(1) A title;
(2) The page number/number of pages in that chapter;

(3) Lines of data (usually six) in two columns, adjoining *line select* keys, each with a title in smaller print;

(4) A *scratch pad*. This is the bottom line of the screen and it is the electronic equivalent of the pupil pilot's knee-pad on his first solo crosscountry. The crew can enter data here (by using the alphanumeric keys) – the only part of the screen where they can do so. A line select key is then used to reposition the data up the screen to an appropriate position.

Annunciators

These are lights which alert the crew when a change of FMS conditions occur, typically being: MSG (Message), DSPY (Display), FAIL, OFST (Offset).

Message (MSG)

The FMS can generate advisory or alert messages which are displayed on the scratch pad and illuminate the MSG light. Any information that was in the scratch pad is temporarily suppressed. When the MSG is cleared by the crew, the data returns and the MSG light goes out. A typical *ALERT* message would be *NO SIGNAL FROM* **** meaning that a particular procedure specified Navaid is not valid, while an ADVISORY message would be for example, NOT IN DATA BASE meaning that the computer has searched the data base and cannot find the entered ident.

Display (DSPY)

This light illuminates white if the page displayed is not related to the active (current) flight plan leg or to the current operational performance mode.

Fail

This illuminates as an AMBER light if certain FMS functions fail.

Offset (OFST)

Illuminates as a white light when a parallel off-set is in use (i.e. the aeroplane is flying parallel to, but a fixed distance from, the pre-programmed FMS track).

Clear and Delete keys (CLR/DEL)

The CLR key only clears data in the scratch pad. Momentarily pressed, it clears the characters one at a time from the right. Held down for a second or so, it will clear the whole entry. The same key will also clear any system-generated messages and extinguish the MSG annunciator.

The DEL key will only operate on certain pages and certain lines and for which a particular drill has to be followed.

Function keys

EXEC (Execute) Used when a change is made to an active V–NAV or L–NAV mode. To make the change effective, the EXEC key must be pressed. The light bar in the key illuminates while the proposed change is being made and by pressing the key the change is incorporated and the light extinguished.

NEXT PAGE and *PREV PAGE*   Used so that the CDU displays respectively, the next higher page number or next lower page number of the selected chapter.

Mode keys

The purpose of these keys is to enable direct selection of certain pages to be made, as opposed to using line select keys. They will probably include:

INIT REF (Initialisation/Reference) – for setting up pre-flight;

RTE (Route) – to display the current segment of route being flown;

CLB (Climb) – to display the page for the active climb mode;

CRZ (Cruise) – to display the page for the active cruise mode;

DES (Descent) – to display the page for the active descent mode;

DIR/INTC (Direct/Intercept) – to display page(s) so the route can be changed to fly direct to a position or intercept a facility;

LEGS – to display the details of each leg of the flight plan;

DEP ARR (Departure/Arrival) – to display SIDs, etc., depending upon the current phase of the flight;

HOLD – to display a page for establishing a holding point;

PROG (Progress) – to display how the flight is progressing, for example distance to and ETA next way point, fuel remaining etc.;

FIX – to display pages which enable the crew to obtain a fix by the interception of the present route with a selected radial from a navigation aid.

Application and use

FMS use may be conveniently divided into Route Management and Performance Management.

Route Management

The automatic lateral navigation (L–NAV) of the aircraft, which consists firstly of continually fixing the aircraft's position, say by INS, VOR and/or DME. When the FMS and the navigation system (say INS) are powered up, the present position data must be fed into the INS via the FMS CDU and the pilot goes on to select the routes or route segments that he wishes to follow. The FMS is then instructed to use this data for navigation. In flight, from the information loaded in the data base, the computer determines any discrepancy between the required track and that actually being made good and provides an *error* signal to the autopilot Flight Director System. The autopilot brings the aircraft back on to the required track to the next way-point by sustaining its correction to the flight planned heading until the *error* signal is zero. If the forecast winds and temperatures are correct, the error signal will be nil and the FMS displayed Heading, Groundspeed and ETAs will be those which were pre-flight planned.

Performance management

This comprises the two elements of automatic vertical navigation (V-NAV) and automatic thrust management (auto-throttle). V-NAV involves the automated climb and descent phases together with the maintenance of optimum flight levels for the most economical fuel consumption. In vertical navigation, whenever any discrepancy is detected between the actual flight path and that required, a correction is fed to the autopilot.

Automatic thrust management maintains power settings for maximum fuel economy during climb, cruise and descent by comparing desired power (engine pressure ratio: EPR) against indicated power and a correction for any *error* there is applied to the autothrottles until the need for further correction is eliminated.

Earlier, the FMS computer was described as akin to a book. Its application and use in the particular aircraft of an airline is subject to a series of drills which soon become as familiar as using the remote control of a domestic television set or video recorder. However the capacity and potential of Flight Management Systems are such that the airline operators provide their pilots with Crew Manuals on their own particular aeroplanes' FMS – usually spelt out in great detail and running to about 100 pages!

Flight Director System (FDS)

As alluded to under *Route Management* above, the purpose of the Flight Director is to ensure that from the instruments' indications or their sensors' inputs, the aircraft is flown manually or by the auto-pilot along the intended flight path. There may be a relatively basic display in which the indicator of the Flight Director looks like a conventional artificial horizon and is usually called an Attitude Flight Director Indicator (AFDI) (Fig. 20.6), or it can be a state-of-the-art system on a full fly-by-wire aeroplane with an Electronic Attitude Director Indicator (EADI).

Amongst the information that a pilot derives from the basic flight in-struments on his panel are the aircraft's attitude and its departure (if any) from the intended flight path. Correlating the information and deciding how best to manoeuvre the aeroplane to achieve and maintain the planned flight path involves accurate and rapid *rate* judgements which have become more pressing for pilots as aircraft performance his improved. A Flight Director assists the pilot in this work-load. It accepts the flight path displacement information, compares it with current attitude information and presents, where necessary, the required attitude change(s) as simple *commands* or *directions* on a single instrument. A basic system and its use is described first, the pilot's task being shown in Fig. 20.7.

The flight director's use of the computer to assimilate the information and

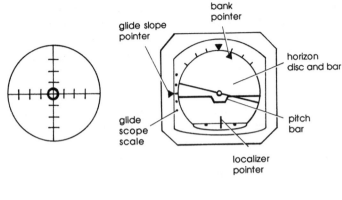

a) simple flight director   b) attitude flight director

Fig. 20.6   Flight director systems indicators

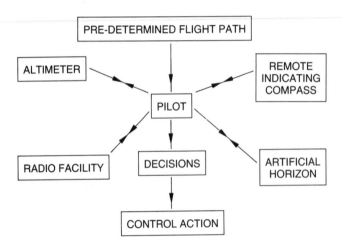

Fig. 20.7   The pilot's task

compute the necessary attitude changes on a continuous basis is shown in Fig. 20.8.

Even on basic displays, Flight Director information can be presented in a variety of ways either for Head-Up or Head-Down depending upon the particular aeroplane's instrument fit. It could be as simple as shown in Fig. 20.9 which is a parallel motion cross-pointer indicator. This directs the pilot to fly up or down, left or right, depending upon the position and attitude of the aeroplane in relation to its pre-determined flight path.

The centre of the small circle, itself at the centre of the dial, represents the zero datum over which the cross wires intersect when the commands of the FDS are being fulfilled. Although initially the required flight path may not

Fig. 20.8   FDS principle

a) simple presentation

b) attitude direction indicator

Fig. 20.9   Indicator 'commands'

Fig. 20.10   EADI

coincide with any pre-selected flight path, provided the pilot obeys the initial commands by manoeuvring the aeroplane to keep the cross wires at zero, he will intercept the pre-selected flight path smoothly and will maintain it with maximum accuracy. When the pilot is acting correctly to achieve the pre-selected flight path the Flight Director will indicate zero demand even though other instruments may be indicating various combinations of attitude, heading and flight path displacement. Even basic FDS indicators are equipped with 'OFF' warning flags for each pointer but the absence of these flags is no guarantee that the display is accurate, as errors in the input sources would not necessarily activate the warning signals.

Consider now a more sophisticated Flight Director being used in conjunction with the autopilot system and with an Electronic Attitude Director Indicator (EADI) (Fig. 20.10).

In the flight director's EADI, the roll and pitch indicating elements are controlled electronically from a remotely located vertical gyro unit. In rolling motion, the horizon bar and roll scale are marked on the background disc which is controlled by roll command signals from the vertical gyroscope and moves about the fore and aft axis. Similarly, the pitch or command bar corresponds to the model aircraft on the conventional artificial horizon and is controlled by pitch command signals to move in the vertical plane above and below the instrument centre-line. Signals from the ILS are fed to independent pointers. A glide slope vertical dot scale, against which a glide slope pointer travels, is located down one side of the instrument and indicates departure of the aircraft above or below the flight path. Similarly, across the bottom of the instrument face is a scale against which a localiser pointer indicates aircraft displacement left or right of the localiser beam (Fig. 20.11).

When the aircraft attitude changes about the gyro unit, signals are transmitted from the pitch and roll synchros which are installed about the axes of the vertical gyro. These signals are amplified and fed to servomotors which

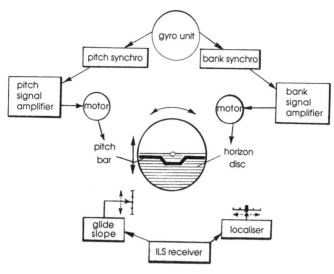

Fig. 20.11   Electrical connections to EADI

move the pitch bar and horizon disc to indicate the change of attitude of the aircraft and return the synchro rotors to their neutral position.

Similarly, during an ILS approach the signals received from the glide slope and localiser transmitters are fed to motors. In turn the motor deflects the pointer and the pitch bar to indicate the correction required to recapture the glide slope. When the aircraft is back on the correct vertical path, the glide slope pointer and pitch bar are returned to the horizontal centre position. In the same way, any departure to one side of the localiser beam causes the corresponding motor to deflect the localiser pointer and when the centre of the beam has been recaptured the pointer is returned to its central position aligned vertically with the centre of the horizon disc.

On the principle of providing the pilot with comprehensive information, on the face of an EADI there may also be displayed a simple ball-in-tube slip and skid indicator (as Fig. 17.6), the aircraft ground speed, its radio altitude and the selected Decision Height.

On its companion Horizontal Situation Indicator (HSI) or Course Deviation Indicator (CDI) (Fig. 20.12), the navigational situation is displayed by a rotatable compass card against a lubber line at centre top of the case and a model aircraft as a reference symbol at the centre. This too will have additional information such as distance to go, counters for selected course (i.e. track) as well as a lateral deviation scale and bar and glide slope pointer and scale. The lateral deviation indication is used in conjunction with the aircraft's VOR receiver as well as with ILS localiser beams. When VOR is selected and the required course is set, a fly left or fly right signal is shown until the aircraft is on track to the VOR station. To avoid error, the display embodies a TO/FROM arrow. To fly a particular heading there is a *heading*

distance to go to   drift angle   ground speed (or TAS)
next waypoint   cursor   display
display

FMC NAV
or VOR / ILS
indicator

course
pointer

to / from
flag

waypoint
bearing
pointer

HSI
data
source

vertical
deviation
pointer

alert   lateral
annunciator   deviation bar

Fig. 20.12   Horizontal situation indicator

selector knob which positions a heading marker against the compass card.
Again the difference between the heading indicated against the lubber line
and the selected desired heading is detected and the command bars show the
manoeuvre required to bring the aircraft on to the desired heading.

Warning flags

Should there be any failure within the Flight Director, the pilot is alerted by a
system of *flags* whether the aircraft is being flown manually or by the autopilot. Typically these flags are labelled with the facility to which they related
and as far as possible, obscure the indication too. They are usually operated
by their own meter mechanisms which are triggered by malfunctions such as
command signals too weak to be reliable or lost altogether. The flags may be:

(a)   GS flag: failure or malfunction of the aircraft's glide slope
                        receiver or the transmitted signal;
(b)   VOR/LOC: failure or malfunction of the transmitted VOR
                        radial signal or localiser signal, or of the aircraft's
                        receiver;
(c)   GYRO flag: failure or malfunction of the vertical gyro unit
                        and/or attitude display systems;
(d)   COMPASS flag: failure of the magnetic compass system;
(e)   COMPUTER flag: failure of the flight director or steering computer
                        and/or its command display systems.

Mode control

In the more advanced flight director systems, there is a mode control panel
(MCP) on the flight-deck which enables the pilot to pre-select the system for
a particular phase of flight. This may be for example to select a climb or

descent profile by means of a knob on the Flight Director itself or a separate MCP. On such a selection, a servomotor drives the command bars to the required position and the aircraft attitude is pitched up/down.

Many switches on mode control panels are operated by push buttons which also illuminate when pushed to ON. They can enable the pilot to fly the aircraft manually following the flight director bars by steering the aircraft to keep the command bars centred. Fully automatic control of the aircraft (Autopilot/Flight Director System, AFDS) is achieved by selecting the autopilot command mode instead of pushing the captain or copilot command button. Although autoland is available, take-off mode is only via a flight director mode.

For vertical navigation, an altitude select mode is provided to control the aircraft to the altitude selected on the MCP and automatically capture this altitude. A Flight Level Change Switch (FLCH) enables the flight director and the aircraft's Thrust Management System (FMS) to combine to increase/ decrease thrust when the aircraft's current altitude is different from the MCP selected altitude. The AFDS controls the aircraft to the airspeed on the MCP and then holds it through the elevators, so the aircraft ascends/descends to the selected altitude at the selected airspeed. Once achieved, the autopilot captures and holds the selected altitude while the autothrottle then holds the airspeed.

Selection of APP (approach) on the MCP sets up the AFDS to carry out an autoland. All the autopilots automatically capture the glide slope and localiser, bring the aircraft down the beams to flare and touchdown. Some MCPs have APP–I and APP–II, where the control is to Category I standard ILS approach or Cat II respectively. If LOC (localiser) is selected, the AFDS only follows the localiser, while pressing the B/CRS (back-course) push button on the MCP selects the mode to capture and maintain lateral flight on the localiser's back beam.

Other switches on the MCP may include V/S and GA. When V/S is selected a particular vertical speed, climb or descent, will be maintained while GA is selected for a go-around after a missed approach.

The more sophisticated Flight Director Systems have Built-In Test Equipment (BITE) which may have its own crew alerting system screen on the flight deck. The equipment continuously monitors the performance of the system and its computer(s) for the flight crew and is also the basis of the system's routine maintenance checks.

Test questions
(1)   An Air Data Computer has
  (a)   an Appleyard Scale
  (b)   an electronic Appleyard Scale
  (c)   no Appleyard Scale.
(2)   An Air Data Computer has inputs from
  (a)   all flying control surfaces

    (b)   all flying control surfaces and pressure and temperature sensors

    (c)   pressure and temperature sensors.

(3)   The usual position in which an Air Data Computer is installed is

    (a)   On the central console of the instrument panel visible to both pilots

    (b)   in the aircraft electronics bay

    (c)   below the electronic indicators on the aircraft's system panel.

(4)   With an Air Data Computer the pilot

    (a)   cannot *key in* specific data relative to the performance of the aircraft during flight such as a revised V_{MO}

    (b)   has to interrrupt the BIT cycle to input revised aircraft performance data

    (c)   can only input revised aircraft performance data when the ADC WARN lamp is on and a malfunction flag is showing on the instrument panel.

(5)   An Air Data Computer has pressure inputs for

    (a)   only static pressure and its rate of change

    (b)   only pitot pressure and its rate of change

    (c)   pitot pressure and static pressure and its rate of change.

(6)   On an EFIS, the meaning of MFD is

    (a)   Master Fuel Display

    (b)   Met Function Display (i.e. Weather Radar)

    (c)   Multi-Function Display.

(7)   The initials EFIS stand for

    (a)   Electronic Flight Inertial System

    (b)   Electronic Flight Instrument System

    (c)   Electronic Flight Integrated System.

(8)   The flight deck presentation of EFIS is

    (a)   standardised for all international flights from 1st January 1993

    (b)   varied on the day of the flight dependent upon whether the aeroplane is being used for *short-haul* or EROPS

    (c)   dependent on the *fit* chosen by the airline operator.

(9)   When CENTRE MAP is selected on the MFD

    (a)   it enables map information located behind the aircraft to be displayed

    (b)   it presents map information orientated with North at the top

    (c)   range rings are introduced on to the display.

(10)   On a 16-colour EFIS, cautionary information is normally shown in

    (a)   cyan

    (b)   magenta

    (c)   amber.

(11)   On a FMS, a function of LINE SELECT keys on the CDU is to

    (a)   select the area of the CRT where the pilot can enter data directly

    (b)   enable the pilot to select the scratchpad

    (c)   transfer data from the scratchpad o the main CRT display.

(12)   An FMS is

    (a)   an inertial navigation system providing route management
    (b)   a pilot-interactive navigational computing and display system
    (c)   a fuel monitoring system.
(13)   To enable display of pages relevant to the particular phase of the flight, instead of using the line select keys, the pilot can use
    (a)   MODE keys
    (b)   EXEC keys
    (c)   FUNCTION keys.
(14)   When the DEL key is used on the FMS, the display is
    (a)   delayed
    (b)   delivered
    (c)   deleted.
(15)   Data is entered by the crew on the FMS by using
    (a)   the function keys
    (b)   the alphanumeric keys
    (c)   the annunciators.
(16)   If an ALERT message is generated by the FMS
    (a)   it appears in the middle of the CRT screen and a red light flashes
    (b)   it appears in the scratch pad and an amber light flashes
    (c)   it appears in the scratch pad and the MSG annunciator illuminates.
(17)   On a Flight Director system, if a 'GS' flag shows it means
    (a)   failure or malfunction of the glide slope receiver or signal
    (b)   the aeroplane has descended by half of a full scale deflection below the glide slope
    (c)   the aeroplane's ground speed has been seriously eroded by windshear and there is danger of stalling.
(18)   If an electronics system is equipped with BITE it means that
    (a)   there is built-in test equipment
    (b)   there are contact breakers available to pilots to correct malfunctions in flight
    (c)   by pressing the BITE buttons in turn, the crew can ascertain that all electronic components are operational.
(19)   If it has to be referred to in a pilot's voyage report, the proper name for the scratchpad on a FMS is
    (a)   scratch pad
    (b)   pilot's memo line on CRT
    (c)   display line nine on the CRT.
(20)   On the Electronic Attitude Director Indicator, the pitch command bar is
    (a)   controlled by the GPWS
    (b)   controlled by the Flight Director
    (c)   controlled by the V-NAV system.

Part 3
MAGNETISM AND COMPASSES

Chapter 21
MAGNETISM: GENERAL AND TERRESTRIAL

Magnetism: general and terrestrial

A magnet has the following properties:

(1) It attracts other pieces of iron and steel, with its powers of attraction concentrated at each end, called its poles. The attraction can be exerted at a distance, the effect decreasing with increasing distance.

(2) When a magnet is freely suspended, one end tends to point in a Northerly direction and is called the North-seeking or RED Pole, the South-seeking end being called the BLUE pole.

(3) With two magnets near each other, the red pole will tend to attract the blue pole of the other, while like poles repel each other.

(4) The amount of possible magnetism is limited by the mass of magnetic material in the magnet. When a magnet can no longer by any means be made more powerful, it is said to be saturated.

(5) No magnet can exist with only one pole: even if broken into pieces, each piece would become a complete magnet with poles of equal strength.

The Molecular Theory supports this last point: any piece of iron consists of molecules, each of which is a magnet but exerting its magnetism haphazardly giving no resultant magnetism to the iron bar. On magnetisation, however, each molecule is lined up so that all of them exert their magnetism in the same direction; with every one lined up, the bar is now a magnet, and magnetically saturated, at its maximum magnetic strength.

The sphere of influence of a magnet is called its magnetic field, composed of its magnetic lines of force. These are the lines the direction of each being the path in which an isolated red pole free to move would travel i.e. from North pole to South pole. They are quite definite, and never cross, since they depend on their position with regard to the attracting blue pole, the repelling red pole. Thus, a magnet lying across the magnetic field of another magnet would tend to take up the direction of the line of force running through it with the opposite poles nearer to each other.

Hard and soft iron

Any metal which can be magnetised at all comes under one of these headings: soft iron can be easily magnetised and will just as readily lose its magnetism when the magnetising influence is removed. Hard iron is difficult to magnetise, but once done tends to remain permanently so. Hard iron magnetism is called *permanent* while soft iron is called *temporary* or *induced*.

The Coercive Force is the power which hard iron has of resisting magnetisation, or if already magnetised, of resisting de-magnetisation.

Terrestrial magnetism

The earth itself is a magnet, with its own magnetic field, with a blue pole in the vicinity of the True North Pole: thus a freely suspended magnetised needle will line itself up with its red pole pointing to the earth's Magnetic North Pole.

The Magnetic Poles are areas on the earth's surface where a freely suspended compass needle, influenced only by the earth's magnetic field will stand vertical.

The Angle of Dip in this case is 90°; the Angle of Dip is defined as the angle between the horizontal and a freely suspended magnetised needle influenced only by the earth's magnetic field. Thus the Magnetic equator or Aclinic Line is an imaginary line on the earth's surface joining all points where the Angle of Dip is Nil, and can be said to be the dividing line between the earth's blue and red polarity. *Isoclinals* are lines on charts joining all places having the same magnetic dip.

The earth's line of total force (T) at any particular place is the line of force in which a freely suspended magnetised needle lies in the earth's magnetic field when influenced only by the earth's magnetic field. It follows that only at the Magnetic equator will the needle be horizontal, only at the Pole will it be vertical. The Directive Force is that component of the earth's total force which acts in a horizontal plane, known as H; likewise the Vertical force in the vertical plane, known as Z. The Magnetic Meridian is simply the direction in a horizontal plane of the freely suspended magnetised needle influenced only by the earth's magnetic field, i.e. the direction of the directive force. Thus, we have a triangle of forces depending on the position of the magnetised needle in the earth's magnetic field which solves the actual horizontal direction and angle from the horizontal which it will actually take up along the line of the earth's total force.

A change of magnetic latitude will thus affect the freely suspended needle: the nearer to the Pole, the greater Z, and the less H: conversely, near to the magnetic equator, Z is small, H is high. The forces are shown in Figs 21.1 and 21.2.

An examination of Figs. 21.1 and 21.2 will reveal the following relationships:

(a) $\text{Tan dip} = \dfrac{Z}{H}$

(b) $Z = H \tan \text{dip}$

(c) $H = \dfrac{Z}{\tan \text{dip}}$

(d) $\text{Sin dip} = \dfrac{Z}{T}$, where T is the total force, and

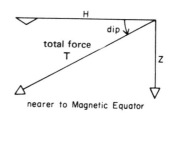

Figs 21.1 and 21.2   Dip, H and Z

(e) $T = \dfrac{Z}{\sin \text{ dip}}$

Now we will introduce a few problems which require use of the above formulae.

(1)   At a place A, the dip is 63° and the value of H is 0.18 units. What is the value of Z and the total force T at this place?

$$Z = H \tan 63°$$
$$= 0.18 \times 1.9626$$
$$= 0.3533$$
$$T = \frac{Z}{\sin 63°}$$
$$= \frac{0.3533}{0.8910}$$
$$= 0.3965$$

(2)   At a place X, the value of H is 0.22 and the value of Z is 0.44 units. What is the angle of dip at this place?

$$\text{Tan dip} = \frac{Z}{H}$$
$$= \frac{0.44}{0.22}$$
$$= 2.000$$
$$\text{Angle of dip} = 63°26'$$

(3)   Given, dip = 60°, Z = 0.27; find the values of H and T.

$$H = \frac{Z}{\tan 60°}$$
$$= \frac{0.27}{1.7321}$$
$$= 0.1559$$

$$T = \frac{0.27}{\sin 60°}$$
$$= \frac{0.27}{0.8660}$$
$$= 0.3118$$

Now try this example – you will need to manipulate the formula a bit.
Given, dip = 61°, H = 0.156, what is the value of T? Check that you are
getting the answer 0.322.

Changes in the earth's magnetic field

The earth's magnetic field at any point is defined from the knowledge of its
three characteristics, that is, variation, intensity and angle of dip. Such a field
is very irregular and seems to be forever changing. There are long-term
changes, periodic changes, local anomalies and a magnetic storm may play
havoc.

Secular change

This is the long-term change and reasonably predictable. At one time it was
thought that this occurred due to the rotation of the magnetic pole round the
geographical pole. Unexpected changes have been recorded at different
places and the overall results do not bear out this theory entirely. Since these
changes are more of a localised nature, they might be caused by changes in
the currents flowing deep within the earth's interior in a particular region.

Of these changes, as aviators we are primarily interested in the changes in
variation. The predicted rate of annual change is given on the maps, either by
a statement in words, e.g. annual change 7'E, or by an arrowed line across
the isogonal with a numeral on it. The arrow head indicates the direction of
the change and the numeral gives the number of nautical miles movement per
year.

Periodic changes

Irregular changes occur daily, annually and every 11 years.

Daily changes appear to be caused by the electric currents flowing in the
ionosphere. These currents are the result of the *atmospheric tides*, the sun's
heating action providing the energy. The tidal currents in the ionosphere then
modify the earth's field. The changes swing between 4' on a quiet day to 12'
on a sun-spot day, the maxima occurring just before sunrise and at noon.

The annual change takes place in the form of a cycle varying between 2'E
to 2'W, the maxima occurring around 21st March and 21st September.
The changes in the southern hemisphere are opposite in sense and it is
thought that the earth's motion round the sun is concerned with this type of
disturbance.

The 11-year changes, like the daily changes are positively associated
with the 11 year sun-spot cycle. When the activity is at a maximum, the
disturbances are also at a maximum.

Local anomalies

Strictly speaking no two places may be expected to have exactly the same field. This is due to the varying rock formation both on the surface and the interior. However, these differences are by no means remarkable and do not draw the attention of the aviator. On the other hand there are places, blessed with an abundance of ferromagnetic substances, which clearly distinguish themselves from the neighbouring regions, causing deviation limited to the locality and only near the surface. Greenland for instance is a tidy magnet in its own right, and there is a small area in mid-Atlantic, a few miles in diameter too. A place near Port Snettisham in Alaska causes a difference of 60° in the compass direction on the surface: it reduces rapidly with height (15° at 3000 ft).

Magnetic storms

Associated with sun-spot activity magnetic storms may last from a few hours to several days. The intensity varies from *small* to *very great* and may envelop the whole earth in a matter of minutes. The effect on the aircraft's compass varies with intensity, but both variation and the horizontal directive force are modified. Generally the effect is more severe in higher latitudes; a deviation of 20° by the needle when flying near Iceland in a magnetic storm is on record.

The regular changes can be allowed for when the isogonals are plotted for an area – those lines joining places of equal magnetic variation, and the amount of annual change of variation forecast: in the UK, the total change is about 7'E, and is hardly likely to be of significance to the pilot until he uses a chart more than 5 years old. Remember the definition of variation? The angular difference between the true and magnetic meridian at a point measured in degrees East or West of True. A line joining places of nil variation is the agonic line. And isoclinals are lines joining all places of equal magnetic dip.

To redefine deviation, it is the angular difference between the magnetic meridian and the direction taken up by a particular compass needle, measured E or W of the magnetic meridian. Aircraft are full of disturbing magnetic influences, and considerable thought is given by constructors and designers to reduce them. Fig. 21.3 should refresh your memory.

Summary of the definitions

Isogonal

A line on the surface of the earth along which all points have the same variation. These lines generally face the magnetic pole but it is not always the case.

Agonic line

A line on the surface of the earth along which all points have nil variation.

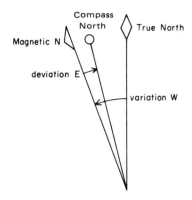

Fig. 21.3   Compass, Magnetic and True North

Variation
This is the angle between the horizontal direction taken up by a freely suspended magnetic needle under the influence of the earth's magnetic field alone, and the direction of true north. It is named east or west according to whether the north-seeking end of the needle lies to the east or west of the true meridian.

Magnetic equator or aclinic line
The line along which all points have zero dip. It runs close to the equator: to the south of the equator in South America and to the north of it in Africa and the Orient.

Isoclinal
It is a line along which all points have equal dip.

Chapter 22
AIRCRAFT MAGNETISM 1

An aircraft contains both hard and soft iron giving rise to permanent and temporary magnetism.

Permanent magnetism in aircraft arises chiefly from hammering whilst under construction and the effect of the Earth's line of total force running through it during building. The molecules in the hard iron tend to line up in the direction of the Earth's line of total force giving red polarity at the north-pointing end. The nature of this permanent magnetism depends on:

(1) Magnetic heading during construction.
(2) The Angle of Dip at the place of construction.
(3) Amount of coercive force of the metals used.
(4) And of course the amount of hammering, battering, vibration and riveting.

Some permanent magnetism can also be set up by the introduction of electro-magnetic material, radio and radar equipment, electric currents. A demagnetising effort called *de-gaussing* is made before an a/c is sent from the workshop, but there is always some residual magnetism.

This permanent magnetism and its effect on the magnetic compass can be measured per aircraft, and a suitable correction card placed nearby. The *Induced* or temporary magnetism in soft iron components of the structure (brought about by the Earth's field, giving these components a changing magnetic value depending on the variable strength of H and Z as the aircraft goes about its business) is not so readily taken care of.

In order to analyse the effect of permanent magnetism, we imagine it to be due to 3 components, acting respectively in the fore and aft, athwartships and vertical line of the a/c:

P is the parameter (or component) acting in the fore and aft line of the compass named + when the blue pole is forward of the compass.

Q is the parameter acting in the athwartships line of the compass, named + when the blue pole is starboard of the compass.

P and Q are horizontal hard iron, then, in the horizontal line of the compass needle itself.

R is the parameter acting in the vertical line of the compass, named + when the blue pole is beneath it. Its effect on the compass in straight and level flight may be taken as negligible.

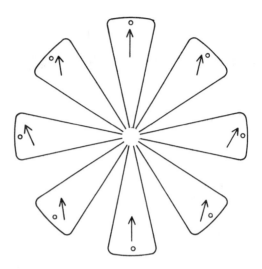

Fig. 22.1   Effect of +P

Analysis of +P

Imagine the aircraft on 8 headings, with a blue pole in the nose, red pole abaft the compass.

Drawing up a table of deviations, and a graph of them:

Hdg (C)	Deviation
N	No deviation; directive force increased
NE	Easterly deviation
E	Max Easterly deviation
SE	Easterly deviation
S	No deviation; directive force decreased
SW	Westerly deviation
W	Max Westerly deviation
NW	Westerly deviation

Fig. 22.2   Deviation due to +P

and we have a sine curve (Fig. 22.2); on the quadrantal Headings Compass the deviation will therefore be 0.7P. A parameter of negative value, −P, would give a Westerly deviation on Easterly Headings Compass. We can summarise then by saying that the deviation due to P is proportional to the sine of the aircraft's Heading Compass, or

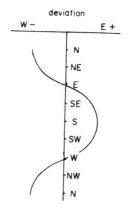

Fig. 22.3   Deviation due to −Q

$$\text{Deviation} = P \sin \text{Hdg(C)}$$

and P is positive or negative depending on Easterly or Westerly deviation with the aircraft on Headings Compass between North and East.

Analysis of −Q

The red pole is to starboard of the compass. Draw it out and check your result against the graph in Fig. 22.3. This is a cosine curve, and the sign of Q is determined by the sign of the deviation obtained on aircraft Hdgs(C) from North to East.

Deviation due to Q is proportional to cos Hdg(C), therefore:

$$\text{Deviation} = Q \cos \text{Hdg(C)}$$

and again the deviation on the quadrantals is 0.7 of the parameter, in this case 0.7Q.

P and Q are horizontal hard iron, permanent: we can conveniently co-relate with them certain soft iron components which act in the same manner on the compass; these induced effects are dependent on the strength of the Earth's magnetic field at the place, and of course on the coercive force of the soft iron itself.

These parameters are 'c' and 'f' ('little c and little f') where 'c' applies to vertical soft iron fore and aft of the compass and 'f' to vertical soft iron athwartships of the compass: 'c', a pair of vertical soft iron rods one before the compass, one behind, each with a pole in the horizontal plane of the compass needle. In the Northern Hemisphere, the bottom pole would be induced with a red magnetism, and in Fig. 22.4 it is assumed that the forward vertical rod has its blue pole level with the needle, the rear rod its red pole so there are effective poles acting on the compass like +P.

Similarly for 'f', this time athwart the compass.

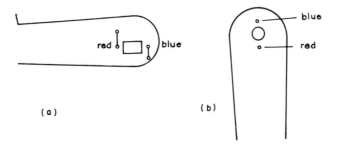

Fig. 22.4   Vertical soft iron

Vertical soft iron will not change its polarity with change of heading; thus, we consider P + c and Q + f at the same time for this analysis.

Proceeding to find a method of correction of the deviations obtained to render the compass as extensively serviceable as possible, the value of the deviations caused by P + c is resolved into Coefficient B, in degrees of deviation.

$$\text{Coefficient B} = P + c$$

which has maximum deviation on Easterly and Westerly Headings: thus, the Coefficient can be rendered as a numerical number of degrees by

$$\text{Coefficient B} = \frac{\text{Deviation on E} - \text{Deviation on W}}{2}$$

for the deviation on Westerly Heading is expected to be of opposite sign to that on Easterly, and we wish to remove the mean maximum deviation. The sign of the deviation is ready for correction on East Compass. Similarly,

$$\text{Coefficient C} = Q + f$$

and is calculated by:

$$\text{Coefficient C} = \frac{\text{Deviation on North} - \text{Deviation on South}}{2}$$

The value is given a sign ready for correction on a North Heading (C). Thus, while not expecting complete perfection of compass reading, we can eradicate the effect of fore/aft and athwartship hard iron magnetism, and vertical soft iron magnetism present.

Once found, coefficients B and C can be to some extent neutralised by setting up a local magnetic field: this correcting device is called the micro-adjuster. With a P-type compass it is placed directly under the compass as an integral part of the instrument while with an E-type, it is usually mounted above the bowl. Two pairs of magnets, one pair fore and aft, the other pair athwartships; the magnets of each pair can be opened like scissors from the

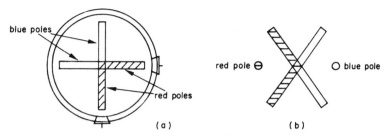

Fig. 22.5   Micro-adjuster

null position to form effective poles at *right angles* to the original line of the magnets. A key is inserted to operate either pair of corrector magnets, and the rule is to use the key hole which lies at right angles to the compass needle.

Figure 22.5(b) illustrates the opening of the fore and aft pair to give an effective blue pole to starboard, which would correct a negative Coefficient C (Q + f).

Coefficient A

This is caused by deviations which are the same on all headings, and nearly always is due to incorrect mounting of the lubber line. The rear of the compass bracket is screwed in against a span of 10° either side of centre, and the mounting of 0° may not be in the fore and aft axis of the aircraft: this would lead to a constant deviation on all headings: a Heading of 000(M) giving a compass reading of 010(C) entirely due to incorrect mounting would give a deviation of −10, which would be repeated on all headings, since the lubber line is displaced to starboard. This is called Apparent A, due to mechanical error. Real A, due to Horizontal soft iron, giving a constant graph of deviation too, is fortunately not part of our study.

Coefficient A is deduced by the deviations on 8 headings, adding them algebraically, and dividing by 8.

Thus, the deviation on any Heading Compass due to the three coefficients discussed is:

A + B sin Hdg + C cos Hdg and the sign of the deviation will
take care of itself.
e.g. A + 3, B + 2, C − 10

What deviation would be expected, (a) on 222(C), (b) on 146(C)?

(a)   +3 + (+2 sin 222) + (−10 cos 222)
= +3 + (2 sin −42) − (10 cos −42)
= +3 − 2 sin 42 + 10 cos 42
= +3 −1.3382 + 7.431
= 9° Easterly

(b) $+3 + (+2 \sin 146) + (-10 \cos 146)$
$= +3 + 2 \sin 34 + (-10 \cos -34)$
$= +3 + 1.11838 + 8.2904$
$= +12°$ or $12°$ East

Now to swing a compass: the methods are legion, and the usual method is to have an engineer with a landing compass mounted accurately on a tripod well in front of the aircraft so that he can sight down the fore and aft line: not as difficult as it sounds, since the tail unit can be sighted as a thin line in the viewer of the landing compass. This ineffably tedious job is now entirely in the hands of a trained Compass Adjuster, and the pilot only gets nobbled to drive occasionally. The procedure is to carry it out in two phases (correcting and check swings) as follows:

(1)   Check compass for serviceability (details of this under the title P type compasses).
(2)   Ensure all equipment not carried in flight is removed.
(3)   Ensure all equipment carried in flight is correctly stowed.
(4)   Take the a/c to a suitable site, at least 50 yards from other aircraft, 100 yards from the hangar. Most airfields have a favourite and magnetically clean area for compass swinging.
(5)   Ensure that all flying controls are in normal flying position, engines on, radios and electrical circuits on.
(6)   Place a/c Hdg South (M) and note deviation.
(7)   Place a/c Hdg West (M) and note deviation.
(8)   Place a/c Hdg North (M) and note deviation.
(9)   Calculate Coefficient C, apply it direct to the compass reading, and set the required corrected reading on the grid ring.
(10) Place the Key across the needle and turn the Key until red is on red. (The Key is turned anti clockwise for + deviation.)
(11) Remove the Key.
(12) Place a/c on Hdg East, note deviation.
(13) Calculate Coefficient B, and correct as before. (Key would be placed in fore and aft position.)
       The correcting swing is complete.
(14) Carry out a *check swing* on 8 headings, starting with SE.
(15) Calculate Coefficient A. Loosen retaining screw on rear bracket of compass, and turn the Instrument *clockwise* if A is +ve, by the quantity found. Re-tighten the screw!

An example:

Correcting swing

	Landing Compass Hdg (M)	P4 Hdg (C)	Deviation	Corrected Reading
S	184	183	+1	180
W	272	268	+4	270
N	000	353	+7	356
E	088	088	0	086

$$\text{Coefficient C} \quad \frac{+7 - 1}{2} = +3$$

$$\text{Coefficient B} \quad \frac{0 - 4}{2} = -2$$

and the corrected readings after these coefficients have been eliminated are as in the end column.

Check swing

L/C	P4	Devn	Residual Devn After Correction	
134	129	+5	+1	
181	177	+4	0	
225	222	+3	−1	
272	270	+2	−2	Coefficient A
314	308	+6	+2	$\frac{+31}{8} = +4$
357	353	+4	0	
048	044	+4	0	
094	091	+3	−1	

Now a deviation card is filled in to be placed next to the compass, so that whoever takes the aeroplane can fly as accurately as possible the required Hdg(M).

FOR (M)	STEER (C)	
000	000	It is necessary in flight to check the
045	045	compass by other means, especially on
090	091	freighters, when unusual loads may be
135	134	carried: and we've already seen that soft
180	180	iron magnetism does change with change
225	226	of magnetic latitude.
270	272	
315	313	

After correction, the residual deviations must be within the tolerances permitted by the *British Civil Airworthiness Requirements* (BCARs) and the *Joint Airworthiness Requirements* (JARs).

JARs

JAR 25 lays down the conditions for instruments. Firstly, it is required that amongst the instruments which must be installed so that it is clearly visible from each pilot's station is a direction indicator in the form of a non-stabilised magnetic compass. Secondly at each pilot station there must be installed, together with an ASI, altimeter, VSI, Turn & Slip indicator and a gyro-stabilised pitch & bank indicator, a Direction Indicator (gyroscopically stabilised, magnetic or non-magnetic).

For a magnetic direction indicator, JARs specify that the installation is such that 'its accuracy is not excessively affected by the aeroplane's vibration or magnetic fields'. It may not have a deviation after compensation, in normal level flight, greater than 10° degrees on any heading. For the Direction Indicator (gyroscopically stabilised, magnetic or non-magnetic) listed with the five other instruments to be located at each pilot's station, JARs specify that they must 'have an accuracy adequate for the safe operation of the aeroplane'. This is then spelt out as:

(1)   After correction the deviation on any heading should not exceed 1°, except that:

    (a)   On aeroplanes with a short cruising range, the limit of 1° may be extended after consultation with the National Authority.

    (b)   A change in deviation due to the current flow in any item of electrical equipment and its associated wiring is permissible but should not exceed 1°. The combined change for all such equipment, with all combinations of electrical load, should not exceed 2°.

    (c)   A change in deviation due to the movement of any component (e.g. controls or undercarriage) in normal flight is permissible, but should not exceed 1°.

(2)   The change in deviation due to the proximity of any item of equipment containing magnetic material should not exceed 1°, and the combined change for all such equipment should not exceed 2°. Common sense should tell a pilot not to stow his torch or his discarded headset on the instrument panel coaming beside the standby compass, but no metallic object should be put within the compass safe distance, i.e. close enough to change the deviation in excess of that permitted under (2) above.

BCARs

In the United Kingdom, for years now BCARs have laid down that the residual deviation:

(1)   of a direct reading compass shall not exceed 3° on any heading, and

(2)   of a remote indicating compass shall not exceed 1° on any heading.

Occasions when a compass should be swung or may require swinging

(1)   On a acceptance of new aircraft from manufacturer.

(2)   When a new compass is fitted.

(3)   Every three months.
(4)   After a major inspection.
(5)   With any change of magnetic material in the aircraft.
(6)   If transferred to another base involving a large change of latitude.
(7)   After a lightning strike or after flying in static.
(8)   After standing on one heading for more than 4 weeks.
(9)   When carrying magnetic freight.
(10)   Whenever specified in the maintenance schedule.
(11)   For the issue of a C of A.
(12)   Following a heavy landing.
(13)   At any time when the compass or recorded deviation is suspect.

The specific requirements for compass swinging are laid down in BCARs.

Change of latitude and its effect on compass deviation

The conclusions arrived at so far are that the deviations leading to the resolution of Coefficients B and C are horizontal hard iron P and Q, and vertical soft iron c and f.

Horizontal hard iron (HHI)

By definition, the deviating force is constant as measured, but with a change of strength of the Earth's horizontal component H, the effect of this deviating force will vary as the directive force on the compass needle varies. As H increases in strength, so the effect of a constant HHI deviating component will decrease, and vice versa. The deviation of the compass will be doubled if H is halved. This can be stated as

$$\text{Deviation due to HHI is proportional to } \frac{1}{H}$$

The value of H anywhere in the world is known, measured in gauss, and a directive force on the needle of 0.25 gauss is resisting a deviating force more strongly than one of 0.15 gauss. The deviation can be resolved then at a new magnetic latitude by the formula:

$$\frac{\text{New deviation}}{\text{Old deviation}} = \frac{\text{Old H}}{\text{New H}}$$

Vertical soft iron (vsi)

Once again, deviation must vary inversely as H, the ability of the needle itself to resist any deviating force. Additionally, the magnetism induced into vertical soft iron will vary as the vertical component of the Earth's magnetic field varies, i.e. it varies as Dip. At the Poles, then, maximum deviation will be caused by vsi where maximum Dip induces maximum magnetism: at the Magnetic Equator, when Z is nil, the value of induced magnetism in vsi will be nil.

Deviation due to vsi is proportional to Z and inversely proportional to H

$\therefore$ Deviation due to vsi is proportional to $\dfrac{Z}{H}$ or tan Dip

Dip, too, is known world wide, as an angular measurement from the horizontal; while Z is measured in gauss, and Z changes its sign as it crosses the Magnetic Equator.

The new deviation due to vsi with change of magnetic latitude can be found from the formula.

$$\frac{\text{New Devn}}{\text{Old Devn}} = \frac{\text{New Tan Dip}}{\text{Old Tan Dip}}$$

Providing clarity is preserved between the two formula, a new deviation can be readily found when magnetic latitude has been changed.

At BERKER, where H = 0.15 gauss, deviation due to P is +3, and due to c − 4; Dip is 48°, what is total deviation due to P + c at POOTLE where H = 0.6, dip 32°?

HHI
$$\frac{\text{New Devn}}{\text{Old Devn}} = \frac{\text{Old H}}{\text{New H}}$$

$$\frac{x}{+3} = \frac{0.15}{0.6}$$

$$= +0.75$$

vsi
$$\frac{\text{New Devn}}{\text{Old Devn}} = \frac{\text{New Tan Dip}}{\text{Old Tan Dip}}$$

$$\frac{x}{-4} = \frac{\text{Tan } 32}{\text{Tan } 48}$$

$$= -4 \tan 32 \cot 48$$

$$= -2.25$$

Total devn due to P + c = −1.5 at POOTLE

Component R

This is vertical hard iron assumed for analysis to be situated above or below the compass. In level flight, its effect on the compass is nil, but tail down or up, the hypothetical magnet is resolved into two parts, one of which introduces a fore and aft effect, as it were a false component P.

In Fig. 22.6(c) components P and R are shown (we can assume the inclusion of 'c') where AC = P and CD = R, $\angle\theta$ = the angle of tail down: the needle remains in the horizontal plane by construction.

Then BC = deviating effect due to P = P cos θ
DE = deviating effect due to R = R sin θ

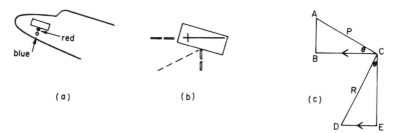

Fig. 22.6   Component R

∴ Total deviating effect = P cos θ + R sin θ; the action in the horizontal plane of component R introducing an additional effect like B (or P).

R is termed + with a blue pole beneath the compass and its deviative value depends on the angular distance of the a/c from the horizontal. It can be readily proved that the actual position of the applied force will change from fore to aft of the needle with change of a/c attitude from climb to descent.

e.g.   In the air, B is −7; on the ground 15° tail down, B is −4. What is the deviation on a Westerly heading climbing at 20°?

$$\text{Total deviating force} = B \cos θ = R \sin θ$$
$$-4 = -7 \cos 15 + R \sin 15$$
$$R = +11$$

In the air,

$$\text{Deviation} = -7 \cos 20 + 11 \sin 20$$
$$= -3, \text{ and this will be on East.}$$
$$∴ +3° \text{ on Westerly Heading.}$$

And another:

Climbing at 10° on East, the deviation due to P and R is +10°, whereas climbing on the same Heading at 20°, the deviation due to P and R is +3°. What is the deviation due to P on Hdg 315(C) in level flight?

$$\text{Total deviation} = P \cos θ + R \sin θ$$
$$10 = P \cos 10 + R \sin 10$$
$$\text{and } 3 = P \cos 20 + R \sin 20$$
$$∴ 10 = 0.98P + 0.17R$$
$$3 = 0.94P + 0.34R$$

which solves into

$$P = +17$$

In level flight, on a Hdg(C) of 315, with R inoperative, the deviation due to P will be 0.7 of −17, or to put it another way, +17 sin 315, an answer of −12°.

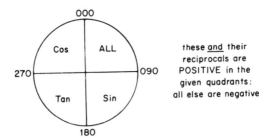

Fig. 22.7   Angles over 90°

Finally, if the aircraft is banked, there will be a resolved component due to R appropriate to the rules of Coefficient C; but the manoeuvre is not sufficiently prolonged or directionally important enough to be worth considering, especially if account is taken of the larger effects of turning errors on the basic magnetic compass.

Sundry tips and reminders

First, are you a bit shaky on how to find cos 324? sin 179? tan 139? Whatever the angle, apply it to 360 or 180 to get below 90: then for the quadrant it falls in, see Fig. 22.7.

For example:

cos 324 = cos 036 and it is positive;
sin 179 = sin 001 and it is positive;
tan 139 = tan 041 and it is negative.

Mathematics and so on

Calculating deviation

Know the formula;

$$B = \frac{E - W}{2} \text{ and } C = \frac{N - S}{2}$$

If the value of B is known, the deviation on any other Heading is found from:

$$\text{Deviation} = B \sin \text{Heading}$$

Similarly,

$$\text{Deviation due to C} = C \cos \text{Heading}$$

If the deviation on a Heading is given, B and C are calculated thus:

$$B = \frac{\text{Deviation}}{\sin \text{Hdg}} \qquad C = \frac{\text{Deviation}}{\cos \text{Hdg}}$$

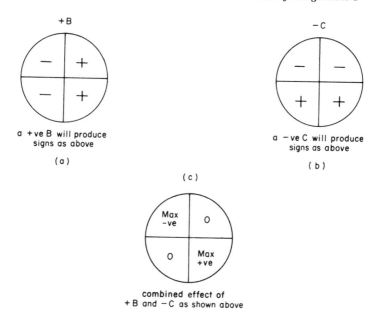

Fig. 22.8   Maximum deviation

and these can be re-written:

$$B = \text{Deviation cosecant Heading}$$
$$C = \text{Deviation secant Heading}$$

If the values of B and C are given and it is required to calculate the deviation on a given Heading, the problem is best solved in two parts: first, calculate the deviation due to B on the Heading given; then calculate the deviation due to C. The algebraic sum of the two is the deviation on that Heading due to the combined effect of both B and C.

$$\text{Deviation} = B \sin \text{Hdg} + C \cos \text{Hdg}.$$

Maximum deviation

Values of B and C are given, and it is required to find the Heading on which maximum deviation will occur, together with its value.

The formula to be used is:

$$\text{Tan Heading} = \frac{B}{C}$$

This will give a Heading between 0 and 90 degrees. It will then be necessary to ascertain the quadrant in which the maximum value occurs and from knowledge of the quadrant, the Heading is converted into that quadrant. The quadrants are easily found from Figs 22.8(a), (b) and (c).

Example

Given B = +4, C = −3, find the Heading on which the deviation will be maximum.

From Fig. 21.8, it is seen that the maximum Westerly deviation will occur between 270 and 360, and maximum Easterly deviation between 090 and 180.

$$\text{Tan Heading} = \frac{B}{C} = \frac{4}{3} = 1.333, \text{ which is the Tan of } 53° \text{ from the tables.}$$

∴ Max westerly devn = 360 − 53 = 307

Max easterly devn = 307 − 180 = 127 (this must be the reciprocal of the
                Hdg which gave maximum
                deviation of opposite sign)

Once the Heading is known, the value of the deviation may be found from the normal formula, e.g. on Hdg 307

$$
\begin{aligned}
\text{Total deviation} &= B \sin Hdg + C \cos Hdg \\
&= 4(-\sin 53) + (-3 \cos 53) \\
&= -4 \times 0.7986 + (-3 \times 0.6018) \\
&= -3.1944 - 1.8054 \\
&= \underline{4.999 \text{ Westerly}}
\end{aligned}
$$

The value may also be found by Pythagoras, since B and C act at right angles to each other and we are interested in their resultant. In the above example:

$$(\text{Maximum value})^2 = 4^2 + 3^2$$
$$= 25$$

∴ max value = 5, and give the sign according to the quadrant.

The whole problem could be solved by scale drawing, but its real virtue lies in the fact that by learning this method, a firmer grasp of aircraft deviations is acquired. We'll do the same problem this way. It looks like Fig. 22.9.

Construction

(a) From a convenient point A, draw AM to represent any Heading of the aircraft.

(b) Along the Heading AM, let AB represent to scale the value of B, in this case +4. If it had been a −ve B, it would have been plotted towards the tail from A.

(c) At A and at right angles to AM draw AC to represent to scale the value of C, in this case −3. Being negative, C acts to the port of the aircraft.

(d) Complete the parallelogram ABDC. AD then represents the maximum deviation, and measures about 5°.

(e) To find the Heading on which this will occur, draw in the magnetic meridian from A, so that it is at right angles to AD, since maximum deviation occurs when the deviating force acts at 90° to the needle.

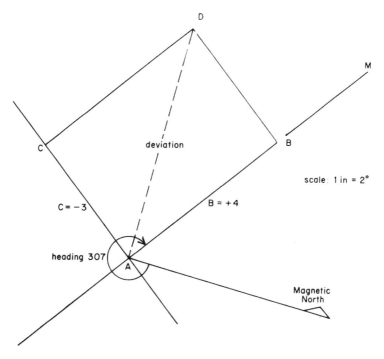

Fig. 22.9   Graphical solution

(f)   Measure the Heading; it is 307.
(g)   The maximum Easterly deviation will occur on the reciprocal, 127.

Maximum deviation – heading given

Another case is when the maximum value and the Heading on which it occurs
are given, and it is required to separate B and C. You will recognise this as a
problem in reverse of the previous one. It is best solved by scale diagram.

Example

Given that the maximum deviation is +5 on a Heading of 127°, find the value
of Coefficients B and C.

   In Fig. 22.10, AM is the given Heading from the Magnetic datum, and
NAP is the aircraft's athwartships axis.

   AD is plotted to scale along the East–West line, and being given as +ve,
in an Easterly direction therefore. The maximum value has in fact been
plotted at 90° to the needle.

   From D, drop two perpendiculars DB and DC to AM and AP respectively.
Measure AB, 4°, and it is +ve since it acts towards the nose of the aircraft.
Measure AC, 3°, and it is −ve since it acts towards the port. The same values
for B and C would have been found if the given maximum deviation was −5
on a Hdg of 307; it's worth the effort of drawing out as a check.

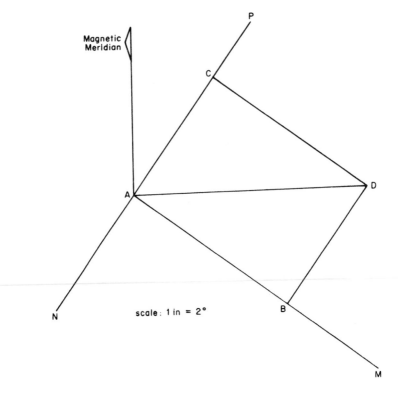

Fig. 22.10   Finding B and C

Zero deviation
If the values of B and C are given, the Heading of zero deviation is found from the formula:

$$\text{Tan Heading} = \frac{C}{B}$$

and its derivation is as follows:

$$\text{Deviation} = B \sin \text{Hdg} + C \cos \text{Hdg} = 0$$

$$\therefore B \sin \text{Hdg} = C \cos \text{Hdg}$$

$$\frac{B}{C} = \frac{\cos \text{Hdg}}{\sin \text{Hdg}} \quad \text{or} \quad \frac{C}{B} = \text{Tan Hdg}$$

In the problem, tan Hdg = $\frac{3}{4}$ = 0.75 = 037° or 217°, the Headings where zero deviation occurs.

Of course, it will be appreciated that once the Heading of maximum deviation is found, the Heading of zero deviation is 90° removed from it. Occasionally, illustrations of zero deviation conditions are called for by means of a scale diagram.

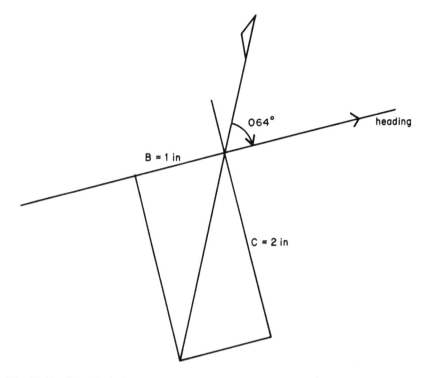

Fig. 22.11   Zero deviation

Example

B is −ve and is half the value of C which is +ve. Draw a diagram to illustrate the heading on which these two forces will cause zero deviation.

The solution is similar to that for finding maximum deviation, except that the magnetic meridian is placed along the resultant and not at right angles to it.

Construction

(a)   Draw in any straight line to represent the aircraft's Heading.
(b)   At a convenient point on that straight line, draw in another straight line at right angles to it to represent the aircraft's athwartships axis.
(c)   From this point plot B and C. B is −ve, so is plotted toward the tail. C is +ve, so is plotted to the starboard.
(d)   Complete the parallelogram and extend the resultant as shown in Fig. 22.11 to represent the Magnetic meridian.
(e)   Measure off the Headings of zero deviation. They are 064° and 244°.

Test questions

(1)   The line on the Earth's surface along which all points have zero dip is known as the

    (a) Agonic line

    (b) Aclinic line

    (c) Isogonal.

(2) The component of permanent magnetism acting in the fore and aft axis of the aircraft is

    (a) P

    (b) Q

    (c) R.

(3) Component Q is +ve when the aircraft's permanent magnetism is equivalent to a blue pole

    (a) forward of the compass

    (b) starboard of the compass

    (c) to the rear of the compass.

(4) Maximum effect of component P occurs on

    (a) quadrantal headings

    (b) North and South headings

    (c) East and West headings.

(5) Coefficient A occurs

    (a) equally on all headings

    (b) on all headings but is greatest on the cardinal points

    (c) on all headings but is greatest on the quadrantal points.

(6) Coefficient B is derived from

    (a) P + c

    (b) Q + f

    (c) P + f.

(7) The formula for determining the heading for maximum deviation is

    (a) sin heading = B/C

    (b) tan heading = B/C

    (c) tan heading = C/B.

(8) The formula for determining the heading for zero deviation is

    (a) tan heading = C/B

    (b) sin heading = C/B

    (c) tan heading = B/C.

Chapter 23
AIRCRAFT MAGNETISM 2

We learnt the theory of aircraft magnetism in the previous chapter. We will now consolidate it by working a few problems. At the start we summarise the properties of aircraft magnetism which should be kept firmly in mind when doing the problems.

	Hard iron (P and Q)	*Vertical soft iron (cZ and fZ)*
Strength	Hard iron is of permanent nature and therefore there is no change in its strength either due to the change of heading or the change of latitude.	The value of Z increases as the latitude increases; decreases as the latitude decreases; it is zero at the magnetic equator.
Polarity	There is no change in the polarity of hard iron either with change of heading or change of latitude.	The polarity reverses on crossing the magnetic equator.
Deviation: *Effect of change of heading*	P varies as sine of the heading Q varies as cosine of the heading	cZ varies as sine of the heading fZ varies as cosine of the heading
Effects of change of latitude	No effect on hard iron. Earth's component H varies with latitude, $\therefore$ deviation $\propto \dfrac{1}{H}$ and $\dfrac{\text{New dev}}{\text{Old dev}} = \dfrac{\text{old H}}{\text{new H}}$	vsi is zero at the magnetic equator, maximum at the poles. $\dfrac{\text{New dev}}{\text{Old dev}} = \dfrac{\text{new}\dfrac{Z}{H}}{\text{old}\dfrac{Z}{H}} = \dfrac{\text{new tan dip}}{\text{old tan dip}}$

Terminology
Landing compass reading means *heading magnetic*. Similarly, *aircraft compass reading* means *heading compass*. A plus (+) deviation is the same as easterly deviation and a minus (−) deviation is the same as westerly deviation.

Compass swing problems

(1)   An aircraft is swung on 4 cardinal headings with the following results. Calculate coefficients A, B and C.

Landing compass	Aircraft compass
000	001
089	092
176	175
271	270

Solution
The first step is to work out the deviation on all four headings. If you have any doubt as to the sign (+ or −) of deviations the golden rule is: make your aircraft compass read magnetic heading by adding or subtracting from the compass heading. That is your deviation, i.e. moving from Hdg (Compass) through Hdg (Magnetic) to Hdg (True), the signs read true. In the above problem make 001 read 000 by subtracting 1; the deviation is −1. Thus, we have:

Landing compass	Aircraft compass	Deviation
000	001	−1
089	092	−3
176	175	+1
271	270	+1

Coefficient A is found by adding algebraically the deviation on all 4 headings (or 8 headings if it is an eight-point swing), and by dividing this total by the number of points on which deviation was checked, (that is, 4 or 8).

Therefore, $$A = \frac{-1 + (-3) + 1 + 1}{4} = -\frac{2}{4} = -\frac{1}{2}$$

Coefficients B and C are found by the formulae

$$B = \frac{\text{dev on east} - \text{dev on west}}{2} = \frac{-3 - (+1)}{2} = -\frac{4}{2} = -2$$

$$C = \frac{\text{dev on north} - \text{dev on south}}{2} = \frac{-1 - (+1)}{2} = -\frac{2}{2} = -1$$

Answer: B = −2; C = −1; A = $-\frac{1}{2}$.

(2)   Calculate coefficients B and C

Hdg(M)	Hdg(C)
359	357
091	089
180	180
271	273

Answer: B = +2, C = +1.

(3)   Calculate coefficients B and C

Hdg(C)	Hdg(M)
357	358
090	087
182	179
268	270

Answer: B = −2.5, C = +2.

(4)   Calculate coefficients A, B and C

Landing compass	Aircraft compass
000	356
045	045
089	096
137	145
178	184
225	224
269	264
313	311

Answer: A = −1°; B = −6°; C = +5°.

(5)   Calculate coefficients A, B and C

a/c compass	Landing compass
001	003
048	043
095	087
136	133
181	175
224	225
268	274
313	317

Answer: A = −1°; B = −7°; C = +4°.

(6)   A compass is found to have following coefficients: A = +1, B = −3, C = −2. Determine the deviation on heading 210°(C).

Solution

The formula for calculating deviations when coefficients are known is:

$$\text{Dev on hdg } \theta = A + B \sin \theta + \cos \theta.$$

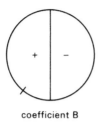

coefficient B   coefficient C

Fig. 23.1   Deciding + or −

Thus,

$$\begin{aligned}
\text{Dev on } 210° &= +1 + (-3 \sin 30°) + (-2 \cos 30°) \\
&= +1 + (-3 \times -0.5) + (-2 \times -0.86) \\
&= +1 + 1.5 + 1.7 \\
&= +4.2°
\end{aligned}$$

Alternative layout:

A =   +1.0
B = 3 sin 30° = 3 × 0.5 =   1.5 (ignore the sign for time being)
C = 2 cos 30° = 2 × 0.86 =   1.7 (ignore the sign for the time being)

Total deviation (when all
signs are known)   ?

   To determine the signs draw up two circles, one representing coefficient B and the other, coefficient C. Mark off roughly 210° points on both circles. Then look up the question again for the signs of B and C. The signs given are correct as follows:

> Coefficient B: the sign is correct for easterly headings.
> Coefficient C: the sign is correct for northerly headings.

   Divide the circle in two halves as shown in the Fig. 23.1. Coefficient B is −3, therefore, we put a minus (−) sign in the eastern half of the circle, a plus sign in the western half. Note that your heading mark falls in the plus (+) half. So, plus is the sign for B. Insert the sign in the above table.
   The coefficient C is negative, therefore a minus (−) sign goes in the northern half, a plus sign in the southern half. The heading mark is in the plus half, so the sign for C is, again, plus.
Thus, the total is: +1° + 1.5° + 1.7° = 4.2°.

(7)   B = +7, C = −6; what is the deviation on heading 200°(C)?

Answer: +3.25°.

(8)   A = −1; B = −2, C = −3; what is the deviation on heading 295°(C)?

Answer: −0.46°.

(9) A =−1, B =+2, C = −2; what is the deviation on heading 315°(C)?

Answer: −3.8°.

(10) A = +2, B =−2, C = +3; calculate the total deviation when the heading indicated by the aircraft compass is 060°(C)?

Answer: +1.8°.

Adjustment of compass

A swing may start on a northerly or southerly heading. If it starts on the north the aircraft heading is compared with the landing compass, the deviation is ascertained for north and then the aircraft is turned on to an easterly heading. The procedure is repeated and the aircraft is then taken on to south. Here we now have sufficient data to calculate coefficient C: that is,

$$\frac{\text{Dev N} - \text{Dev S}}{2}$$

Let us say that we have these deviations:

a/c comp	L/C	Dev
004	001	−3
175	180	+5

These readings give the coefficient C of −4°. Since we are already on a southerly heading we might as well correct for C here. What must be remembered here is that the sign of the coefficient C is valid on north; therefore if the correction is made on south the sign must be reversed.

The aircraft is heading on 175°; coefficient is −4°, the correction to apply is +4; therefore, the compass must be made to read 179°. This adjustment is made by use of the compass corrector key in conjunction with the micro-adjuster mounted on the compass.

Coefficient C is corrected when the aircraft is heading north or south.

Positive (+) C is corrected by turning the key in one of the two keyholes in the athwartships axis in an *anti-clockwise direction*.

Negative (−) C corrected by turning the key in one of the two keyholes in the athwartships axis in a *clockwise* direction.

Thus, in our case the key is turned clockwise until the compass reads 179°.

Had the swing commenced on south the correction for C would be made when heading north. The coefficient would then be applied without change of sign, that is, the compass is made to read: 004° − 4° = 000°.

Now on to west and let us assume the deviation to be:

a/c comp	L/C	Dev
085	087	+2
274	270	−4

to give us the coefficient B of +3, which when corrected on a westerly heading, must have the sign reversed to obtain the correct required reading i.e. 271°.

Fig. 23.2   Coefficient A

To correct positive (+) B insert the key in one of the two keyholes in the fore-and-aft axis and turn in an anti-clockwise direction.

To correct negative (−) B insert the key in one of the two keyholes in the fore-and-aft axis and turn in a clockwise direction.

In our illustration the key is turned anti-clockwise until the compass reads 274° − 3° = 271°. If the swing had commenced on south the correction would be made when on an easterly heading and the corrected compass heading would be 085° + 3° = 088°.

Coefficient A may be corrected on any heading whatsoever and there is no question of any sign change since A is a constant value deviation throughout 360°. Thus, for example if A is −3°, then if adjusting on heading 212° you make the compass read 209°; on 050° you make it read 047° and so on. Coefficient A arises mainly due to the misaligned lubber line (although there is some A due to magnetic causes) and the correction is purely mechanical. Fig. 23.2 illustrates the cause of A due to a misaligned lubber line and explains the following rules of correction.

To remove positive (+) A, turn the compass bowl clockwise.
To remove negative (−) A, turn the compass bowl anti-clockwise. This can be seen in Fig. 23.2 which illustrates a −ve A.

(11)   An aircraft compass was swung on 8 points with the following results.

a/c comp	L/C
000	003
046	044
090	084

135	129
179	174
227	223
270	270
315	319

(a) Calculate coefficients A, B and C.
(b) If B is compensated on east, what would you make the compass read?
(c) If C is corrected on south, what would you make your compass read?
(d) If A is corrected on 315°, what would you make your compass read?
(e) List the residual deviations that you would expect after compensation for coefficients A, B and C.

a/c comp	L/C	Dev
000	003	+3
046	044	−2
090	084	−6
135	129	−6
179	174	−5
227	223	−4
270	270	0
315	319	+4

$$A = \frac{+7 - 23}{8} = -\frac{16}{8} = -2°$$

$$B = \frac{-6 - (0)}{2} = -\frac{6}{2} = -3°$$

$$C = \frac{+3 - (-5)}{2} = +\frac{8}{2} = +4°$$

(a) A = −2°, B = −3°, C = +4°.
(b) a/c hdg   = 090°
    Coeff B   = −3°

    Make compass read = 087°
(c) a/c hdg   = 179°
    Coeff C   = −4° (change sign)

    Make compass read = 175°
(d) a/c hdg   = 315°
    Coeff A   = −2°

    Make compass read = 313°

(e) In a magnetic compass there are altogether five coefficients: A, B, C, D and E. Coefficients D and E are not in your syllabus but when you zero A, B and C, you still have some residual deviation left in the compass due to D and E. To work this question quickly and without getting bogged down in unnecessary calculations, the following layout is recommended.
    ● Make columns under the following headings and enter the information available from the question: aircraft headings and landing compass readings. The aim is to complete all the columns for all eight headings.
    ● Columns under Hdg(C) and Hdg(M) will give you the deviations; enter them in the third column.

• Now complete the column under A; it's the same number all the way through with the same sign: $-2°$ in our illustration.

• Column under B. On north and south the value of B is 0; on east, it is the value calculated $(-3°)$; on the west, enter $+3°$. As for the deviations on the quadrantal headings, they are all functions of sine of $45°$. The value to enter in our case is $3° \times 0.7 = 2.1°$. Having entered $2.1°$ on all quadrantal points, determine the sign from the deviation circle.

• Repeat the process for the figures under C. North is $+4°$, south is $-4°$ and 0 on the east and west. The cosine of $45°$ is also 0.7 and the value to enter for quadrantal headings is $4° \times 0.7 = 2.8°$, the signs extracted from the circle for C.

• Add the values of A, B and C for each heading and complete the next column *total*. The figure in this column under each heading indicates the amount by which each heading was corrected when we compensated for A, B and C. Thus, on north: A $= -2°$, B $= 0$, C $= 4°$, Total $+2°$, and this is the correction applied to the compass heading which is 000°.

• After the compensation, the compass on north reads 000° $+2°$ = 002°. This is entered in the column under 'compass reads'. Complete the column.

• Finally the column under *residual* is the answer. This is the remaining deviation after compensation. The values for this column are obtained by comparing *what the compass reads now* with *what it ought to read*, that is, the magnetic heading. After the compensation on north the compass reads 002° whereas the landing compass reads 003°. The residual deviation for this heading is $+1°$. Complete the remainder of the column and your work should read as in the table below – the answer to the question (e) being the figures under *residual*.

Hdg(C)	Hdg(M)	Dev	A	B	C	Total	Comp reads	Residual
000	003	+3	−2	0	+4	−2	002	+1
046	044	−2	−2	−2.1	+2.8	−1.3	044.7	−0.7
090	084	−6	−2	−3	0	−5	085	−1
135	129	−6	−2	−2.1	−2.8	−6.9	128.1	+0.9
179	174	−5	−2	0	−4	−6	173	+1
227	223	−4	−2	+2.1	−2.8	−2.7	224.3	−1.3
270	270	0	−2	+3	0	+1	271	−1
315	319	+4	−2	+2.1	+2.8	+2.9	317.9	+1.1

(12) There follows the result of a compass swing.

Hdg(C)	Hdg(M)
001	004
045	047
091	088

$$\begin{array}{cc} 134 & 130 \\ 181 & 176 \\ 226 & 224 \\ 271 & 270 \\ 315 & 317 \end{array}$$

(a) Determine the coefficients, A, B and C.
(b) Determine the residual deviations existing on all eight headings.

Answer: (a)   A = −1; B = −1; C = +4
        (b)   0, +0.9, −1, +0.5, 0, +1.1, −1, −0.5.

(13) There follows the result of an aircraft's compass swing.

Hdg(C)	Hdg(M)
002	357
047	044
092	090
137	135
182	181
227	228
272	272
317	313

(a) Give the values of the coefficients A, B and C.
(b) Explain how you would compensate for coefficients B and C.
(c) Explain how you would compensate for coefficient A.

Answer: (a)   A = −2, B = −1, C = −2.
        (b)   Since the swing commenced on a northerly heading, the coefficient C will be the first to be corrected on a southerly heading.

a/c hdg	182°(C)
Coeff C	+ 2° (change sign)
Make compass read	184°(C)

This adjustment is made by inserting the micro-adjuster key in either of the keyholes in the athwartships axis and turning the key clockwise until the new heading is obtained.

Coefficient B is corrected on heading 272°(C)

a/c hdg	272°(C)
Coeff B	+ 1° (change sign)
Make compass read	273°(C)

To make this adjustment the compass key is inserted in either hole in the fore-and-aft axis and turned clockwise until the required heading is indicated.

(c) Coefficient A is usually corrected in the hangar after the field operation is complete. Therefore the aircraft may be on any heading when the correction is being made. Assuming the aircraft is on 220°(C). Coefficient A is −2°. Loosen the retaining screws at the base of the compass and rotate the base anti-clockwise through 2° against the scale at the base provided specifically for this purpose. The effect of this is to rotate the lubber line anti-clockwise through the same amount, thus reducing the heading. Set up the new reading against the lubber line (thus upsetting the red/red relationship). After the bowl has been rotated through the requisite angle note that red is again aligned with red. The new heading is then being indicated and coefficient A has been removed. Fasten down the base screws.

(14) During a swing of a direct reading magnetic compass the following readings were obtained.

Landing compass	a/c compass
268	270
357	352
089	085
176	175

(a) Determine the values of coefficients A, B and C.

(b) If coefficient B is corrected on heading 089°(C) which keyhole would you use, and which way would you turn the key?

Answer: (a)   A = +2, B = +3, C = +2.

(b)   Using either keyhole in the fore-and-aft axis, turn the key anti-clockwise.

(15) An aircraft compass swing gives the following readings;

H(C)	H(M)
002	001
091	096
183	186

At this stage when the aircraft is on the southerly heading, coefficient C was compensated.

(a) What should the compass be made to read?

Assuming the coefficients present in the compass are A, B and C only

(b) what deviation would you expect to find when on the compass heading of 272°(C)?

(a) 185°(C).

(b) The only coefficients present are A, B and C. On a southerly heading, there can be no deviation due to coefficient B; therefore, the only coefficients present are A and C. After adjusting for C on south, we note that the aircraft heading is 185°(C) whereas the magnetic heading is 186°(M). This difference is due to coefficient A, +1°.

Before we arrive at the deviation on 272° we must establish the value of coefficient B. On east and west there can be no coefficient C. Therefore the only coefficients present on these headings are A and B. On east, the deviation measured is +5°. We know that we have +1° of coefficient A, therefore, deviation +5° is made up as follows:

Fig. 23.3   Hard iron and latitude change

+1° of coefficient A

+4° of HI and/or vsi (P and/or cZ)

Therefore, +4° is the coefficient B we are looking for. Any other figure for coefficient B may give you +5° deviation on the east, but not without producing a residual. This may be checked in the following.

Hdg(C)	Hdg(M)	Dev	A	B	Total	Comp reads	Residual
091	096	+5	+1	?	_____	096	0

In the above, we know that after compensating for A and B the residual must be 0 (there is no C on east and there are no other coefficients present). If the residual is to be 0, the compass, after the compensation, must read the same as the magnetic heading, which is 096°. This can only be achieved if the total compensation is +5° (091° + 5° = 096°). This +5° is the total of coefficients A and B. Therefore, if A is +1, B has to be +4°.

$$\text{Now, } B = \frac{E - W}{2} \quad \text{or} \quad 2B = E - W$$

and
$$W = E - 2B$$
$$= +5° - 8°$$
$$= -3°$$

So the answer is −3°, but you need not go through this process of shifting the equation. Notice that B is +4°; on the west it changes the sign: −4°; to this apply the coefficient A to give you the total deviation, which is −3°.

Change of deviation with latitude

Fig 23.3 shows the effect on deviations due to a change of latitude, where the deviations are caused by hard iron only. A hard iron component, HI, is shown acting at right angles to the directive force, H: firstly, in the very close vicinity of the two poles, secondly, at intermediate latitudes in both the hemispheres and thirdly at the magnetic equator. Note from this diagram that

(a)   The magnitude of the hard iron present in the aircraft does not change with latitude. The HI vectors shown in the diagram are of a constant length.

(b)   The earth's component H is least at the vicinity of the poles, and greatest at the equator. The needle takes up the position resultant of these two vectors, causing changes in deviations. And since HI remains constant throughout, the amount of deviation at any place is dependent upon the strength of the component H only. The relationship is

$$\tan D = \frac{HI}{H}$$ and since HI is constant and the rate of change of tangent is almost linear at small angles

$$D \propto \frac{1}{H}$$

This is the basic relationship. When we connect the deviations at two latitudes (and that's what we are interested in) the formula becomes:

$$\frac{D_1}{D_2} = \frac{H_2}{H_1}$$

and from this since we always seem to want the deviation at the second place, D_2,

$$D_2 = \frac{D_1 H_1}{H_2} \quad \text{(hard iron formula)}$$

(c)   In Fig. 23.3 the deviation is easterly all the way through. Although with change of latitude the value of deviation changes, the sign of the deviation does not change. If the deviation due to HI at X was negative, it would still be a minus quantity at Y no matter where Y was situated.

Now for the vertical soft iron, vsi. vsi is induced by the component Z of the earth's field. Z varies with magnetic latitude, growing weaker away from the magnetic poles, and the induced fields similarly vary in proportion. Therefore, if an aircraft's compass deviations are caused entirely by vsi, both the vectors that influence the needle, that is, H and vsi are variable with change of latitude. The effect of these two variables on deviation is shown in Fig. 23.4. Nearer the two magnetic poles the value of Z is very large, the value of H very small with consequent very large deviations. Approaching the magnetic equator, Z decreases, H increases until the magnetic equator is reached where Z completely disappears, H is maximum and no deviations are present. Note from Fig. 23.4 that on crossing the magnetic equator from one hemisphere to another the vsi reverses its polarity. (In Fig. 23.5 we show why this occurs.) From Fig. 23.4,

$$\tan D = \frac{cZ}{H} \quad \text{and} \quad D \propto \frac{Z}{H}$$

Since $\dfrac{Z}{H}$ also equals tangent of dip, the formula linking the deviations at

Fig. 23.4   vsi and latitude change

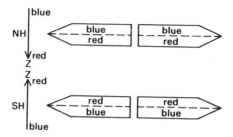

Fig. 23.5   Change of hemisphere

two places may be written down in two ways:

(a) $\dfrac{D_1}{D_2} = \dfrac{Dip_1}{Dip_2}$ (vertical soft iron formula)

(b) $\dfrac{D_1}{D_2} = \dfrac{Z_1/H_1}{Z_2/H_2}$; reversing this: $\dfrac{D_2}{D_1} = \dfrac{Z_2/H_2}{Z_1/H_1}$ and

$$D_2 = D_1 \times \frac{H_1}{Z_1} \times \frac{Z_2}{H_2}$$

$$D_2 = \frac{D_1 H_1 Z_2}{H_2 Z_1}$$ (vsi formula).

You have perhaps noted that the hard iron formula is multiplied by Z_2/Z_1 to arrive at the vsi formula.

In Fig. 23.5 vertical soft iron is shown on easterly and westerly headings in both hemispheres. The earth's component Z is shown acting downward in the northern hemisphere and upward in the southern hemisphere. This component Z induces magnetism in the vsi. Note from Fig. 23.5 that

(a) In the northern hemisphere the lower end of the vsi becomes red, upper end blue.

(b) In the southern hemisphere the lower end is blue, the upper end red. Thus there is a reversal of polarity with change of hemisphere.

(c) Note also that there is no change of polarity with change of heading (east and west polarities). This fact enables us to combine vsi with HI in calculating coefficients B and C.

In dealing with the problems where the compass was left completely un-corrected, you simply calculate the new deviation using the HI and vsi formulae as appropriate.

If the compass is corrected at X, calculate the deviation at Y as follows:

(a) If it was entirely due to HI, and completely compensated, then the deviation at X is 0 and the deviation at Y will also be 0. If it was partially compensated, say 2° out of +4°, then you have 2° of easterly deviation uncompensated and treat this as if the compass has not been corrected.

(b) Total or partial correction of vsi holds good only for the particular values of H and Z. Therefore, where the deviation is entirely due to the vsi and corrected, the new deviation can be calculated in two steps:
   - Calculate the effect of the micro-adjuster at Y using the hard iron formula and remembering that this HI of the micro-adjuster is of opposite polarity to the deviation it corrected at X. Thus, if the deviation at X was +2°, then when correcting for this, you inserted a micro-adjuster HI polarity of −2° to neutralise it.
   - Then calculate the dev due to vsi at Y, using the vsi formula.
   The sum of the two above is the new deviation.

(c) If the deviation at X is due to both HI and vsi, do the problem in three steps:
   - Calculate the micro-adjuster effect at Y using the HI formula;
   - Calculate the new deviation due to HI part using the HI formula;
   - Calculate the new deviation due to vsi part using the vsi formula.
   The sum of the three is the new deviation at Y.

Latitude change problems

(1) The values of H and Z at two places X and Y are these:

	H	Z
X	0.4	0.3
Y	0.3	−0.2

The coefficient B at place X is made up HI of +2° and vsi of −2°. What is the value of coefficient B at Y?

Solution

$$\text{Dev due to HI at Y} = \frac{D_1 H_1}{H_2} = \frac{+2 \times 0.4}{0.3} = +\frac{8}{3} = +2.66°$$

$$\text{Dev due to vsi at Y} = \frac{D_1 H_1 Z_2}{H_2 Z_1} = \frac{-2 \times 0.4 \times -0.2}{0.3 \times 0.3} = \frac{16}{9} = +1.77°$$

$$\text{Total dev at Y (coeff B)} = +4.43°$$

(2)   At position X(H = 0.3, Z = 0.3) the coefficient B of $+1\frac{1}{2}°$ is entirely due to vertical soft iron. If this has been entirely compensated at X, determine the deviation on heading 315°(C) due to coefficient B at Y (H = 0.15, Z = −0.4)

Answer: +4.9°

Solution
Coefficient B of +1.5° has been compensated by means of a micro-adjuster. Therefore, at X, a hard iron of −1.5° has been introduced, and although at X, it neutralised the vsi, at Y it will produce deviation of its own.

$$\text{Micro-adjuster: } D_2 = \frac{D_1 H_1}{H_2} = \frac{-1.5 \times 30}{15} = -3°$$

$$\text{vsi: } D_2 = \frac{D_1 H_1 Z_2}{H_2 Z_1} = \frac{+1.5 \times 30 \times -4}{15 \times 3} = -\frac{180}{45} = -4°$$

$$\text{Coefficient B} = \overline{-7°}$$

$$\text{Dev on } 315° = \text{B sin } 315°$$
$$= -7° \times (-\sin 45°)$$
$$= +4.9°$$

Max min deviations, polarity, relative bearings
When dealing with these problems keep these points firmly in your mind.

(a)   If a blue or red pole is located in the fore-and-aft axis, it can only produce coefficient B. Similarly, poles lying in the athwartships axis produce only coefficient C. A pole lying in the intermediate position will produce both B and C coefficients.

(b)   When the aircraft (or deviascope) turns, these poles which are fixed in the frame turn with the aircraft, and therefore their relative position with regard to the needle alters, altering the deviation.

(c)   When the blue pole is aligned with the needle, maximum directive force results. When the red pole is aligned with it, minimum directive force results.

(d)   When the poles are located at 90° to the needle, maximum deviation results.

(1)   A vertical soft iron bar is carried in an aircraft, fore of the fore-and-aft axis, and produces a coefficient of magnitude 4. The compass is in the southern hemisphere and the lower end of the bar is level with the magnet system. What deviation will be caused by this bar when on heading 300°(C)?

Solution
The problem basically involves identification of the pole giving a coefficient of 4.
   Since the bar is placed in the fore-and-aft axis, the coefficient is B. And since the lower end of the bar is level with the compass and the compass is in the southern hemisphere, the polarity in front of the needle is blue.

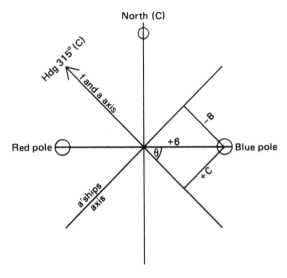

Fig. 23.6   Deviation 6°E due to HI on 315°(C)

And lastly, a blue pole in line with the needle in the fore position in the fore-and-aft axis gives a positive coefficient B.

Now the problem is solved in the normal way.

$$Dev_{300} = B \sin 60°$$
$$= +4° \times (-0.87)$$
$$= -3.48°$$

(2)   A hard iron source on a deviascope produces a maximum easterly deviation of 6° when on a heading of 315°(C).

Show the locations of the blue and red poles causing this deviation in a diagram.

Solution
In Fig. 23.6 the poles have been placed at 90° to the needle as the deviation is maximum. Since the deviation is easterly, in order that the needle be pulled clockwise, the blue pole is placed to the right of it, red pole to the left.

(3)   For the data in question 2, what is the deviation on heading 210°(C)?

Solution
To be able to calculate the deviation on 210°(C) (or any other heading for that matter) we must have both the value and the signs of coefficients B and C.

The values of B and C are worked out by trigonometry. In Fig. 23.6 drop perpendiculars from the blue pole to the fore-and-aft and athwartships axes of the aircraft. These represent coefficients C and B respectively.

Since we know the aircraft heading we are able to work out the value of angle θ in the figure. This angle is 45°. Now we have sufficient information to calculate B and C.

$$\text{Sin } 45° = \frac{C}{+6°} \quad \text{and} \quad C = 4.2°$$

$$\text{Cos } 45° = \frac{B}{+6°} \quad \text{and} \quad B = 4.2°$$

As for the signs, looking at the figure once again, we notice that in the fore-and-aft axis B is acting aft of the compass position in the fore-and-aft axis, and therefore it is −ve B. Similarly, C is acting to the right of the centre line in the athwartships axis; therefore, C is positive. Thus, the coefficients are

$$B = -4.2°$$
$$C = +4.2°$$
$$\begin{aligned}
\text{Dev}_{210} &= B \sin 210° + C \cos 210° \\
&= (-4.2° \times -0.5) + (+4.2° \times -0.87) \\
&= +2.1° - 3.7° \\
&= -1.6°
\end{aligned}$$

(4)   For the data in question 2, on what heading is the directive force (a) maximum? (b) minimum?

Solution

(a)   For maximum directive force, the blue pole must lie in front of the red point of the needle. Referring to Fig. 23.6, the blue pole will come in this position if the heading is altered to port through 90°. Thus, the heading for maximum directive force = 315° − 90° = 225°(C).

(b)   For minimum directive force, the red pole must lie against the red point of the needle. This heading is 225° − 180° = 045°(C).

(5)   Given: B = +3°, C = +2°.
(a)   On what heading is the directive force maximum?
(b)   On what heading is the directive force minimum?
(c)   On what heading is the deviation maximum?

Answer: (a) 326°19′; (b) 146°19′; (c) 236°19′ and 056°19′.

Test questions

(1)   Because magnetism due to hard iron is of a permanent nature, the change in its strength due to change of
(a)   heading is nil but it varies as sine latitude
(b)   latitude is nil but it varies as sine heading
(c)   latitude and of heading is nil.
(2)   Vertical soft iron magnetism
(a)   strength increases with increase of magnetic latitude
(b)   strength varies as cosine magnetic latitude

      (c)   has the same polarity in both hemispheres.

(3)   Deviation due to vertical soft iron fZ varies as
      (a)   sine heading
      (b)   cos heading
      (c)   tan heading.

(4)   In an aeroplane where deviation is due only to hard iron permanent magnetism, with change of latitude the new deviation is derived from
      (a)   old deviation × old H/new H
      (b)   old deviation × new H/old H
      (c)   new H × old H/old deviation.

(5)   In an aeroplane where deviation is due only to vertical soft iron magnetism, with change of magnetic latitude the new deviation is derived from
      (a)   old deviation × old tan dip/new tan dip
      (b)   old tan dip × new tan dip/old deviation
      (c)   old deviation × new tan dip/old tan dip.

(6)   To remove a positive (+) coefficient A the compass bowl should be
      (a)   turned anti-clockwise
      (b)   moved away from the pilot towards the aircraft's nose
      (c)   turned clockwise.

(7)   If deviation is −3° and magnetic variation is 3°E
      (a)   compass, magnetic and true headings are all the same value
      (b)   true heading is greater than magnetic heading
      (c)   compass heading is greater than true heading.

(8)   It is noted that the brass mounting of a compass has been secured with steel bolts. The effect would be that
      (a)   the mounting would affect the compass reading but the bolts would not
      (b)   both the mounting and the bolts would affect the compass reading
      (c)   the bolts would affect the compass reading but the mounting would not.

(9)   British Civil Airworthiness Requirements state that the residual deviation of a direct reading compass shall not exceed on any heading
      (a)   1°
      (b)   2°
      (c)   3°.

(10)   The value of magnetic variation
      (a)   cannot exceed 90°
      (b)   has a maximum value of 180°
      (c)   must be 0° at the magnetic equator.

Chapter 24
DIRECT READING (STANDBY) COMPASS; P-TYPE, E2-TYPE

The basic compass is simply a needle which points to the North, adapted for aerial use. It is mandatory to carry in civil transport aircraft a compass which does just this, so that if the splendidly refined direction-indicating gear goes for a burton, you are down to basics. The P-type is rather bulky and is seldom selected nowadays by sophisticated operators, but it is still in use world-wide nevertheless, although generally the card type (E-type) compass is now preferred as a standby.

A freely suspended magnet would settle along the earth's line of total force, providing it were clear of other magnetic influences, which means it would point to Magnetic North in the horizontal plane, and dip from the horizontal in the vertical plane (66° in the UK): the latter effect must be got rid of somehow, for we are interested only in the earth's horizontal force H.

For the compass to function efficiently it must:

(1) Lie horizontal
(2) Be sensitive
(3) Be aperiodic or dead-beat.

The first requirement is obtained by making the magnet system pendulous. Up to four magnets may be used in fact, and they are mounted close together below the pivot, so that when tilted by the earth's vertical force Z, the centre of gravity moves out from below the point of suspension bringing a righting force into action: the magnet will take up a position which is the resultant of the two equal and opposite forces, the tilting of the needle due to Z being counteracted by the weight of the magnet system acting through the C of G (Fig. 24.1). The final inclination of the compass to the horizontal is actually about 2°/3°, but it will increase with increased Z until 70N or S where H is so weak and Z so strong as to render the instrument useless.

In the N. hemisphere, the C of G would be considered to be southwards of the point of suspension, since the correcting force must be away from the north seeking end which is trying to dip: it must be stressed right now that this displacement of the C of G is a factor brought into play by the system's pendulosity: there is not, repeat not, some built-in mechanical adjustment to the pivoting of the needle which would render such a compass useless in the other Hemisphere. The C of G is displaced automatically from beneath the pivot to correct for dip whichever end of the needle does the dipping.

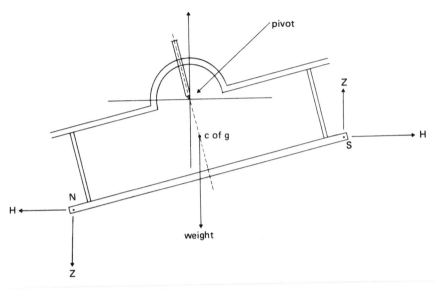

Fig. 24.1   C of G below the pivot

The second requirement of sensitivity can only be done by increasing the pole strengths of the magnets used so that the needle stays firmly fixed along the magnetic meridian. This is helped by keeping pivot friction to a minimum by using iridium for the pivot which is suspended in a sapphire cup. All this is suspended in liquid which reduces the effective weight of the system and lubricates the pivot.

The third requirement of aperiodicity is a trifle more complex. If a suspended magnet is deflected from its position of equilibrium and released, it oscillates between positions on either side of the equilibrium position for some time before coming to rest. *Period* of oscillation is the time taken in seconds to travel from one extreme position to the other and back again. A period is undesirable in a compass, and the ideal compass would stop without oscillation, when it could be said to be *aperiodic*. In the air, the compass needle is readily moved from its alignment with the magnetic meridian by acceleration and turns. Aperiodicity is attained in aircraft compasses by the following means:

(1)   The bowl is filled with methyl alcohol or a silicone fluid, and damping filaments are fitted to the magnet system.

(2)   Several short powerful magnets are used instead of one large one, thereby increasing the righting force, and reducing the moment of inertia.

(3)   The apparent weight of the system is reduced by the buoyancy of the liquid, and that weight is concentrated near the centre, by mounting close to the pivot. The moment of inertia is even further reduced.

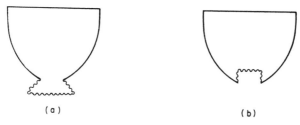

Fig. 24.2   Provision for liquid expansion

Fig. 24.3   Magnet system and split sleeve

The liquid should be transparent; have wide temperature range, say −50° to +50°C; low coefficient of expansion – in practice it hasn't, it's about 12% over the full temperature range; low viscosity and low specific gravity – not too bad; non-corrosive – not so important with plastic bowls, but it can eventually get at the rubber gasket of the verge ring of a P-type compass. Since the liquid will change in volume with temperature variations, some expansion device is necessary. At the bowl base, an expansion chamber is fitted in the larger types or a sylphon tube in the smaller, of thin corrugated metal (Fig. 24.2).

One disadvantage of the use of liquid is that in a prolonged turn it will turn with the aircraft, taking the magnet system with it tending to affect indicated readings on completion. This is offset to some extent by keeping a good clearance between the damping wires and the wall of the bowl; the effect is small, since the viscosity of the liquid used is low, too, but liquid swirl does prevent an immediate settling down on a new heading compass.

P-type compass

The magnet system (Fig. 24.3)
The split sleeve overlaps the ledge surrounding the dome and prevents the whole works falling apart when the aircraft and hence the compass is inverted.

The bowl

The lubber line on the bowl is fixed on the aircraft's fore and aft axis precisely, and we have already seen the effect of any displacement of it, as well as the ease of correction. The suspension of the bowl and its expansion device is such that vibration which would harm the pivot is reduced to a minimum: it stands on 4 bronze helical springs which are attached to the outer case spaced at 90° apart, and a floating ring, to which friction springs are attached, supports the bowl in slots to prevent azimuth movement.

The grid ring fits over the verge ring which seals the liquid in the bowl, and has direction marked every 10° graduated in 2° divisions, luminous. Additionally, the North point is a red triangle, hence the expression *red on red*, and parallel lines are marked across the plate, to be lined up with the needle precisely: the locking device is put to *lock* once the desired heading is set against the lubber line, and the aircraft turned till *red is on red*. The North pointer of the needle is crossed to prevent error.

Serviceability checks

(1) Check liquid is free from bubbles, discoloration, sediment.
(2) Examine all parts for luminosity.
(3) Ensure that grid ring rotates freely through 360°, and that locking device functions positively.
(4) Test suspension of bowl by moving gently in all directions and that there is no metal to metal feeling.
(5) Test for pivot friction: deflect the magnet system through 10–15° each way, and note the reading on return: each should be within 2° of the other.
(6) Test for damping: deflect system through 90°, hold for 30 seconds to allow liquid to settle and time its return through 85°. The maximum and minimum times are laid down in the manufacture's Instrument Manual, usually about 6.5 seconds to 8.5 seconds.

The E2 compass

A small compass, vertical reading, which is the favourite as a standby compass: invariably fitted between the two pilots above the windscreen. It has correctors built in for Coefficients B and C and R (there is another model, the E2A, which omits the R corrector), on top of the bowl.

The bowl is of transparent plastic, and the lubber line is simply a luminous line in the window; the magnet is a steel circle around the base of a dome, and from the dome a pivot is dropped which rests in a sapphire cup on a stem fixed to the base of the bowl (Fig. 24.4). The centre of gravity is below the pivot so dip is minimised as in the P-type. The bowl is filled with a silicone fluid, non-corrosive, of low viscosity, and with a low coefficient of expansion – but there is a sylphon tube at the rear of the compass bowl.

The compass card is a light metal ring, marked off every 30°, graduated in 10° or 5°, attached to the circular magnet, and the dome of the bowl prevents the system falling off when inverted. The E2 suffers from turning and

Fig. 24.4   E-type compass principle

acceleration errors, and could in extreme climb or dive positions not be free
to rotate.

Test questions
(1)   In a direct-reading compass, the magnet system is made aperiodic by the
      use of
      (a)   the damping action of the compass liquid
      (b)   magnets with a large magnetic moment
      (c)   a pendulous suspension.
(2)   The modern stand-by direct reading compass has
      (a)   no lubber line
      (b)   no facility for setting the heading
      (c)   no pendulous suspension.
(3)   The sensitivity of a direct reading compass varies
      (a)   directly with Z
      (b)   inversely with both H and Z
      (c)   directly with H.
(4)   The compass card of an E-type direct reading compass is shaped to the
      inside profile of the bowl in order to
      (a)   increase sensitivity
      (b)   minimise parallax error
      (c)   permit clearer calibrations to be marked on it.
(5)   In a modern stand-by direct reading compass, there is
      (a)   a non-pendulously mounted magnet system
      (b)   a single pendulously mounted bar magnet
      (c)   a circular magnet or pair of bar magnets pendulously mounted.
(6)   Compared to the P-type compass, a modern stand-by direct-reading
      compass is
      (a)   unaffected by dynamic errors
      (b)   so located as to reduce dynamic errors
      (c)   still affected by dynamic errors.

Chapter 25
TURNING AND
ACCELERATION ERRORS

We're still on about compasses where a magnet system is fitted pendulously to counteract the effect of Dip: the residual angle from the horizontal is around 3° in UK latitudes, and in the reduction from 66° to 3° the C of G has been displaced from below the pivot to South of the pivot to pull the dipping North-seeking end up towards the horizontal. This displacement will vary with Z, and clearly in the S. Hemisphere the displacement will be of opposite sign, i.e. the C of G will displace itself to the North of the pivot to counter-balance the dipping South seeking compass pole.

This displacement, however, has a marked effect on the compass needle in turns, accelerations and decelerations, except at the Magnetic equator where Z is nil.

Acceleration errors

On a Westerly heading, if speed is increased, the pivot and the magnet system will move forward with the aircraft: there will also be an equal and opposite force acting on the centre of gravity, which in the horizontal plane is South of the Pivot: the resultant of this horizontal couple will rotate the needle in an anticlockwise direction, i.e. the North seeking end will be moved to the west. Additionally since the C of G is placed below the pivot in the vertical plane, the pivot assembly going forward while the C of G lags behind will cause a vertical tilt to the needle, since the needle, the pivot and the C of G are no longer in line with the magnetic meridian: the counteracting C of G against dip will thus be lost to some extent and the North end of the needle will be under some influence from Z, causing further rotation of the North seeking end in the direction of the acceleration. In fact, it is this part of the action which contributes the major amount of the total error (Fig. 25.1).

Fig. 25.1 Effect of acceleration

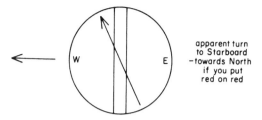

Fig. 25.2   Acceleration error

Accelerating on an Easterly Hdg, with similar resultant forces, the needle would turn clockwise, showing an apparent turn to port, i.e. to the North. In all changes of speed, where the aircraft's heading is across the needle there will be a compass error until constant speed is regained (Fig. 25.2).

Summary of acceleration and deceleration errors

HDG	SPEED	NEEDLE TURNS	EFFECT
E	Increase	Clockwise	Apparent Turn to N.
W	Increase	Anticlockwise	Apparent Turn to N.
E	Decrease	Anticlockwise	Apparent Turn to S.
W	Decrease	Clockwise	Apparent Turn to S.

N.B.

(1)   In Southern Hemisphere, above errors are opposite.
(2)   No errors on Northerly and Southerly headings as the force acts along the needle.
(3)   They can occur in bumpy conditions.
(4)   No errors on the Magnetic Equator, as the pivot and the C of G are coincident.

Turning errors

These are maximum on N and S headings, and are important within 35° of these headings.

Consider a turn through N to starboard: the centripetal force acting on the pivot directed inwards towards the centre of the turn should balance the centrifugal force acting outwards: but the centrifugal force acts on the centre of gravity, which we known in the N. Hemisphere to be displaced south of the pivot. Thus the needle will be pulled outwards from its centre of gravity, turning the needle in the direction of turn, Easterly: and the compass will indicate less than the turn actually accomplished. Additionally, the unbalanced centrifugal/centripetal forces will set up a vertical pull on the slightly tilted North-seeking pole, accentuated by the fact that the needle has left the magnetic meridian; this vertical pull in the turn will manifest itself as

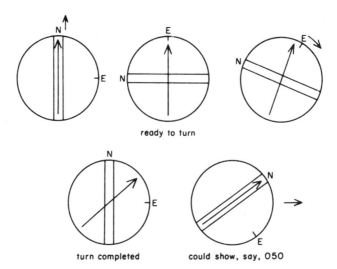

ready to turn

turn completed   could show, say, 050

Fig. 25.3   Turn to starboard from north

a rotation of the magnet system in the direction of the turn, to the East: again, this is the major contribution to the error.

In the turn we are considering, the needle can turn at the same rate as the aircraft, and indicate no turn at all: it can turn slower than the aircraft, indicating a smaller turn than actually accomplished: it can, in high rates of turn, move quicker than the aircraft and indicate a turn in the wrong direction. In turns through South (we're in the N. Hemisphere) the reverse will take place, and the compass will rotate in the opposite direction to the aircraft, indicating a greater turn than that actually made: but as the needle turns as it were to meet the aircraft, the result always is an overreading, and always in the right direction.

No fixed figure can be laid down to any of these errors, as so many variables are involved: but errors of up to 60° are not unusual in a prolonged turn, and only experience of a particular aircraft with its particular compass type can avoid the fiddling and twiddling to get settled down on the precise compass heading required as soon as possible.

In the Southern Hemisphere, with the C of G displaced to the North of the pivot, the reverse results will be obtained. The swirl of the liquid which tends to turn in the same direction as the aircraft will, in the Northern Hemisphere, be additive to the error in turns through North, and subtractive in turns through South.

To summarise:

TURN	NEEDLE	EFFECT	LIQUID SWIRL	CORRECTION
Through North	Same as aircraft	Under Indication	Adds to Error	Turn less than needle shows
Through South	Opp. to aircraft	Over Indication	Reduces Error	Turn more than needle shows

N.B.

(1)   In Southern Hemisphere, above errors are of opposite value.
(2)   In turns about East and West, no errors to speak of, since forces act along the needle.
(3)   Northerly turning error is greater than Southerly, since liquid swirl is additive.
(4)   For accurate turns, use the DI. All dynamic errors last only for the period of speed changes or turns: once a constant speed or level flight is resumed the compass needle finds North again.

Check the pictures in Fig. 25.3, for a turn to starboard from North, where the needle turns slower than the aircraft. Repeat them for a variety of turns through N and S, in both hemispheres.
      And for rules of thumb, see Fig. 25.4.

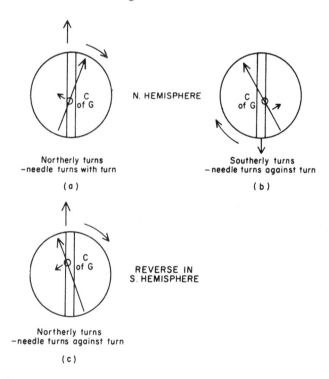

Fig. 25.4   Summary of effects

So, if you visualise in flight the amount of turning you need to do to achieve a particular change of heading, it can be encapsulated as shown in Fig. 25.5.

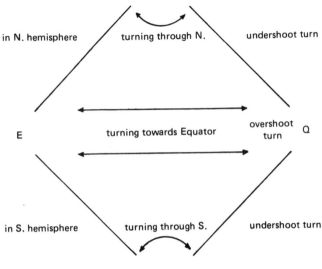

Fig. 25.5   Rules of thumb

Test questions

(1) In the holding pattern at Barcelona (41°N 02°E) an aircraft using a direct reading compass for heading reference turns anti-clockwise from 032°M to 310°M. At the end of the turn the compass will
   (a) overread the amount of turn
   (b) underread the amount of turn
   (c) correctly read the amount of turn.

(2) When accelerating after take-off towards the West at Entebbe (00°30′N 32°30′E) the direct reading compass will show
   (a) a significant apparent turn towards North
   (b) a significant apparent turn towards South
   (c) no significant error arising from the acceleration.

(3) When approaching runway 10R at Heathrow the aircraft decelerates as gear and flaps are lowered. The direct reading compass would be seen to show
   (a) a turn towards South
   (b) a turn towards North
   (c) no apparent turn due to the deceleration.

(4) When approaching Copenhagen (55°42′N 12°34′E) on a Westerly heading the aircraft decelerates whilst on the approach. The direct reading compass
   (a) will indicate an apparent turn towards South
   (b) will indicate an apparent turn towards North
   (c) magnet system will turn anti-clockwise.

(5) While carrying out a turn at the magnetic equator, whith a direct reading compass there would be

(a) no turning error
(b) a tendency to overread turns through North and underread turns through South
(c) a tendency to underread all turns due to the liquid swirl.

Chapter 26
REMOTE INDICATING COMPASS (RIC)

A remote indicating compass combines the use of a gyro with the earth's magnetic lines of force, thus giving the best of both DI and direct reading compasses. As for the magnetic part the system does not align itself with the meridian; it *senses* it, as we shall soon see. Since it is a remote indicating compass, the detector unit which senses the meridian can be placed outside the cockpit. In fact it is usually tucked away in the wing tip or other remote part of the fuselage where the magnetic interference is the least. This gives it a high accuracy of $\pm\frac{1}{2}°$. The compass incorporates a facility to set variation, thus giving true headings, if required. Finally, the heading information may be transferred to a number of repeaters in the cockpit or other equipment requiring heading information e.g. RMI, Doppler, etc.

Principle of direction sensing

If you expose a highly permeable magnetic bar to the earth's field the bar will acquire magnetic flux. The amount of flux thus produced will depend on two factors: latitude which governs the strength of the earth's component H (assuming the bar is horizontal) and the direction of the bar relative to the direction of the component H. This second part is the key to the heading sensing.

In Fig. 26.1(a) a bar is placed having its axis directly in line with the magnetic meridian as defined by the direction H. Since H goes right through the length of the bar the flux produced is maximum. If this bar was fixed in the fore-and-aft axis of the aircraft, maximum flux will result when the aircraft is on heading 000(M). In Fig. 26.1(b) the aircraft carrying the bar is on heading 090(M). Since component H acts at 90° to the axis of the bar, no flux will be induced. This is a cosine relationship. If the aircraft was on heading 030(M), the flux intensity would be H cos 30°. Now, on heading 150(M) the flux intensity will be the same as on 030(M) but the direction of the flux flow will have reversed (cosine of 150° is negative).

This, therefore, gives us a basic principle which may be adapted to give direction measurements. The flux intensity is the measure of the heading. The problem is to convert flux into electrical voltage and current. Now, this is an easy matter if the flux so produced was *changing* flux, for, according to Faraday, 'Whenever there is change of flux linked with a circuit, an EMF is induced in the circuit'. It will be appreciated that in an aircraft at any given

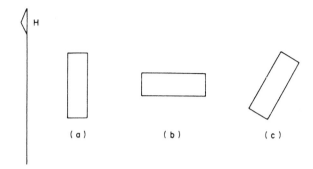

Fig. 26.1   Change of flux

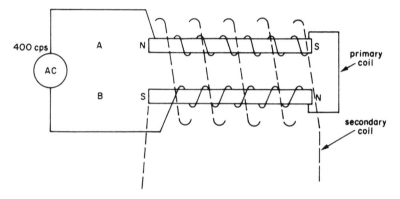

Fig. 26.2   Flux valve

position the flux produced will be a steady, constant quantity. If this steady flux could be converted to changing flux, a current representing heading would flow. This is what we want, a current representing aircraft's heading. In the description below, the Sperry CL2 is taken as a typical RIC.

Flux Valve
This is achieved in the RIC by a device called the Flux Valve. It consists of two bars of highly permeable magnetic material – bars A and B in Fig. 26.2.

Both the bars are wound with a coil and connected to an AC source in series. The coil is called the Primary Coil. Over the primary coil and going round both the bars is a pick-up coil, called the Secondary Coil. The effect of passing AC through these wirings is shown in Fig. 26.3. The AC passed is of such strength that at the peak it saturates both the coils, as seen in the figure. However, the flux produced in Fig. 26.3 will have no effect on the secondary coil since at any given instant two bars produce flux of equal intensity and opposite polarity. But in practice this situation does not arise, since a bar placed horizontally on the earth's surface or at an altitude (as in an aircraft)

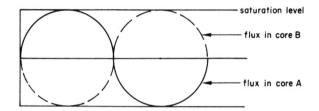

Fig. 26.3   Effect of AC

Fig. 26.4   Static flux due to H

Fig. 26.5   Saturation reached

Fig. 26.6   Changing flux

has always present in it the earth's component H (unless the aircraft is flying in the close vicinity of either Pole). This component H produces a static flux in both the bars which is shown in Fig. 26.4.

The effect of this static flux is to saturate the cores before AC reaches the peak, as seen in Fig. 26.5. The coils are saturated and AC is still rising. The effect will be that from now on, as the saturation occurs, the intake of the earth's flux will start reducing and on a combined figure it will appear as a curve – a changing flux.

This changing flux will now produce voltage and current will flow in the secondary coil.

Basic components of the compass

An RIC comprises five basic units as follows:

(1) Detector Unit
(2) Master Indicator
(3) Amplifier
(4) The Gyro Unit
(5) Control Panel

Detector unit

This is a very small unit in size and contains the sensing element. A simple flux valve as explained above would do as a sensing element but there are two disadvantages to its use. First, at varying latitudes, varying current will flow; second, an ambiguity exists. With relation to Fig. 26.1 above, we said that the flux on headings 030(M) and 150(M) will be of the same intensity but of opposite polarity. This means, then, we can differentiate. On heading 330(M), however, as the cosine of 330 is also positive, the flux will be of the same intensity and polarity as on heading 030(M).

These disadvantages are overcome by the use of three simple flux valves instead of just one. They are placed 120° apart and all six cores (or bars) are excited by a common primary coil. To improve sensitivity, six curved collector horns are attached to the outer ends of the bars. They collect the flux and feed into their respective spokes (Fig. 26.7).

Signal selsyn

This unit, located in the master indicator, receives the current from the detector unit. The selsyn unit consists of three legs similar to the spokes of the detector unit and a moveable coil, called the *rotor*, at the centre. The stators having received signals from the respective three secondary coils resolve the field produced in a final resultant direction. Detector unit and signal selsyn are shown in Fig. 26.8.

Operation

Follow the operation with reference to Fig. 26.9.

(1) On switching on, the detector unit will produce voltages in three secondary coils. These voltages are a direct measure of the heading.
(2) These voltages are fed to three respective stators of the signal selsyn. The stators resolve these voltages into a resultant field.
(3) That resultant field is a definite direction. If the pointer of the master

Fig. 26.7   Detector unit

Fig. 26.8   Detector unit and signal selsyn

indicator is indicating that very heading at this time the rotor of the signal selsyn will be at *null* position, that is, it will be lying at 90° to the direction of the resultant field. In this state no voltage is induced in the rotor.

(4)   If the heading is not synchronised, the rotor will not be at null and voltage will be induced in the rotor.

(5)   This voltage is fed to the precession amplifier where –

   (a)   it will be phase detected,

   (b)   rectified (i.e. converted from AC to DC), and

   (c)   amplified.

(6)   This DC signal is then passed to the precession coil in the Gyro Unit where the precession of the gyro takes place in the horizontal plane and in correct direction due to arrival of this signal. How this is done is explained later.

(7)   As gyro turns, the horizontal bevel gear turns, turning the vertical bevel gear with it. The vertical bevel gear carries a shaft on which are mounted the gyro unit pointer (this is the pilot's indicator) and the *rotor* of the gyro unit data selsyn. Therefore, as the vertical gear and

Fig. 26.9   RIC operation

the shaft rotate, the pointer and the rotor of the data selsyn must rotate too.

(8)   This data selsyn rotor of the gyro unit is continuously energised by AC and therefore, has a standing field in it affecting its stators. When the rotor rotates, this field must rotate, producing new signals in its stators.

(9)   These new signals are passed to the respective stators of the data selsyn in the master indicator, altering the field in them.

(10)   This new field in the stators will affect the rotor and an AC will be induced in it.

(11)   This AC or error signal is passed to the follow-up amplifier where it is amplified and then sent out to a two-phase follow-up motor.

(12)   This will energise the motor and it will start turning the central shaft in the MI (Master Indicator) via the gear train. Mounted on this shaft are the rotors of the two selsyns. They will continue to rotate until the rotor of the signal selsyn is at null position to the resultant field in that selsyn.

(13)   At this instant, signal selsyn rotor will stop sending error signals to the amplifier and to the rest of the system. The gyro is now aligned with the magnetic meridian, both the pointers are similarly synchronised with the meridian, and the system comes to rest.

Let's go over the whole thing again, this time taking some figures. Say, on switching on, the nose of the aircraft is pointing to 060(M). This is the field the detector unit will produce and the stators of the signal selsyn will resolve. Say, at this time the pointers of the two indicators are indicating 050(M).

Field in the stators – 060; pointers are not indicating this heading, therefore signal selsyn rotor is not at null. It sends off an error signal to the precession amplifier where three things noted above happen. The signal is then passed on to the precession mechanism of the gyro.

This turns the gyro, horizontal and vertical bevel gears. The shaft in the gyro unit rotates, rotating with it the rotor of the gyro unit data selsyn. This rotor was initially aligned with 050 indication. Now, say, at a given instant it has rotated to be aligned with 058 (in the course of its turn in the direction of 060). This turning will cause a new field in its stators which will be repeated in the stators of the data selsyn in the master indicator.

This rotor was aligned to indicate 050; now the field in its stators equals 058. A signal will be raised in the rotor, amplified and passed to the motor. The motor turns, turning the shaft and the rotors with it. Signal selsyn rotor turns to align with 058 – all rotors are in synchronism but the signal selsyn rotor has not gained the null position: it still has two degrees to go and therefore, it continues to send out error signals.

When all three rotors are aligned with 060, no more error signals are raised, and the compasses are synchronised.

Manual synchronising

In above illustration, the pointer will take exactly 5 minutes to move round from 050 to 060 since the rate of precession of the gyro is limited to 2° per minute. This slow rate of precession is quite adequate to keep the gyro in the magnetic meridian throughout the flight – i.e. to check the gyro's apparent wander. But where a large discrepancy between the nose of the aircraft and the indicated heading is present, e.g. on initial switching on, the pointers are synchronised manually. This is done by use of the *synchronising knob* on the Gyro Unit (Fig. 26.10).

The fact that the pointers are not indicating synchronised heading will be brought to your attention by the presence of a dot or a cross in the middle of the annunciator window on both the gyro unit indicator and the master indicator. This indication is removed by depressing the synchro knob on the gyro unit and turning it in the direction shown by the arrow until both symbols appear. When it is so depressed the gyro itself is disconnected and only the shaft and the pointers are turned.

Behaviour of an RIC in a turn

Earlier, we said that the normal precession operation is adequate to take care of the gyro wander etc. This might give an impression that the pointers would get desynchronised during a turn. This is not so, because during a turn the gyro, due to its rigidity, drives the pointers and keeps them aligned with the instantaneous heading. This is what takes place.

The aircraft, and therefore the gyro case, rotates about the horizontal bevel wheel and the gyro. Thus, the vertical bevel gear goes round the horizontal bevel gear, and the shaft in the gyro unit rotates. Error signals

Fig. 26.10   RIC presentation

raised in the stators of the gyro unit data selsyn are repeated in the stators of the master indicator data selsyn. The rotor in that data selsyn raises an error signal, the motor turns and the shaft in the master indicator turns. This keeps the rotors of the signal selsyn and data selsyn in synchronism with the instantaneous heading during a turn.

During all this time the detector unit is also turning with the aircraft. Therefore the field in the signal selsyn stators is also rotating. Both this field and the rotor rotate at the same speed and in the same direction. Therefore, continuous synchronism is maintained.

In a steep and prolonged turn a slight desynchronisation may be expected. This is due to the fact that the detector unit is no longer horizontal and a small component of Z will enter in it, giving rise to a false field. However, on coming out of the turn, the needle will be brought to correct reading by the normal precession process. Apart from this small error there are no turn and acceleration errors.

Variation setting
The system incorporates a facility for setting variation on the compass so that true headings may be flown. This is done by turning the stators of the signal selsyn which has the effect of rotating the field in the stators by an equivalent amount. The facility for setting variation is located on the master indicator and as the knob is turned a scale in the variation window rotates behind a lubber line to indicate the amount of variation being set.

Precession mechanism
The precession mechanism consists of a coil, called the precession coil, mounted in the outer gimbal, and a pair of horn shaped permanent magnets mounted on the inner gimbal. See Fig. 26.11. The polarity of the permanent magnets is as shown in the figure. When desynchronisation occurs, a DC is

Fig. 26.11   Precession mechanism

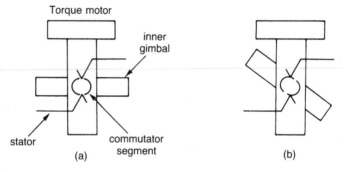

Fig. 26.12   Erection mechanism

passed from the amplifier via the annunciator circuit to the precession coil. (As a matter of interest AC models are also available). Depending on the direction of the current, two ends of the precession coil will acquire magnetic polarity. At one end this polarity will be in attraction and at the other end in repulsion to the polarity of the permanent magnet. This attraction and repulsion will apply a torque on the inner gimbal in the vertical plane and the gyro will precess in the horizontal plane, that is, the horizontal bevel gear will turn.

Erection mechanism

It will be appreciated that, as with the DI, the gyro in an RIC must be maintained horizontal. Erection mechanism ensures this. It consists of a two-phase torque motor with its stators mounted on the outer gimbal and a levelling switch mounted on the inner gimbal – see Fig. 26.12.

The levelling switch is made up of a commutator split in two segments by an insulating strip. When the gyro axis is horizontal the stators rest on the insulated strip and the switch to the motor is off – Fig. 26.12(a). When the axis is tilted the stator will come in contact with the commutator and the circuit to the torque motor is complete. The direction of the current to the

Fig. 26.13   Annunciator

torque will depend on the direction of the tilt, as is seen in Fig. 26.12(b). The direction of the current decides the direction the torque will be applied, that is, clockwise or anti-clockwise. The torque so applied about the vertical axis will precess the gyro axis until it is once again horizontal when the stator will slip off the commutator and rest on the insulated strip, switching off the motor.

The annunciator

This unit gives the indication of synchronisation state, i.e. the gyro alignment with the magnetic meridian, and consists of a pivoted arm carrying a flag marked with dot and cross at one end and a permanent magnet at the other. The magnet is held between two annunciator coils connected in series. When the pointers are desynchronised from the magnetic meridian, DC flows from precession amplifier to the precession coil. Use is made of this current flow which passes through the annunciator circuit. As it passes through the two annunciator coils (connected in series) the two ends nearest to the permanent magnet will acquire the same polarity, one end attracting the magnet and the other end repelling. As the magnet is drawn towards one end of the coil the flag arm will turn about its pivot, the flag with be displaced from the centre and one of its ends, carrying either a dot or a cross, will appear in the window. Whether the dot or a cross will appear in the centre of the window depends on which end of the magnet is drawn towards the coils, which in its turn depends on the direction of the DC (Fig. 26.13).

Control panel

With an RIC system there are two gyro units, one for each pilot, together with the master indicator. But as we saw above only one gyro unit could be run together with the detector unit. In Fig. 26.9 we have no accommodation for two gyro units. Therefore, the other gyro must run as a DI. On the control panel there is a three-position switch on which you may select gyro off, gyro on port, or gyro on the starboard side. In the off position, both gyros operate as a DI, that is, unmonitored by the detector unit. In flight, the appearance of a DG *flag* on a gyro unit indicates that that unit is no longer being monitored by the detector unit.

Adjustment and calibration
Having done a normal swing and calculated coefficients A, B and C, proceed as follows to correct for them.

Equipment required
A centre reading voltmeter (CRV). This is plugged in at the jack socket in the amplifier. This then by-passes the annunciator circuit; the CRV acts as a more sensitive annunciator. If no current flows through the CRV the system is synchronised. You also require a stable DC supply of 24–28V and a Compass Corrector Key.

Correction for B and C
(1) Having worked out the heading you want the compass to read, press the manual synchro knob on the gyro unit, turn it and give the required reading to the pointer.
(2) Keep the knob depressed. If the knob is released the pointer will be precessed back to the original reading.
(3) The CRV needle is now displaced from its zero position to one side or the other.
(4) On the corrector box there is a two-position switch. In one position corrections up to 3° may be made; in the other, corrections over 3° may be made. If your correction for B and C does not exceed 3° place the switch to 3° position, otherwise on to 15° position.
(5) Insert the compass corrector key in B or C socket as appropriate and turn the key until CRV reads 0.
(6) Correction is complete; release the synchro knob.

Coefficient A over 2°
(1) Steps 1, 2 and 3 are as per B and C above.
(2) Turn the detector unit physically until CRV reads 0.
(3) Release the synchro knob.

Coefficient A of 2° and below
This is simply taken out on the Variation scale on the master indicator as follows:
(1) Set the value of the coefficient A on the VSC as if you are setting variation. If A is positive set easterly variation of equivalent amount. If it is negative set westerly variation. For example you wish to correct for A, value −1. Set 1° westerly variation.
(2) Insert compass corrector key in the groove on the side of the master indicator (approximately at the 8 o'clock position) and turn the key until the lubber line of the VSC moves and covers 0 variation. The lubber line was displaced by you when you carried out step 1 above.

Advantages of a remote indicating compass

The advantages of a remote indicating compass over a DI are these:
(1)   DI suffers from slow drift and has to be reset frequently in a flight. Further, when resetting, the aircraft must be flown straight and level to be able to take reading of a magnetic compass. A remote indicating compass does away with this, since its indicators are monitored by a detector unit.
(2)   The detector unit can be installed in a remote part of the aircraft where influences due to aircraft magnetism are least. This gives a better accuracy to a remote indicating compass whereas a magnetic compass from which the DI is reset is exposed to these influences.
(3)   The flux valve used in the detector unit *senses* the meridian instead of *seeking* it increasing the instrument's sensitivity.
(4)   The compass can be detached from the detector unit by a flick of a switch and the gyro then works as normal DI. This entirely does away with the requirement of a pure DI in the cockpit (A remote indicating compass is used as a DI when flying in extreme northerly/southerly latitudes where H is very feeble.)
(5)   It may be used in providing heading information to other equipments, e.g. autopilot, RMI, Doppler, etc.
(6)   It enables repeaters to be provided for each crew position.
(7)   By the incorporation of a variation setting control, true heading information can be presented.
(8)   The low rate of control of the detector unit over the gyro *almost* eliminates turning and acceleration errors.

Disadvantages compared with a direct reading compass
(1)   It is heavier.
(2)   It is more expensive.
(3)   It is electrical in operation and therefore less reliable.
(4)   It is more complicated mechanically.

  Despite these disadvantages, of which 2, 3 and 4 are of particular concern to the operator as 3 and 4 are also more expensive in maintenance, the advantages heavily outweigh the disadvantages for airline operations.

Test questions
(1)   The detector unit of a remote indicating compass is normally
  (a)   fixed in the vertical plane only
  (b)   fixed in azimuth
  (c)   free in both the vertical and horizontal planes.
(2)   Compensation for coefficient A in a remote indicating compass is carried out by
  (a)   rotation of the detector unit
  (b)   electro-magnetic corrector coils
  (c)   the permanent magnets of a corrector device.

(3) In a remote indicating compass, the rotor of the slaved gyro is auto-matically prevented from wandering in the vertical plane by means of
  (a) its pendulous suspension
  (b) the bevel gears and gimbals
  (c) a levelling switch and torque motor.

(4) In a remote indicating compass the rotor of the slaved gyro is auto-matically prevented from wandering in the horizontal plane by means of
  (a) a levelling switch and motor
  (b) a commutator-type alignment switch
  (c) a precession circuit.

(5) In a remote indicating compass the rate of precession of the gyro is limited to
  (a) 2° per minute
  (b) 5° per minute
  (c) 10° per minute.

(6) In a remote indicating compass, the function of the *follow-up* system is to
  (a) maintain the master indicator aligned with the gyro unit
  (b) exercise a low rate of control over the gyro unit
  (c) hold the two gyro units in mutual alignment.

(7) The appearance of a DG flag on the gyro unit of a remote indicating compass when in flight indicates to the pilot that the unit is
  (a) unserviceable
  (b) no longer monitored by the detector unit
  (c) misaligned from the magnetic meridian.

(8) In a remote indicating compass in clear air turbulence conditions, the annunciator will
  (a) remain steady
  (b) alternate regularly
  (c) alternate irregularly.

(9) On a remote indicating compass, variation can be set by
  (a) offsetting the master indicator from the gyro unit
  (b) displacing the stators of the signal selsyn
  (c) physical rotation of the detector unit.

(10) British Civil Airworthiness Requirements state that the residual deviation of a remote indicating compass shall not exceed on any heading
  (a) 1°
  (b) 2°
  (c) 3°.

Part 4
SOLAR SYSTEM

Chapter 27
SOLAR SYSTEM: TIME

The Solar System consists of the Sun, nine major planets of which the earth is one, and about 2000 minor planets or asteroids. All members of the solar system are controlled by the Sun which is distinguished by its immense size and its radiation of light and heat; for all practical purposes, it may be considered as the stationary centre round which all the planets revolve.

Unlike the Sun, the planets and their satellites are not self-luminous, but reveal their presence by reflecting the Sun's light. The planets revolve about the Sun in elliptical orbits, each one taking a period of time about the job: Mercury takes 88 days, for example, while Pluto which is rather a long way from the parent body, is thought to take about 248 years. The planetary satellites in the meantime are revolving about their own parents.

Certain laws relating to the motion of planets in their orbits were evolved by the astronomer Kepler, who died in abject poverty as a reward:
- Each planet moves in an ellipse, with the Sun at one end of its foci;
- The radius vector of any planet sweeps out equal areas in equal intervals of time.

These are the important laws for our purpose in studying the Earth's motion, as we shall see.

The Earth rotates on its axis in a West to East direction, resulting in day and night. It revolves round the Sun along a path or orbit which is inclined to the Earth's axis at about $66\frac{1}{2}°$, resulting in the seasons of the year. When the Earth is inclined towards the Sun, we get the Summer Solstice (about June 21); when the axis is away from the Sun, we get the Winter Solstice (about Dec 22). When the Earth's axis is at right angles to the Sun, days and nights are equal, the Spring and Autumn Equinox (March 21 and Sept 23) (Fig. 27.1). The point where the planet is nearest to the Sun is called perihelion, and where farthest aphelion; it is worth noting that in obeying Kepler's second law, the speed of the Earth at perihelion is faster along its orbit than at aphelion; and that the Earth is nearer to the Sun in British winter.

Measurement of time

The instant at which a heavenly body is directly over a meridian is called a *transit*. The earth rotates on its axis from West to East and to us on its crust, the heavenly bodies appear to revolve about the Earth from East to West. The period of this apparent revolution is measured by the time elapsing

Fig. 27.1   Earth's orbit

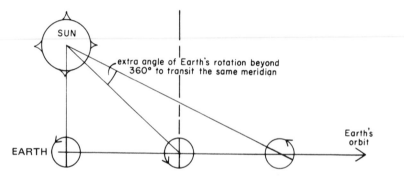

Fig. 27.2   Apparent solar day

between two successive transits of a heavenly body, called a *day*. If a star were the heavenly body, since stars are such immense distances away, the *sidereal* day would be of constant length, for only the Earth's axial movement of rotation would affect the star's apparent movement. The Earth is 8 light minutes from the Sun, but $4\frac{1}{3}$ light years from the nearest star. We measure the day by the Sun, of course, and must needs investigate the problems that result, without involving ourselves with the vast academic matters of the Universe.

An *apparent solar day* is the time interval between two successive transits of the real or apparent Sun at the same meridian, the word 'apparent' signifying that is how it appears to us as we move with the Earth. Seen from above the North Pole, the Earth rotates on its axis at an even speed in an anti-clockwise direction, and also revolves round the Sun in its orbit in an anti-clockwise direction; since the direction of axial rotation is the same as orbital revolution, West to East, it follows that it must rotate on its axis through more than 360° to produce successive transits (Fig. 27.2).

Furthermore, since the Earth's orbit is elliptical, the Earth's speed of revolution in its orbit varies continuously and the length of an Apparent Solar Day will not be constant.

The time of transit is called Local Apparent Noon; but these facts and their unequal variations would make human working life difficult.

Mean Solar Time

In order to have a constant measurement of time which will still have the Solar Day as a basis, the average length of an apparent solar day is taken, called the *Mean Solar Day*, divided into 24 hours of mean solar time. This is arrived at as follows:

The time of orbital revolution of the Earth in one year is constant at 365 days 5 hours 48 minutes 45 seconds. A mean sun is imagined to travel once round a circular path in the same plane as the Equator at a constant speed in the same time as the True Sun travels round its apparent elliptical path at its varying speeds: thus, the time of two successive transits of the Mean Sun over any given meridian is constant, as both the Earth and Mean Sun are rotating in the same plane at constant speeds. In other words, we keep time by an imaginary or Mean Sun which leaves a meridian and returns to it 24 hours later of mean time.

The discrepancy between the transit of the Apparent Sun and the Mean Sun over the Greenwich meridian is not large enough to affect the working day (Mean noon at Greenwich is approximately $16\frac{1}{3}$ minutes later than Apparent noon in November; and $14\frac{1}{3}$ minutes earlier in February).

The year of 365 days 5 hours 48 minutes 45 seconds (again measuring in Mean Solar Time) is itself an inconvenient measure: the Calendar year is 365 days, so to even things up, a leap year of 366 days is inserted every 4 years, and to round things off, 3 leap years are suppressed every 4 centuries. (1700, 1800 and 1900 were not leap years, but 2000 will be.)

Time in arc

Time can also be measured in arc since in one day of mean solar time, the Sun is imagined to travel in a complete circle round the Earth, a motion of 360°. The measurement of 24 hours then is the same measurement as 360° of longitude. Really, that is the only thing to remember, for any conversion of one to the other is mental arithmetic; for reference:

$$24 \text{ hours} = 360° \text{ of longitude}$$
$$1 \text{ hour} = 15° \text{ of longitude}$$
$$1 \text{ minute} = 15' \text{ of longitude}$$
$$1 \text{ second} = 15'' \text{ of longitude}$$

Conversely:

$$360° = 24 \text{ hours of time}$$
$$1° = 4 \text{ minutes of time}$$
$$1' = 4 \text{ seconds of time}$$
$$1'' = 1/15 \text{ second of time}$$

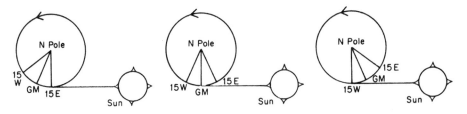

Fig. 27.3   LMT – GMT

Local Mean Time

The beginning of the day at any place is midnight, or 0000 hours LMT, e.g. 0000 hours at a place in longitude 50°W will be when the Mean Sun is in transit with the ante meridian 130°E. This means that the LMT of places in different longitudes varies by an amount corresponding to the change in longitude. A standard meridian has to be chosen to which all LMTs can be referred, and the meridian at Greenwich is internationally accepted as this standard. Local Mean Time at Greenwich is called Greenwich Mean Time.

The Greenwich Day commences when the Mean Sun is in transit with the ante meridian of Greenwich and as the Sun appears to travel from East to West, it will be in transit with Easterly meridians before it is in transit with Greenwich. Thus, LMT of places East of Greenwich will be ahead of GMT and places West of Greenwich will be behind GMT.

Consider the diagrams in Fig. 27.3 for a Sunrise at 0600 hrs LMT, to establish the relationship of LMT to time on the Greenwich meridian. The rule is:

Longitude East, Greenwich Time Least

Longitude West, Greenwich Time Best

All flying is done on GMT, no matter whereabouts on the globe a pilot is operating, but the Sun rises and sets at different times on the same meridian, depending on the declination of the Sun and the Earthly latitude of the observer. The times of the phenomena are listed in the Air Almanac in LMT, so the conversion from one to the other is very necessary knowledge indeed. The Air Almanac is published 6-monthly by HMSO. Its preface and explanation are located after the main tabulated ephemeral data called the *daily pages* and before the miscellaneous diagrams and tables. Its contents are listed on the back cover. A few examples of conversions GMT/LMT:

(a)   GMT 1200 hrs, then LMT at 60°E = 1600 hrs (60° arc = 4 hrs time)
        and LMT at 80°W = 0640 hrs (80° arc = 5 h 20 m time)

(b)   What is the GMT and GD of a place in longitude 46°25′E where LMT is 14 h 23 m 15 s and LD is 2nd June?

46°25′ in time =   3 h 05 m 40 s

LMT and LD = 14 h 23 m 15 s   2nd June

GMT least   = 11 h 17 m 35 s and GD still
                                    2nd June

(c) If GD and GMT are 2nd Dec 21 h 02 m 24 s, give LD and LMT in
longitude 96°47′E.

$$96°47' \text{ in time} = \quad 6\text{ h } 27\text{ m } 08\text{ s}$$
$$\text{GMT least} \quad = 21\text{ h } 02\text{ m } 24\text{ s} \quad \text{2nd Dec GD}$$
$$\text{LMT} \quad = 03\text{ h } 29\text{ m } 32\text{ s} \quad \text{3rd Dec LD}$$

The Air Almanac, on one of the last odd pages of the book gives a table for
the conversion of arc to time from 1° to 360°, so that 341° for example is at
once read off as 22 h 44 m; the end column gives minutes of arc into minutes
and seconds of time e.g. 17′ of arc is 1 m 08 s of time.

Co-ordinated Universal Time
UTC is gradually replacing GMT in aviation. For all practical purposes it is
the same as GMT.

Standard Time
Standard Time is the set time used for a particular country or part of a
country. In general, it is based on the LMT $7\frac{1}{2}°$ on either side of a regular
meridian divisible by 15°, but this of course often conflicts with political and
national requirements, and has finally become arbitrary. The UK normally
kept GMT as its Standard Time, but now has added one hour to GMT
throughout the duration of British Summer Time. A country like the USA is
longitudinally too vast to keep one standard time, and divides itself up, so
that the Atlantic Seaboard keeps Eastern Standard Time, 5 hours behind
GMT, while Hawaii is 10 hours slow on GMT. Currently the states are listed
individually in the Air Almanac.

All Standard Times are listed in the Air Almanac, in three tables: (1)
Places East of Greenwich, fast on GMT, (2) Places on GMT, (3) Places West
of Greenwich, slow on GMT. With many local adjustments and diverse
boundaries of separation, there is an abundance of footnotes to be watched: a
pleasant note is that the adjustment one to the other of GMT to ST is
explained in each table (see end of chapter).

Dateline
When travelling Westward from Greenwich, an observer would eventually
arrive at longitude 179 59 W, where the LMT is about to become 12 hours less
than GMT. An observer travelling Eastward from Greenwich would
eventually arrive at 179 59E where the LMT is about to become 12 hours
more than GMT. Thus there is a full day of 24 hours difference between the
two travellers, although they are both about to cross the same meridian.
When the antemeridian of Greenwich is crossed, one day is gained or lost,
depending on the direction of travel (Fig. 27.4): the Dateline is the actual line
where the change is made, and is mainly the 180 meridian, with some slight
divergences to accommodate certain groups of South Sea Islands and regions
of Eastern Siberia. The problem readily resolves itself in flying – your watch
is always on GMT: the place whose Standard Time you want is listed in the
Air Almanac: apply the correction to GMT, and the date will take care of

itself. Crossing the dateline always seems to excite passengers in aircraft much more than crossing the equator: you will want to let them know when, on a leg from HONOLULU to TOKYO, the date changes from the 2nd to the 3rd.

For example:

(a) Give the standard time and date of arrival in TOKYO (JAPAN) of a flight of 9 hours duration which departed from ANCHORAGE (ALASKA, USA) at 10.00 hrs ST on 14th March.

ANCHORAGE (ALASKA, USA)	ATD	14th:	10 00 ST
ST/GMT correction (List III)			+ 9
	ATD	14th:	19 00 GMT
Flight time			9 00
TOKYO (JAPAN)	ETA	14th:	28 00 GMT
		= 15th:	04 00 GMT
GMT/ST correction (List I)			+ 9
TOKYO (JAPAN)	ETA	15th:	10 00 ST

(b) Give the standard time and date of ETA VANCOUVER (BRITISH COLUMBIA, CANADA) of an aircraft scheduled to depart BRISBANE (QUEENSLAND, AUSTRALIA) at 20 30 hrs on 5th November, if the flight is planned to take 13 hr 50 min.

BRISBANE	ETD	5th:	20 30 ST
ST/GMT correction List I (Queensland, Australia)			− 10
	ETD	5th:	10 30 GMT
Flight time			13 50
VANCOUVER	ETA	5th:	24 20 GMT
GMT/ST correction List III (B.Col., Canada)			− 08
VANCOUVER	ETA	5th:	16 20 ST

Sunrise (S/R) and sunset (S/S)

We are only concerned with the visible phenomenon, when the upper edge of the Sun is coincident with the observer's horizon: at the moment of this vision, the centre of the Sun is about 1° below the horizon, but due to refraction we see it as higher than it really is. All this is mercifully built into the Tables (reproduced at the end of the chapter) to let the pilot cope with what he sees, and let the theory look after itself.

The times of S/R and S/S at any place change by only a minute or two each day except in high latitudes; so the time of the occurrences at specified Latitudes on the Greenwich meridian may be taken as the same for all longitudes. A tabulation of 0708 for a certain date and latitude is in fact the LMT of the phenomenon on the Greenwich meridian, it will also be the LMT

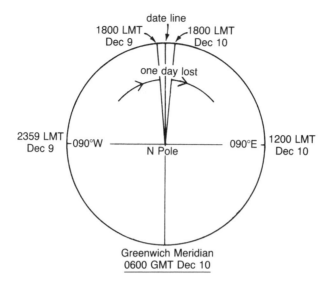

Fig. 27.4 Crossing the date line

on any other longitude on the same local date and Latitude: by the time 0708 LMT comes along at 30°W, the time on the Greenwich meridian is by now 0908. And if you are at 30°W in an aeroplane with your watch set to GMT as usual, you will look up the Air Almanac for your Latitude, find 0708 LMT and apply the usual rule to find the GMT at the time of the rising. Check again with Fig. 27.3.

The tabulation in the Air Almanac covers every band of Latitude for dates three days apart: the bands of Latitude are sometimes 10° apart, sometimes 2°. The times of S/R and S/S vary considerably as the Latitude of the observer increases. The interpolation from the tables for the date required on the observer's Latitude may be done without tedious calculation: take the nearest tabulated day, and interpolate on that day for the Latitude required.

Figures 27.5 to 27.7 will explain the effect of Latitude; and, bearing in mind that the Sun's declination is a maximum $23\frac{1}{2}°$N or $23\frac{1}{2}°$S approximately, how it comes about that the Sun can be above or below the horizon all day in some Latitudes. CH is the observer's horizon.

With a midsummer's day N Hemisphere, the length of the day from S/R to S/S from Fig. 27.5 increases with the observer's latitude Z until eventually, in Fig. 27.6, he is Northerly enough to have the Sun above his horizon all day: this particular observer gets his come-uppance as the Sun makes its way South, for then it is continuous Northern night (Fig. 27.7). The symbols in the Tables for such occasions are explained at the beginning of the Air Almanac, after the daily pages.

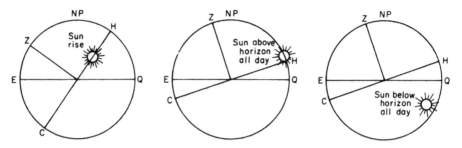

Figs 27.5, 27.6 and 27.7   Effect of latitude

Example

What is GMT of S/S in Position 32°00′S 172°15′W on 13th Jan LD? The extract from the Air Almanac looks like this:

	Jan 11	Jan 14
Lat. S30°	1906	1905
Lat. S35°	1918	1917

and 13th Jan is thus as for 14th Jan. Interpolate for 32°S, 2/5 of 12 minutes = 5 minutes. Thus

```
13th Jan at 32°00′S = 1910 LMT
172°15′W to time        1129
          GMT          3039   best
                     = 0639   14th Jan GMT & GD
```

i.e. the time and date on the Greenwich meridian when the sun sets in 32°00′S 172°15′W.

Twilight

When the Sun is below the horizon, an observer will still receive light which has been reflected and scattered by the atmosphere. It is divided into three stages: Astronomical (Sun 12° to 18° below Horizon. It is completely dark with no natural light at 18°); Nautical (6°–12° below the Horizon, and has to do with the sea horizon being indistinct, and artificial light is still required) and Civil Twilight when the Sun's centre is actually between 1° and 6° below the horizon, when work is possible without artificial light, and the stars are not clearly visible. This last is the one we're concerned with.

The Air Almanac tabulates in exactly the same form as S/R and S/S the beginning of morning civil twilight and the end of evening civil twilight, all in LMT as before. The duration of morning twilight is then simply the difference between S/R and the twilight tabulation for that place on that day. Just as in high latitudes we had occasions of 24 hours daylight or darkness, so again we shall have occasions where twilight lasts all night. The symbol is explained in the same place as before in the Air Almanac.

The whole period of twilight has particular significance to pilots beyond the obvious transition of light and dark, and the impairment of visual judgments at that time. It is around twilight that the ionosphere starts to move, with the consequent reduction of the effective range of MF radio aids especially, and of HF aids to some extent. The ADF can become sluggish and even HF RTF suffers increased noise with the altering properties of the atmosphere for radio transmission as the Sun's powers change. If a navigator is carried meanwhile, he is denied the heavens for astro-navigation. It is worth a thought that in fast aircraft and long range radio aids, a twilight zone can exist between the aircraft and the station for quite a long time, most noticeable on Easterly and Westerly flights.

Effect of height
The tabulations in the Air Almanac for risings and settings and twilight are all for an observer at sea level; in flight, the visible horizon is extended, and the phenomena will occur earlier in the morning and later in the evening. The rate of movement of the Sun through the angle of depression varies with the latitude of the observer and the time of year as well as with the observer's height, and the calculation of the time difference, though measurable, takes the pilot into matters at present outside his syllabus of study. However, an explanation and all the necessary figures are in the Air Almanac, should in-flight times be required.

The Moon
The Moon is a perfect sphere which travels round the Earth according to Kepler's Laws 1 and 2, but due to the Earth's own orbit its apparent path is somewhat irregular though calculable. It rotates on its axis West to East in exactly the same time as it takes to get round the Earth, so that we are always presented with almost the same face (actually, over a period, 59% of the Moon's surface has been seen by the Earthbound observer). One half of the Moon is always illuminated by the Sun, and as the Moon revolves round the Earth, the sunlit half is presented in varying amounts, the phases of the Moon.

When the Moon passes between the Earth and the Sun, it is said to be in conjunction, and its sunlit half is away from the Earth, a new Moon. It is in opposition when the Earth lies between the Sun and Moon, the illuminated face is straight towards us, a full Moon. When the direction of the Moon is 90° to that of the Sun, it is in quadrature, when half of the disc is visible from the Earth, called the first and last quarter; crescent phases are less than half full, gibbous more than half. The age of the Moon is the number of days which have elapsed since it was last new, and even that is recorded in the daily pages of the Air Almanac, together with an illustration of how the moon will appear, e.g. crescent, gibbous.

In Fig. 27.8 which illustrates the phases, it must be borne in mind that the three bodies are not in a straight line; if they were, then an eclipse, total or

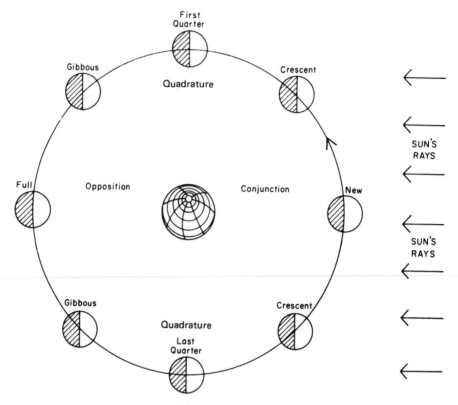

Fig. 27.8   Moon's orbit and phases

partial, solar or lunar, would be seen from the Earth. In simple terms, a North/South value similar to a latitude projected into the celestial sphere is called the declination of a heavenly body, and the declinations of the Sun and Moon must be nearly equal to give a solar eclipse; and there must be a relationship for a lunar eclipse when the Moon passes through the Earth's shadow.

Moonrise (M/R) and moonset (M/S)

The Moon revolves on its orbit West to East round the Earth once in $29\frac{1}{2}$ days: its average daily movement =

$$\frac{360}{29\frac{1}{2}} = 12\frac{3}{4}^{\circ} \text{ which is 51 minutes of time.}$$

If the declination of the Moon were constant, it would rise and set on the average 51 minutes later each day (Fig. 27.9).

But the declination changes very rapidly, and the difference between M/R or M/S on successive days is marked and inconstant. The extra amount of

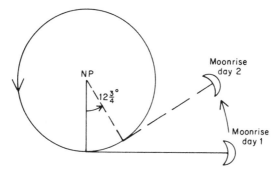

Fig. 27.9   Moonrise

revolution required to transit the same meridian successively is known as the DAILY LAG, and it varies with the latitude of the observer and the declination of the Moon. So the daily changes of the M/R and M/S are great enough to prevent figures tabulated in the Air Almanac for the phenomenon on the Greenwich Meridian to be regarded as LMTs for other meridians.

Precise times of M/R and M/S are seldom required however: and a tabulation of two different daily lags for correction to Easterly or Westerly longitude is avoided in the Almanac by inserting under the term *Difference*, half the daily lag. This *difference* is found against the observer's latitude, on the daily pages, with the LMT of M/R of M/S. This difference is then taken to the *Interpolation* of Moonrise/Moonset (on the loose flap usually), and entering with difference and observer's longitude, the correction is read off: this correction is added to LMT M/R or M/S if Longitude W, subtracted if Longitude E. A thumbnail sketch would illustrate why – the lag is progressive, and East of Greenwich the phenomenon will occur at an earlier LMT than at Greenwich, so the correction is subtracted: on Westerly meridians, the correction is additive since the Moon will have moved further on its orbit.

As the time interval between successive phenomena is more than 24 hours, it follows that in each month there will be one day when there will be no M/R and another when there will be no M/S.

This will occur when M/R or M/S is near to local midnight. The tabulations are for the phenomena on the Greenwich meridian; in Fig. 27.10, it is clear that the effect of the lag for M/S on Easterly meridians may not have caused the jump from local Friday to local Sunday, i.e. the M/S could have occurred on late local Saturday. To allow for this, the Air Almanac gives the time as 2400+, as a basis for calculation of the occurrence in other longitudes; the point to watch is the date. 2431 as the tabulated time on 7th Jan is really 0031 on 8th Jan, the date at Greenwich.

It can happen that the times found are for the day before, or day after, the one required: in which case, it is quite in order to add or subtract twice the difference, watching the date carefully, as:

Fig. 27.10   Determining M/R and M/S

Fig. 27.11   M/R at Greenwich   Fig. 27.12   M/R at 150°E

Required GMT of M/R 8th March, at 52°N, 150°E.

From daily Page M/R 8th March	0958	diff. 25
From Flap Table 25 vs 150	− 22	for E long. diff.
LMT 8th March	0936	
Long. 150°E	1000	
GMT	2336	(Greenwich Least) 7th GD
Also, twice diff.	+ 50	
GMT + one day	0026	9th March GD.

In other words, there was no M/R in this position on 8th March, GD.

Fig. 27.11 is a sketch of the tabulated M/R for the Greenwich meridian with times at the occurrence for Greenwich meridian and 150°E. Knowing then that the M/R takes place (Fig. 27.12), 10 hours (approx.) earlier for 150°E than on the Greenwich meridian, the Greenwich time will be 2336, 7th March GD and no moonrise will take place at 150°E on the 8th, for the lag (or double the difference) will whip the next occurrence there to the 9th March, *the calculations being all for GD.*

A final touch about the tabulations of M/R and M/S on the daily pages. With the moon so near the Earth that it has been circumnavigated and landed on, there is plenty of parallax and refraction, all of which are allowed for in the Tables, so that the usual rule of visible rising and setting is obeyed: the differences in higher latitudes are often too erratic to be reasonably measured, and an asterisk is inserted to warn you. If the difference is noted as negative the correction duly found from the Interpolation table on the flap is applied in the opposite direction, as the footnote points out. On this table, too, it is accurate enough to take the nearest noted figure for difference v longitude without interpolation.

Practice problems

Use the tables at the end of this chapter to extract the times of sunrise, sunset and twilight. You will need to interpolate between the dates and the latitude bands. The answers should be correct to the nearest minute.

(1) If the LMT in position 47°30′N 00°00′ is 12 00 hr what is the LMT in the position 54°20′S 00°00′?

   (a) 06 h 47 m 50 s   (b) 12 h 00 m 00 s   (c) 18 h 47 m 50 s.

(2) LMT in position 54°40′S 00°00′ is 15 25 hr, what is the GMT in position 15°S 180°?

   (a) 18 h 00 m 00 s   (b) 20 h 03 m 40 s   (c) 15 h 25 m 00 s.

(3) If the GMT is 10 27 30 hr what is the LMT at 47°32′W?

   (a) 07 h 17 m 22 s   (b) 10 h 27 m 30 s   (c) 13 h 27 m 38 s.

(4) At 08 00 hr GMT, what is the LMT at 40°30′N 117°15′E?

   (a) 00 h 11 m 00 s   (b) 07 h 49 m 00 s   (c) 15 h 49 m 00 s.

(5) What is the LMT in Istanbul (41°N 29°E) when

   5.1 the LMT in Paris (long 02°30′E) is 08 00 hr?

      (a) 09 h 46 m 00 s   (b) 09 h 56 m 00 s   (c) 05 h 54 m 00 s.

   5.2 the LMT in Rome (long 12°E) is 19 00 hr?

      (a) 20 h 08 m 00 s   (b) 17 h 52 m 00 s   (c) 18 h 12 m 00 s.

   5.3 the LMT in Baghdad (long 44°17′E) is 00 13 00 hr on 1st May?

      (a) 23 h 11 m 52 s on 30 April

      (b) 21 h 15 m 52 s on 30 April

      (c) 03 h 10 m 08 s on 1st May.

(6) The LMT at Hamilton, Ontario (43°09′N 79°56′W) is 21 16 00 hr on 17th June. What are the GMT and ST (standard time)?

   (a) 02 h 35 m 44 s 18th June GMT 21 h 35 m 44 s 18th June ST;

   (b) 21 h 35 m 44 s 17th June GMT 02 h 35 m 44 s 18th June ST;

   (c) 02 h 35 m 44 s 16th June GMT 21 h 35 m 44 s 17th June ST.

   (Note: Hamilton ST is 5 hr behind GMT.)

(7) The LMT at Gibraltar (36°07′N 05°21′W) is 11 15 hr on 4th July. What are the GMT and ST?

   (a) 13 h 39 m 28 s 4th July GMT 12 h 39 m 28 s 4th July ST;

   (b) 11 h 36 m 24 s 4th July GMT 12 h 36 m 24 s 4th July ST;

   (c) 10 h 54 m 36 s 4th July GMT 11 h 54 m 36 s 4th July ST.

   (Note: Gibraltar ST is 1 hr ahead of GMT.)

(8) The GMT at El Aovina, Tunisia (36°50′N 10°14′E) is 19 47 hr on 28th April. What are the LMT and ST?

(a)   19 h 06 m 04 s 28th April LMT 20 h 06 m 04 s 28th April ST;

(b)   20 h 27 m 56 s 28th April LMT 21 h 27 m 56 s 28th April ST;

(c)   20 h 27 m 56 s 28th April LMT 20 h 47 m 00 s 28th April ST.

(Note: Tunisia ST is 1 hr ahead of GMT.)

(9)   The ETA in ST and SD (corrected for summer time) for a 14 hour flight departing Honolulu (Hawaii, USA) at 0030 hrs ST for Sydney (NSW Australia) will be:

(a)   11.30 hrs next day

(b)   11 30 same day

(c)   17 30 previous day

(10)   An aircraft is making for Rawalpindi, West Pakistan (32°25′N 76°20′E) on 9th February and pinpoints over Lahore at 11 42 GMT. If the distance to go is 173 nm and W/V is Light and Variable, what RAS must be maintained at FL 60 temp. +30°C to make the destination by sunset?

(a)   300 kt   (b)   150 kt   (c)   176 kt (by computer).

(Note: time of sunset Rawalpindi is 17 h 39 m 37 s.)

(11)   If the GMT is 12 00 hr, in what longitude is the LMT 20 00 hr?

(a)   120°W   (b)   120°E   (c)   80°E.

(12)   Find the ST of sunset at Leningrad, Russia (59°46′N 30°20′E) on local date 22nd January.

(a)   16 h 46 m 26 s ST;

(b)   09 h 36 m 24 s ST;

(c)   15 h 49 m 00 s ST.

(Note: USSR, West of longitude 40°E, ST is 3 hr ahead of GMT.)

(13)   Give the GMT of sunrise at Auckland, New Zealand (36°50′S 174°48′E) on local date 3rd February.

(a)   17 h 37 m 46 s 2nd Feb;

(b)   17 h 37 m 46 s 3rd Feb;

(c)   17 h 37 m 46 s 4th Feb.

(14)   Give the GMT sunset at Taranto (40°26′N 17°16′E) on local date 6th February.

(a)   17 h 23 m 15 s 6th Feb;

(b)   16 h 23 m 15 s 6th Feb;

(c)   16 h 13 m 44 s 6th Feb.

(15)   An aircraft wishes to arrive at Sydney, NSW (33°52′S 151°23′E) one hour before sunset on 9th January. The flight is planned to take 5 hr 13 min. What is the latest time LMT it can depart from 35°S 172°17′E?

(a)   14 h 25 m 52 s LMT;

(b)   15 h 25 m 52 s LMT;

(c)   16 h 25 m 52 s LMT.

The following pages are reproduced from the Nautical Almanac Office Air Almanac 1985 with the permission of the Controller of Her Majesty's Stationery Office.

SUNRISE

Times are given in h m. A solid bar (■) denotes that the Sun does not rise.

Lat.	Dec. 30	Jan. 2	Jan. 5	Jan. 8	Jan. 11	Jan. 14	Jan. 17	Jan. 20	Jan. 23	Jan. 26	Jan. 29	Feb. 1	Feb. 4	Feb. 7	Feb. 10
N 72	■	■	■	■	■	■	■	11 14	11 06	10 48	10 27	10 35	10 11	09 49	09 30
70	■	■	■	■	■	■	■	10 14	10 08	10 01	09 47	09 51	09 34	09 18	09 03
68	■	■	11 37	11 15	10 57	10 42	10 28	09 40	09 34	09 30	09 20	09 21	09 09	08 56	08 43
66	10 32	10 27	10 22	10 15	10 07	09 59	09 50	09 16	09 10	09 08	09 00	09 00	08 49	08 38	08 27
64	09 52	09 49	09 46	09 41	09 36	09 30	09 23	08 57	08 51	08 50	08 43	08 42	08 33	08 24	08 14
62	09 24	09 23	09 20	09 17	09 13	09 08	09 03	08 41	08 36	08 35	08 29	08 28	08 20	08 12	08 03
N 60	09 03	09 02	09 00	08 58	08 55	08 51	08 46	08 28	08 23	08 23	08 18	08 16	08 09	08 01	07 54
58	08 46	08 45	08 44	08 42	08 39	08 36	08 32	08 16	08 12	08 12	08 07	08 06	07 59	07 53	07 46
56	08 32	08 31	08 30	08 28	08 26	08 23	08 20	08 06	08 02	08 02	07 58	07 57	07 51	07 45	07 39
54	08 19	08 19	08 19	08 17	08 15	08 12	08 10	07 57	07 54	07 54	07 50	07 49	07 43	07 38	07 32
52	08 08	08 08	08 08	08 06	08 05	08 02	08 00	07 49	07 46	07 46	07 43	07 42	07 37	07 32	07 26
N 50	08 08	08 08	07 58	07 57	07 56	07 54	07 52	07 49	07 39	07 43	07 27	07 35	07 30	07 26	07 21
45	07 58	07 58	07 38	07 38	07 37	07 36	07 34	07 32	07 24	07 27	07 14	07 21	07 18	07 14	07 10
40	07 38	07 38	07 22	07 22	07 22	07 21	07 20	07 18	07 12	07 14	07 03	07 09	07 07	07 03	07 00
35	07 21	07 22	07 08	07 08	07 08	07 08	07 07	07 06	07 02	07 03	06 54	07 00	06 57	06 55	06 52
30	06 55	06 56	06 57	06 57	06 57	06 57	06 57	06 56	06 53	06 54	06 53	06 51	06 49	06 47	06 45
N 20	06 34	06 35	06 36	06 37	06 37	06 38	06 38	06 38	06 37	06 37	06 37	06 36	06 35	06 34	06 32
N 10	06 16	06 17	06 18	06 19	06 20	06 21	06 22	06 22	06 23	06 23	06 24	06 23	06 22	06 22	06 21
0	05 59	06 00	06 01	06 03	06 05	06 06	06 07	06 07	06 07	06 09	06 09	06 10	06 10	06 11	06 11
S 10	05 41	05 43	05 44	05 46	05 47	05 49	05 51	05 52	05 53	05 55	05 56	05 57	05 58	05 59	06 00
20	05 22	05 24	05 26	05 28	05 30	05 32	05 34	05 36	05 38	05 40	05 42	05 43	05 45	05 47	05 49
S 30	05 00	05 02	05 05	05 07	05 09	05 12	05 14	05 17	05 20	05 23	05 25	05 28	05 30	05 33	05 35
35	04 48	04 50	04 52	04 55	04 57	05 00	05 03	05 06	05 09	05 12	05 15	05 19	05 22	05 25	05 28
40	04 33	04 35	04 38	04 40	04 43	04 47	04 50	04 53	04 57	05 01	05 04	05 08	05 11	05 15	05 19
45	04 15	04 17	04 20	04 23	04 27	04 30	04 34	04 38	04 42	04 47	04 51	04 55	05 00	05 04	05 09
50	03 53	03 55	04 00	04 02	04 06	04 10	04 15	04 20	04 25	04 30	04 35	04 40	04 45	04 51	05 00
S 52	03 42	03 45	03 48	03 52	03 56	04 01	04 06	04 11	04 16	04 22	04 27	04 33	04 38	04 44	04 56
54	03 30	03 33	03 37	03 41	03 45	03 51	03 55	04 01	04 07	04 13	04 19	04 25	04 31	04 37	04 50
56	03 16	03 19	03 23	03 28	03 32	03 38	03 44	03 50	03 56	04 03	04 09	04 16	04 23	04 29	04 43
58	02 59	03 03	03 07	03 12	03 18	03 24	03 30	03 37	03 44	03 51	03 58	04 06	04 13	04 20	04 36
S 60	02 39	02 43	02 48	02 54	03 00	03 07	03 14	03 21	03 29	03 37	03 45	03 54	04 02	04 10	04 19

SUNSET

Lat.	Dec. 30	Jan. 2	Jan. 5	Jan. 8	Jan. 11	Jan. 14	Jan. 17	Jan. 20	Jan. 23	Jan. 26	Jan. 29	Feb. 1	Feb. 4	Feb. 7	Feb. 10
	h m	h m	h m	h m	h m	h m	h m	h m	h m	h m	h m	h m	h m	h m	h m
N 72	■	■	■	■	■	■	■	■	■	■	13 21	13 53	14 18	14 40	15 00
70	■	■	■	■	■	■	■	13 09	13 37	13 59	14 19	14 38	14 55	15 11	15 27
68	■	■	12 34	12 59	13 18	13 36	13 52	14 08	14 24	14 38	14 53	15 07	15 20	15 34	15 47
66	13 33	13 40	13 49	13 58	14 09	14 19	14 31	14 42	14 54	15 05	15 17	15 28	15 40	15 51	16 02
64	14 13	14 18	14 25	14 32	14 40	14 48	14 57	15 06	15 16	15 26	15 36	15 46	15 56	16 05	15 15
62	14 40	14 45	14 50	14 56	15 03	15 10	15 18	15 26	15 34	15 42	15 51	16 00	16 09	16 17	16 26
N 60	15 01	15 05	15 10	15 15	15 21	15 28	15 34	15 41	15 49	15 56	16 04	16 12	16 20	16 28	16 35
58	15 19	15 22	15 26	15 31	15 36	15 42	15 48	15 54	16 01	16 08	16 15	16 22	16 29	16 36	16 44
56	15 33	15 36	15 40	15 45	15 49	15 55	16 00	16 06	16 12	16 18	16 25	16 31	16 37	16 44	16 51
54	15 46	15 49	15 52	15 56	16 01	16 06	16 11	16 16	16 22	16 27	16 33	16 39	16 45	16 51	16 57
52	15 56	15 59	16 03	16 07	16 11	16 15	16 24	16 25	16 30	16 35	16 41	16 46	16 52	16 57	17 03
N 50	16 06	16 09	16 12	16 16	16 20	16 24	16 28	16 33	16 38	16 43	16 48	16 53	16 58	17 03	17 08
45	16 27	16 29	16 32	16 35	16 39	16 42	16 46	16 50	16 54	16 58	17 02	17 07	17 11	17 15	17 19
40	16 43	16 46	16 48	16 51	16 54	16 57	17 00	17 04	17 07	17 11	17 14	17 18	17 21	17 25	17 29
35	16 57	16 59	17 02	17 04	17 07	17 10	17 13	17 16	17 19	17 22	17 25	17 28	17 31	17 34	17 37
30	17 10	17 12	17 14	17 16	17 18	17 21	17 24	17 26	17 29	17 31	17 34	17 36	17 39	17 41	17 44
N 20	17 30	17 32	17 34	17 36	17 38	17 40	17 42	17 44	17 46	17 48	17 50	17 51	17 53	17 55	17 57
N 10	17 49	17 50	17 52	17 53	17 55	17 57	17 58	18 00	18 01	18 02	18 03	18 05	18 06	18 07	18 07
0	18 06	18 07	18 09	18 10	18 11	18 12	18 13	18 14	18 15	18 16	18 17	18 17	18 17	18 18	18 18
S 10	18 23	18 25	18 26	18 27	18 28	18 28	18 29	18 29	18 30	18 30	18 30	18 30	18 29	18 29	18 28
20	18 42	18 43	18 44	18 45	18 45	18 46	18 46	18 46	18 45	18 45	18 44	18 43	18 42	18 41	18 40
S 30	19 04	19 05	19 05	19 06	19 06	19 05	19 05	19 04	19 03	19 02	19 01	18 59	18 57	18 55	18 53
35	19 17	19 17	19 18	19 18	19 18	19 17	19 16	19 15	19 14	19 12	19 10	19 08	19 06	19 03	19 00
40	19 32	19 32	19 32	19 32	19 31	19 31	19 29	19 28	19 26	19 24	19 21	19 19	19 16	19 12	19 09
45	19 49	19 50	19 49	19 49	19 48	19 47	19 45	19 43	19 40	19 37	19 34	19 31	19 27	19 23	19 19
50	20 12	20 12	20 11	20 10	20 08	20 06	20 04	20 01	19 58	19 54	19 50	19 46	19 41	19 37	19 32
S 52	20 22	20 22	20 21	20 20	20 18	20 16	20 13	20 10	20 06	20 02	19 58	19 53	19 48	19 43	19 37
54	20 34	20 34	20 33	20 31	20 29	20 26	20 23	20 20	20 15	20 11	20 06	20 01	19 56	19 50	19 44
56	20 48	20 48	20 46	20 44	20 42	20 39	20 35	20 31	20 26	20 21	20 16	20 10	20 04	19 57	19 51
58	21 05	21 05	21 02	21 00	20 56	20 53	20 48	20 43	20 38	20 32	20 26	20 20	20 13	20 06	19 59
S 60	21 25	21 23	21 21	21 18	21 14	21 09	21 04	20 59	20 52	20 46	20 39	20 31	20 24	20 16	20 08

MORNING CIVIL TWILIGHT

Lat.	Dec.	January										February				Lat.
°	30	2	5	8	11	14	17	20	23	26	29	1	4	7	10	°
	h m	h m	h m	h m	h m	h m	h m	h m	h m	h m	h m	h m	h m	h m	h m	
N 72	10 50	10 42	10 33	10 22	10 11	09 59	09 47	09 35	09 22	09 09	08 56	08 43	08 29	08 16	08 02	N 72
70	09 53	09 49	09 44	09 38	09 31	09 23	09 14	09 05	08 55	08 45	08 34	08 23	08 12	08 01	07 49	70
68	09 19	09 17	09 13	09 09	09 04	08 58	08 51	08 43	08 35	08 27	08 18	08 08	07 59	07 48	07 38	68
66	08 54	08 53	08 50	08 47	08 43	08 38	08 32	08 26	08 19	08 12	08 04	07 56	07 48	07 38	07 29	66
64	08 35	08 34	08 32	08 29	08 26	08 22	08 17	08 12	08 06	08 00	07 53	07 45	07 38	07 30	07 21	64
62	08 19	08 19	08 17	08 15	08 12	08 08	08 04	08 00	07 55	07 49	07 43	07 36	07 29	07 22	07 15	62
N 60	08 06	08 05	08 04	08 02	08 00	07 57	07 54	07 50	07 45	07 40	07 34	07 29	07 22	07 16	07 09	N 60
58	07 54	07 54	07 53	07 52	07 50	07 47	07 44	07 40	07 36	07 32	07 27	07 22	07 16	07 10	07 04	58
56	07 44	07 44	07 44	07 42	07 41	07 38	07 36	07 33	07 29	07 25	07 20	07 15	07 10	07 05	06 59	56
54	07 36	07 36	07 35	07 34	07 33	07 31	07 28	07 25	07 22	07 18	07 14	07 10	07 05	07 00	06 55	54
52	07 27	07 28	07 27	07 26	07 25	07 23	07 21	07 19	07 16	07 12	07 09	07 05	07 00	06 56	06 51	52
N 50	07 20	07 20	07 20	07 19	07 18	07 17	07 15	07 13	07 10	07 07	07 04	07 00	06 56	06 52	06 47	N 50
45	07 04	07 05	07 05	07 04	07 04	07 03	07 01	07 00	06 58	06 55	06 53	06 50	06 46	06 43	06 39	45
40	06 51	06 52	06 52	06 52	06 52	06 51	06 50	06 49	06 47	06 45	06 43	06 41	06 38	06 35	06 32	40
35	06 39	06 40	06 40	06 41	06 41	06 40	06 40	06 39	06 38	06 37	06 35	06 33	06 31	06 29	06 26	35
30	06 29	06 30	06 30	06 31	06 31	06 31	06 31	06 30	06 29	06 29	06 27	06 26	06 24	06 22	06 20	30
N 20	06 10	06 11	06 12	06 13	06 14	06 14	06 14	06 14	06 14	06 14	06 13	06 13	06 12	06 11	06 10	N 20
N 10	05 53	05 54	05 55	05 56	05 57	05 58	05 59	06 00	06 00	06 01	06 01	06 01	06 00	06 00	06 00	N 10
0	05 36	05 38	05 39	05 41	05 42	05 43	05 45	05 45	05 46	05 47	05 48	05 48	05 49	05 49	05 49	0
S 10	05 18	05 20	05 21	05 23	05 25	05 26	05 28	05 30	05 31	05 33	05 34	05 35	05 36	05 37	05 38	S 10
20	04 58	05 00	05 02	05 04	05 06	05 08	05 10	05 12	05 14	05 16	05 18	05 20	05 22	05 24	05 26	20
S 30	04 33	04 35	04 37	04 40	04 42	04 45	04 48	04 51	04 53	04 56	04 59	05 02	05 05	05 07	05 10	S 30
35	04 18	04 20	04 23	04 25	04 28	04 31	04 34	04 38	04 41	04 44	04 48	04 51	04 54	04 58	05 01	35
40	04 00	04 02	04 05	04 08	04 11	04 15	04 18	04 22	04 26	04 30	04 34	04 38	04 42	04 46	04 50	40
45	03 38	03 40	03 43	03 47	03 51	03 55	03 59	04 03	04 08	04 12	04 17	04 22	04 27	04 31	04 36	45
50	03 08	03 11	03 15	03 19	03 24	03 28	03 33	03 39	03 44	03 50	03 56	04 02	04 08	04 14	04 19	50
S 52	02 53	02 57	03 01	03 05	03 10	03 15	03 21	03 27	03 33	03 39	03 46	03 52	03 58	04 05	04 11	S 52
54	02 36	02 39	02 44	02 49	02 54	03 00	03 06	03 13	03 20	03 27	03 34	03 41	03 48	03 55	04 02	54
56	02 14	02 18	02 23	02 29	02 35	02 42	02 49	02 57	03 04	03 12	03 20	03 28	03 36	03 44	03 52	56
58	01 45	01 50	01 56	02 03	02 11	02 19	02 28	02 37	02 46	02 55	03 04	03 13	03 22	03 31	03 40	58
S 60	00 58	01 06	01 15	01 26	01 37	01 48	01 59	02 11	02 22	02 33	02 44	02 55	03 05	03 16	03 26	S 60

EVENING CIVIL TWILIGHT

Lat.	Dec. 30	January										February				Lat.
		2	5	8	11	14	17	20	23	26	29	1	4	7	10	
	h m	h m	h m	h m	h m	h m	h m	h m	h m	h m	h m	h m	h m	h m	h m	°
N 72	13 15	13 26	13 38	13 51	14 05	14 19	14 33	14 48	15 03	15 17	15 31	15 46	16 00	16 14	16 28	N 72
70	14 12	14 18	14 26	14 35	14 45	14 55	15 06	15 17	15 29	15 41	15 53	16 05	16 17	16 29	16 41	70
68	14 46	14 51	14 57	15 04	15 12	15 20	15 30	15 39	15 49	15 59	16 09	16 20	16 30	16 41	16 52	68
66	15 10	15 15	15 20	15 26	15 33	15 40	15 48	15 56	16 05	16 14	16 23	16 32	16 42	16 51	17 01	66
64	15 29	15 33	15 38	15 44	15 50	15 56	16 03	16 10	16 18	16 26	16 34	16 43	16 51	17 00	17 08	64
62	15 45	15 49	15 53	15 58	16 04	16 09	16 16	16 22	16 29	16 37	16 44	16 52	16 59	17 07	17 15	62
N 60	15 58	16 02	16 06	16 11	16 15	16 21	16 27	16 33	16 39	16 46	16 52	16 59	17 06	17 13	17 21	N 60
58	16 10	16 13	16 17	16 21	16 26	16 31	16 36	16 42	16 48	16 54	17 00	17 06	17 13	17 19	17 26	58
56	16 20	16 23	16 27	16 31	16 35	16 40	16 45	16 50	16 55	17 01	17 06	17 12	17 18	17 24	17 30	56
54	16 29	16 32	16 35	16 39	16 43	16 47	16 52	16 57	17 02	17 07	17 12	17 18	17 23	17 29	17 35	54
52	16 37	16 40	16 43	16 47	16 50	16 54	16 59	17 03	17 08	17 13	17 18	17 23	17 28	17 33	17 39	52
N 50	16 44	16 47	16 50	16 53	16 57	17 01	17 05	17 09	17 14	17 18	17 23	17 28	17 32	17 37	17 42	N 50
45	17 00	17 03	17 06	17 08	17 12	17 15	17 19	17 22	17 26	17 30	17 34	17 38	17 42	17 46	17 50	45
40	17 14	17 16	17 19	17 21	17 24	17 27	17 30	17 33	17 36	17 40	17 43	17 47	17 50	17 54	17 57	40
35	17 25	17 27	17 30	17 32	17 35	17 37	17 40	17 43	17 46	17 49	17 52	17 54	17 57	18 00	18 03	35
30	17 36	17 38	17 40	17 42	17 44	17 47	17 49	17 52	17 54	17 57	17 59	18 02	18 04	18 06	18 09	30
N 20	17 54	17 56	17 58	18 00	18 02	18 04	18 06	18 08	18 09	18 11	18 13	18 14	18 16	18 18	18 19	N 20
N 10	18 12	18 13	18 15	18 16	18 18	18 19	18 21	18 22	18 23	18 24	18 26	18 27	18 28	18 28	18 29	N 10
0	18 28	18 30	18 31	18 33	18 34	18 35	18 36	18 37	18 37	18 38	18 38	18 39	18 39	18 39	18 39	0
S 10	18 46	18 48	18 49	18 50	18 50	18 51	18 52	18 52	18 52	18 52	18 52	18 52	18 51	18 51	18 50	S 10
20	19 07	19 08	19 08	19 09	19 09	19 10	19 10	19 09	19 09	19 08	19 08	19 06	19 05	19 04	19 02	20
S 30	19 31	19 32	19 32	19 33	19 33	19 32	19 32	19 31	19 29	19 28	19 26	19 25	19 22	19 20	19 18	S 30
35	19 46	19 47	19 47	19 47	19 47	19 46	19 45	19 44	19 42	19 40	19 38	19 36	19 33	19 30	19 27	35
40	20 04	20 05	20 05	20 04	20 03	20 02	20 01	19 59	19 57	19 54	19 52	19 49	19 45	19 42	19 38	40
45	20 27	20 27	20 26	20 25	20 24	20 22	20 20	20 18	20 15	20 12	20 08	20 04	20 00	19 56	19 51	45
50	20 56	20 56	20 55	20 53	20 51	20 48	20 45	20 42	20 38	20 33	20 29	20 24	20 19	20 13	20 08	50
S 52	21 11	21 10	21 09	21 07	21 04	21 01	20 57	20 53	20 49	20 44	20 39	20 34	20 28	20 22	20 16	S 52
54	21 28	21 27	21 25	21 23	21 20	21 16	21 12	21 07	21 02	20 57	20 51	20 44	20 38	20 31	20 25	54
56	21 50	21 48	21 46	21 43	21 39	21 34	21 29	21 23	21 17	21 11	21 04	20 57	20 50	20 42	20 35	56
58	22 19	22 16	22 12	22 08	22 02	21 56	21 50	21 43	21 35	21 28	21 20	21 12	21 03	20 55	20 46	58
S 60	23 05	22 59	22 52	22 44	22 36	22 26	22 17	22 08	21 59	21 49	21 39	21 29	21 20	21 10	21 00	S 60

STANDARD TIMES (Corrected to September 1985)

LIST I—PLACES FAST ON G.M.T. (mainly those EAST OF GREENWICH)

The times given ⎱ *added* to G.M.T. to give Standard Time.
below should be ⎰ *subtracted* from Standard Time to give G.M.T.

	h	m
Admiralty Islands	10	
Afghanistan	04	30
Albania*	01	
Algeria	01	
Amirante Islands	04	
Andaman Islands	05	30
Angola	01	
Annobon Island	01	
Australia		
Australian Capital Territory*	10	
New South Wales[1]*	10	
Northern Territory	09	30
Queensland	10	
South Australia*	09	30
Tasmania*	10	
Victoria*	10	
Western Australia*	08	
Austria*	01	
Bahrain	03	
Balearic Islands*	01	
Banaba	11	30
Bangladesh	06	
Belgium*	01	
Benin (Dahomey)	01	
Botswana, Republic of	02	
Brunei	08	
Bulgaria*	02	
Burma	06	30
Burundi	02	
Cameroon Republic	01	
Caroline Islands, west of long. E. 135°	09	
long. E. 135° to E. 150°	10	
long. E. 150° to E. 160°	11	
east of long. E. 160°	12	
Central African Republic	01	
Chad	01	
Chagos Archipelago[2]	05	
Chatham Islands	12	45
China[3]	08	
Christmas Island, Indian Ocean	07	
Cocos Keeling Islands	06	30
Comoro Islands (Comoros)	03	
Congo Republic	01	
Corsica*	01	
Crete*	02	
Cyprus, Ercan*	02	
Larnaca*	02	
Czechoslovakia*	01	
Denmark*	01	

	h	m
Djibouti	03	
Egypt, Arab Republic of	02	
Equatorial Guinea, Republic of	01	
Estonia	03	
Ethiopia	03	
Fernando Pó	01	
Fiji	12	
Finland*	02	
France*	01	
Friendly Islands	13	
Gabon	01	
Germany, East*	01	
West[4]*	01	
Gibraltar*	01	
Greece*	02	
Guam	10	
Holland (The Netherlands)*	01	
Hong Kong	08	
Hungary*	01	
India	05	30
Indonesia, Republic of		
Bali, Bangka, Billiton, Java,		
Madura, Sumatra	07	
Flores, Kalimantan, Lombok,		
Sulawesi, Sumba, Sumbawa, Timor	08	
Aru, Irian Jaya, Kai, Moluccas,		
Tanimbar	09	
Iran	03	30
Iraq*	03	
Israel*	02	
Italy*	01	
Japan	09	
Jordan*	02	
Kamchatka Peninsula	12	
Kampuchea, Democratic	07	
Kenya	03	
Kiribati Republic[5]	12	
Korea, North	09	
Republic of (South)	09	
Kuril Islands	11	
Kuwait	03	
Laccadive Islands	05	30
Laos	07	
Latvia	03	
Lebanon*	02	

* Summer time may be kept in these countries.
[1] Except Broken Hill Area which keeps 09h 30m.
[2] Except Diego Garcia which keeps 06h.
[3] All the coast, but some areas may keep summer time.
[4] Including West Berlin.
[5] Except Banaba which keeps 11h 30m.

STANDARD TIMES (Corrected to September 1985)

LIST I—(*continued*)

	h	m		h	m
Lesotho	02		Sicily*	01	
Libya*	01		Singapore	08	
Liechtenstein	01		Socotra	03	
Lord Howe Island*	10	30	Solomon Islands...	11	
Luxembourg*	01		Somalia Republic	03	
			South Africa, Republic of ...	02	
Macao	08		South West Africa (Namibia) ...	02	
Madagascar, Democratic Republic of ...	03		Spain*	01	
Malawi	02		Spanish Possessions in North Africa		
Malaysia			(Ceuta, Melilla)*	01	
Malaya, Sabah, Sarawak	08		Spitsbergen (Svalbard)	01	
Maldives, Republic of The	05		Sri Lanka	05	30
Malta*	01		Sudan, Republic of	02	
Mariana Islands	10		Swaziland	02	
Marshall Islands[1]	12		Sweden*	01	
Mauritius	04		Switzerland*	01	
Monaco*	01		Syria (Syrian Arab Republic) ...	03	
Mongolia, West	07				
Central*	08		Taiwan*	08	
East	09		Tanzania	03	
Morocco	01		Thailand	07	
Mozambique	02		Tonga Islands	13	
			Truk	10	
Namibia (South West Africa)	02		Tunisia	01	
Nauru	12		Turkey*	02	
Netherlands, The*	01		Tuvalu Islands	12	
New Caledonia*	11				
New Zealand*	12		Uganda	03	
Nicobar Islands	05	30	Union of Soviet Socialist Republics[2]*		
Niger	01		west of long. E. 40°	03	
Nigeria, Republic of	01		long. E. 40° to E. 52° 30′ ...	04	
Norfolk Island	11	30	long. E. 52° 30′ to E. 67° 30′ ...	05	
Norway*	01		long. E. 67° 30′ to E. 82° 30′ ...	06	
Novaya Zemlya	05		long. E. 82° 30′ to E. 97° 30′ ...	07	
			long. E. 97° 30′ to E. 112° 30′ ...	08	
Okinawa	09		long. E. 112° 30′ to E. 127° 30′ ...	09	
Oman	04		long. E. 127° 30′ to E. 142° 30′ ...	10	
			long. E. 142° 30′ to E. 157° 30′ ...	11	
Pakistan	05		long. E. 157° 30′ to E. 172° 30′ ...	12	
Papua New Guinea	10		east of long. E. 172° 30′ ...	13	
Pescadores Islands	08		United Arab Emirates	04	
Philippine Republic	08				
Poland*	01		Vanuatu, Republic of*	11	
			Vietnam, Socialist Republic of ...	07	
Réunion	04				
Romania*	02		Wrangell Island	13	
Rwanda	02				
Ryūkyu Islands	09		Yemen	03	
			Yugoslavia*	01	
Sakhalin	11				
Santa Cruz Islands	11		Zaire		
Sardinia*	01		Kinshasa, Mbandaka	01	
Saudi Arabia	03		Haut-Zaire, Kasai, Kivu, Shaba ...	02	
Schouten Islands	09		Zambia, Republic of	02	
Seychelles	04		Zimbabwe	02	

* Summer time may be kept in these countries.
[1] Except the islands of Kwajalein and Eniwetok which keep a time 24ʰ slow on that of the rest of the islands.
[2] The boundaries between the zones are irregular; the longitudes given are approximate only.

STANDARD TIMES (Corrected to September 1985)
LIST II—PLACES NORMALLY KEEPING G.M.T.

Ascension Island	Ghana	Ireland, Northern[1]	Mauritania	Sierra Leone
Bourkina-Faso	Great Britain[1]	Irish Republic*	Portugal*	Tangier
Canary Islands*	Guinea Bissau	Ivory Coast	Principe	Togo Republic
Channel Islands[1]	Guinea Republic	Liberia	St. Helena	Tristan da Cunha
Faeroes*, The	Iceland	Madeira*	São Tomé	
Gambia	Ifni	Mali	Senegal	

*Summer time may be kept in these countries.
[1] Summer time, one hour in advance of G.M.T., is kept from March $27^d 01^h$ to October $23^d 01^h$ G.M.T.

LIST III—PLACES SLOW ON G.M.T. (WEST OF GREENWICH)
The times given } *subtracted* from G.M.T. to give Standard Time.
below should be } *added* to Standard Time to give G.M.T.

	h	m		h
Argentina...	03		Cape Verde Islands	01
Austral Islands[1]	10		Cayman Islands ...	05
Azores*	01		Chile*	04
			Christmas Island, Pacific Ocean	10
Bahamas*...	05		Colombia ...	05
Barbados ...	04		Cook Islands*, except Niue	10
Belize	06		Costa Rica	06
Bermuda*	04		Cuba*	05
Bolivia	04		Curaçao Island	04
Brazil, eastern[2]	03			
Territory of Acre	05		Dominican Republic	04
western	04			
British Antarctic Territory[3]	03		Easter Island (I. de Pascua)*	06
			Ecuador ...	05
Canada				
Alberta*	07		Falkland Islands[4]	04
British Columbia*	08		Fanning Island ...	10
Labrador*	04		Fernando de Noronha Island	02
Manitoba*	06		French Guiana ...	03
New Brunswick*	04			
Newfoundland*	03 30		Galápagos Islands	06
Northwest Territories*			Greenland[5], Scoresby Sound*	01
east of long. W. 68°	04		Angmagssalik and west coast*	03
long. W. 68° to W. 85°	05		Thule area	04
long. W. 85° to W. 102°	06		Grenada ...	04
west of long. W. 102°	07		Guadeloupe	04
Nova Scotia* ...	04		Guatemala*	06
Ontario*, east of long. W. 90°	05		Guyana, Republic of	03
west of long. W. 90°	06			
Prince Edward Island*	04		Haiti*	05
Quebec*, east of long. W. 63°	04		Honduras...	06
west of long. W. 63°	05			
Saskatchewan*			Jamaica ...	05
east of long. W. 106°	06		Jan Mayen Island	01
west of long. W. 106°	07		Johnston Island ...	10
Yukon*...	08			

*Summer time may be kept in these countries.
[1] This is the legal standard time, but local mean time is generally used.
[2] Including all the coast and Brasilia.
[3] Except South Georgia which keeps 02^h.
[4] Except Port Stanley which may keep summer time.
[5] Danmarkshavn and Mesters Vig keep G.M.T.

STANDARD TIMES (Corrected to September 1985)

LIST III—*(continued)*

	h	m
Juan Fernandez Islands...	04	
Leeward Islands...	04	
Low Archipelago	10	
Marquesas Islands[1]	09	30
Martinique	04	
Mexico[2]	06	
Midway Islands	11	
Miquelon...	03	
Nicaragua...	06	
Niue Island	11	
Panama Canal Zone	05	
Panama, Republic of	05	
Paraguay*...	04	
Peru	05	
Puerto Rico	04	
Rarotonga	10	
St. Pierre and Miquelon	03	
Salvador, El	06	
Samoa	11	
Society Islands[1]	10	
South Georgia	02	
Surinam	03	
Tobago	04	
Trindade Island, South Atlantic ...	02	
Trinidad	04	
Tuamotu Archipelago[1]	10	
Tubuai Islands[1]	10	
Turks and Caicos Islands* ...	05	

United States of America

	h
Alabama[3]	06
Alaska[3], east of W. 169° 30'	09
Aleutian Islands, west of W. 169° 30'	10
Arizona...	07
Arkansas[3]	06
California[3]	08
Colorado[3]	07
Connecticut[3]	05
Delaware[3]	05
District of Columbia[3]	05
Florida[3,4]	05

United States of America *(continued)*

	h
Georgia[3]	05
Hawaii	10
Idaho[3,4]	07
Illinois[3]	06
Indiana[4]	05
Iowa[3]	06
Kansas[3,4]	06
Kentucky[3,4]	05
Louisiana[3]	06
Maine[3]...	05
Maryland[3]	05
Massachusetts[3]	05
Michigan[3,4]	05
Minnesota[3]	06
Mississippi[3]	06
Missouri[3]	06
Montana[3]	07
Nebraska[3,4]	06
Nevada[3]	08
New Hampshire[3]	05
New Jersey[3]	05
New Mexico[3]	07
New York[3]	05
North Carolina[3]	05
North Dakota[3,4]	06
Ohio[3]	05
Oklahoma[3]	06
Oregon[3,4]	08
Pennsylvania[3]	05
Rhode Island[3]...	05
South Carolina[3]	05
South Dakota[3], eastern part ...	06
western part... ...	07
Tennessee[3,4]	06
Texas[3,4]	06
Utah[3]	07
Vermont[3]	05
Virginia[3]	05
Washington, D.C.[3]	05
Washington[3]	08
West Virginia[3]...	05
Wisconsin[3]	06
Wyoming[3]	07
Uruguay*...	03
Venezuela...	04
Virgin Islands	04
Windward Islands	04

*Summer time may be kept in these countries.
[1] This is the legal standard time, but local mean time is generally used.
[2] Except the states of Sonora, Sinaloa, Nayarit and the Southern District of Lower California which keep 07ʰ, and the Northern District of Lower California which keeps 08ʰ*.
[3] Summer (daylight-saving) time, one hour fast on the time given, is kept in these states from the last Sunday in April to the last Sunday in October, changing at 02ʰ 00ᵐ local clock time.
[4] This applies to the greater portion of the state.

ANSWERS TO MULTICHOICE TEST QUESTIONS

Chapter 4: Q3(b), Q4(c), Q5(a), Q6(a), Q7(a), Q8(c), Q9(c), Q10(b), Q11(b), Q12(c), Q13(c), Q14(a), Q15(a).

Chapter 8: Q1(b), Q2(b), Q3(c), Q4(b), Q5(a), Q6(b).

Chapter 10: Q1(a), Q2(c), Q3(c), Q4(c), Q5(c), Q6(a), Q7(c), Q8(b), Q9(b), Q10(c).

Chapter 11: Q1(c), Q2(b), Q3(a), Q4(c), Q5(b), Q6(b), Q7(a), Q8(a), Q9(c), Q10(b), Q11(a), Q12(c).

Chapter 12: Q1(b), Q2(c), Q3(b), Q4(b), Q5(c).

Chapter 13: Q1(c), Q2(a), Q3(b), Q4(c), Q5(b), Q6(b), Q7(b), Q8(c).

Chapter 14: Q1(b), Q2(a), Q3(c), Q4(a), Q5(a), Q6(a), Q7(b), Q8(c), Q9(c), Q10(b).

Chapter 15: Q1(a), Q2(b), Q3(c), Q4(a), Q5(b).

Chapter 16: Q1(b), Q2(c), Q3(a), Q4(b), Q5(c).

Chapter 17: Q1(a), Q2(b), Q3(c), Q4(c), Q5(b), Q6(a).

Chapter 18: Q1(b), Q2(b), Q3(c), Q4(a), Q5(b).

Chapter 19: Q1(a), Q2(a), Q3(a), Q4(a), Q5(a), Q6(b), Q7(a), Q8(b), Q9(d), Q10(c), Q11(d), Q12(b), Q13(a), Q14(a), Q15(c).

Chapter 21: Q1(c), Q2(c), Q3(b), Q4(a), Q5(c), Q6(c), Q7(b), Q8(c), Q9(a), Q10(c), Q11(c), Q12(b), Q13(a), Q14(c), Q15(b), Q16(c), Q17(a), Q18(a), Q19(a), Q20(b).

Chapter 22: Q1(b), Q2(a), Q3(b), Q4(c), Q5(a), Q6(a), Q7(b), Q8(a).

Chapter 23: Q1(c), Q2(a), Q3(b), Q4(a), Q5(c), Q6(c), Q7(b), Q8(c), Q9(c), Q10(b).

Chapter 24: Q1(a), Q2(b), Q3(c), Q4(b), Q5(c), Q6(c).

Chapter 25: Q1(b), Q2(c), Q3(a), Q4(a), Q5(c).

Chapter 26: Q1(b), Q2(a), Q3(c), Q4(c), Q5(a), Q6(a), Q7(b), Q8(c), Q9(b), Q10(a).

Chapter 27: Q1(b), Q2(c), Q3(a), Q4(c), Q5.1(a), 5.2(a), 5.3(a), Q6(a), Q7(b), Q8(c), Q9(a), Q10(c), Q11(b), Q12(a), Q13(a), Q14(c), Q15(a).

GLOSSARY OF ABBREVIATIONS

a/c	aircraft
ADC	Air Data Computer
ADI	Attitude Director Indicator
agl	above ground level
A/H	alter heading
alt or ALT	altitude
amsl	above mean sea level
APP	approach
ASI	Airspeed Indicator
ASR	Altimeter Setting Region
ATD	actual time of departure
BCAR	British Civil Airworthiness Requirements
BIT or BITE	built in test (equipment)
Brg	Bearing
°C	degrees Celsius
°(C)	degrees Compass
CA	conversion angle
CAA	Civil Aviation Authority
CAS	Calibrated Airspeed
CAVOK	weather, in general terms, fine and clear (cf Volume 4)
CDU	Control and Display Unit
CH	celestial horizon
ch lat	change of latitude
ch long	change of longitude
CL	chart length
CLB	climb
CLR	clear
cm	centimetre(s)
CM	central meridian
COAT	corrected outside air temperature
C of G or CG	centre of gravity
CP	critical point
CRS	course
CRT	cathode ray tube
CRV	centre reading voltmeter
CRZ	cruise

c/s or C/S	call-sign
DEL	delete
DEP	departure
DES	descent
Dev	deviation
DH	decision height
DI	Direction Indicator
dist	distance
DME	Distance Measuring Equipment
DR	dead reckoooning
EADI	Electronic Attitude Director Indicator
EAS	equivalent airspeed
ECAM	Electronic Centralised Aircraft Monitor
ED	Earth distance
EFIS	Electronic Flight Instrument System
EHSI	Electronic Horizontal Situation Indicator
EL	Electronic Library
EMF or emf	electro-motive force
ETA	estimated time of arrival
ETD	estimated time of departure
EXEC	execute
FD(S)	Flight Director (System)
FL	flight level
FMC	Flight Management Computer
FMS	Flight Management System
FOB	fuel on board
FT or ft	feet
ft/min	feet per minute
g	normal acceleration due to gravity
°(G)	degrees Grid
GC	great circle
GD	Greenwich date
GMT	Greenwich mean time
GN	Grid North
Griv	grivation
GS	ground speed *or* glide slope
HDG or Hdg	heading
HHI	horizontal hard iron
h, m, s	hours, minutes, seconds
HT or ht	height
hP	hectoPascals
IAS	indicated airspeed
ICAO	International Civil Aviation Organization
IFR	Instrument Flight Rules
ILS	Instrument Landing System
in	inch(es)

INS	inertial navigation system
ISA	international standard atmosphere
JAR	joint airworthiness requirements
kg	kilogram(s)
kg/h	kilograms per hour
km	kilometre(s)
km/h	kilometres per hour
KT or kt	knot(s)
Lat	latitude
LCD	liquid crystal display
LD	local date *or* landing distance
LMT	Local Mean Time
L-NAV	lateral navigation system
Long	longitude
LV	light and variable wind
M	Mach
°(M)	degrees Magnetic
MB/mb	millibar(s)
M_{crit}	critical Mach number
MFD	multi function display
MI	master indicator
min	minute(s)
M_{ind}	indicated Mach number
mm	millimetre(s)
M_{MO}	maximum operating Mach number
MN	Mach number *or* North (Magnetic)
mph	miles per hour
M/R	moonrise
M/S	moon set
MSG	message
msl	mean sea level
ND	navigation display
NH	northern hemisphere
NM/nm	nautical mile(s)
NP	north pole
PA	pressure altitude
PE	pressure error
PFD	primary flight display
P/L	position line
posn	position
QDM	Hdg(M) to station with zero wind
QDR	Brg(M) from station
QFE, QFF, QNH	defined in text
QNE	altimeter reading with subscale set to 1013.2 mb
QTE	Brg(T) from station
RAS	rectified airspeed

RAT	ram air temperature
Rel	relative
RIC	remote indicating compass
RL	rhumb line
RLG	ring laser gyro
RNAV	area navigation
rpm	revolutions per minute
RTE	route
RWY or R/W	runway
SAT	static ambient (air) temperature
SH	southern hemisphere
S/H	set heading
sm	statute miles
SP	south pole
S/R	sunrise
S/S	sunset
ST	standard time
$°(T)$	degrees True
TAS	True airspeed
TAT	total air temperature
TK	track
TKE	track error
TMG	track made good
TN	True North
T/O	take-off
TOC	top of climb
TOD	top of descent
UTC	co-ordinated universal time
Var	magnetic variation
VFR	visual flight rules
V_{MO}	maximum operating speed
V-NAV	vertical navigation
V_{NE}	never exceed speed
VSC	variation setting corrector
vsi	vertical soft iron
VSI	Vertical Speed Indicator
WC	wind component
WPT	waypoint
WS	wind speed
WV	wind velocity

INDEX

acceleration, 183
  errors, 167, 264–9
accelerometer, 183
aclinic line, 222
age (moon), 293
agonic line, 221
Air Almanac, 289
Air Data Computer (ADC), 194–6
aircraft magnetism, 223–255
airspeed indicator, 103–9
algebra, 7
alphanumeric, 202
Altimeter Setting Regions (ASR), 114
altimeters, 110–123
altitude, 114
Angle of Attack systems, 127–9
angle of dip, 218
annunciator, 279
aperiodic, 259
aphelion, 285
apparent A, 227
apparent solar day, 286
artificial horizon, 164–70
astronomical twilight, 292

barometric error, 112
BCARs, 230
bearings, 30, 57, 74, 79
blocked pitot, 108, 113
blocked static, 108, 113, 125
Bonne's projection, 42
Bourdon tube, 179
built-in test equipment (BIT/BITE)
  194–5

caging gyro, 150
calculators, 11
Calibrated Airspeed (CAS), 106
change lat, 24, 231, 251
change long, 24
chart, 41
chart symbols, 49
circles, properties of, 8
civil twilight, 292
  tables, 301–2
coercive force, 218
colour coding, 106, 206
compass, direct reading, 259–263

compass, remote indicating, 270–282
compass swing, 228, 230, 242
composite RL track, 56
compressibility error, 107
compressibility factor, 108, 133
compression, 18
conformal, 42, 44–5, 69, 79, 84, 87
conical orthomorphic, 68–75
conic projections, 65–70
conjunction, moon, 293
constant of the cone, 67
convergence, convergency, 28–40, 55,
  70, 79, 84, 88, 90
conversion angle, 29–40, 57
co-ordinated universal time, 289
corrected outside air temperature
  (COAT) 112, 181
crew alerting system, 197
critical mach number, 131
cylindrical projection, 52

daily lag, 295
dateline, 289
datum, grid, 90
declination, 294
degaussing, 223
density altitude, 116
density error, 106–7, 132
departure, 36
deviation, 223–57
dip, 218
direction indicator, 149–163
directive force, 224
d lat, 20
d long, 20
drift (gyro), 144, 147

eclipse, 294
electronic attitude director indicator
  (EADI), 208–9
electronic flight instrument system
  (EFIS), 196–200
electronic horizontal situation indicator
  (EHSI), 209–210
electronic library, 197
equivalent airspeed (EAS), 108
erection error, 168
erection mechanism, 278
E-type compass, 262–3

flag, malfunction, 120, 129, 135, 212
flight director system (FDS), 205–211
flight level, 214
flight management system (FMS),
    200–205
flux, 270
flux valve, 271
fraction representative, 45

gauss, 231
geoid, 18
geometric conic, 68
geometric cylindrical, 51
gibbous, 293
gimbal, 142
gimballing errors 156
graticle, 19, 20, 53, 56, 76, 83, 85
great circles, 22, 29, 55, 71, 79, 84, 88
Greenwich meridian, 20, 288
grid, 90–100
grivation, 92
gyro-compassing, 187
gyro drift, 144, 151
gyroscope, 140–148

hard iron, 217, 231
horizontal situation indicator (HSI), 210
horizontal soft iron (hsi), 217

Indicated Airspeed (IAS), 107
induced magnetism, 223
inertia, 183
Inertial navigation system (INS),
    183–193
Inertial reference system (IRS), 189
Instantaneous Vertical Speed Indicator
    (ISVI), 126–7
international nautical mile, 24
International Standard Atmosphere
    (ISA), 104, 111, 121
isoclinal, 218, 222
isogonal, 221
isogriv, 92

JARs, 105, 230

Kepler, 285
kilometre, 26

Lambert's projection, 65–75
lapse rate, 111, 112
latitude (definition), 19
latitude nut, 154
line keys, 202
L-NAV, 203
local apparent noon, 287
local mean time, 288
longitude (definition), 20

machmeter, 130–9
mach number, 130

magnetic meridian, 218
magnetism, 217–58
  aircraft, 223–58
  terrestrial, 217–22
map, 35–41
  topographical, 43
maths reminders, 3–17, 234
mean solar time, 287
Mercator, 51–64
  oblique, 85–9
  transverse, 82–5
meridian, 19, 20, 45
meridional parts, 51, 54
metering unit, 124
micro-adjuster, 226
millibar subscale, 112
mode keys, 204
molecular theory, 217
moon, 293
moonrise, moonset, 294

nautical mile, 24
  international, 24
nautical twilight, 292
normal cylinder, 52

oblique Mercator, 85–89
opposition (moon), 293
origin, parallel, 65
orthomorphic projection, 42, 53
orthomorphism, 42, 44–5, 69, 79, 84, 87

parallel of origin, 65
parallels, 19, 45
pendulosity error, 168
perihelion, 285
period of a needle, 260
percentages, 5
permanent magnetism, 223
pitot pressure, 103
pitot, blocked, 108, 113
plotting,
  on Lambert, 74
  on Mercator, 55, 57
polar stereographic, 76–81
poles, 18, 218
position error, 105–6
precession, 141, 277
  secondary, 172
pressure altitude (PA), 114, 121
pressure error, 105–6, 112, 125
primary precession, 172
prime meridian, 20
projections, 41–50
  classification, 42
  cylindrical, 42, 51
  orthomorphic, 42
properties of a circle, 8
proportion, 3
P-type compass, 259–263

quadrature, 293
QFE, QFF, QNH, 113–4

radial error, 189
radio position lines, 57, 74, 79
ram air temperature (RAT), 180
ratio, 3
rectified airspeed (RAS), 106
reduced earth, 18, 41
regional QNH, 114
relief, 49
remote indicating compass (RIC), 270–282
representative fraction, 45
rhumb line, 23, 29, 55, 72, 79, 85, 88
rhumb line track, 29
rigidity, 140
ring laser gyro, 143

scale, 45
    factor, 47
    Lambert, 69
    line, 46
    Mercator, 55
    oblique Mercator, 87
    polar stereographic, 76
    transverse, 84
Schuler-tuned platform, 184
scientific calculator, 11
secant cone, 68
secondary precession, 172
secular change, 220
sidereal day, 286
signal selsyn, 273
small circle, 23
soft iron, 217
solar system, 285–306
solstice, 286
speed of sound, 130, 133
spot QNH, 114
square root, 13
stable element, 184
standard parallel, 65, 68
standard time, 289, 303–6
standby compasses, 259–263
static air temperature, 179
static, blocked, 108, 113, 125
static pressure, 103
static vent, 105
statute mile, 26
stereographic, polar, 76–81
sunrise/sunset, 290
    tables, 299–300
symbols, chart, 49
synchronising knob, 276

take-off errors, 167
temperature deviation, 116
temperature error, 112
temperature, measurement of air, 178–82
temporary magnetism, 218
terrestrial magnetism, 218
test questions,
    acceleration and turning errors, 268–9
    altimeters, 121–3
    artificial horizon, 170
    ASI, 108–9
    DI, 163
    direct reading compasses, 263
    electronic displays & systems, 211–213
    gyroscopes, 147–8
    inertial navigation, 191–3
    machmeter, 138–9
    magnetism, 239–40, 257–8
    oblique/transverse Mercator, 88–9
    phenomena and time, 297–8
    remote indicating compasses, 281–2
    turn and slip indicator, 177
    VSI/IVSI, 129
thermometry, 178–82
tilt, 146–7
time, 285–306
time lag error, 112, 125
topographical maps, 43
topple, 146–7
total air temperature (TAT), 180
track, composite rhumb line, 56
transit, 285
transverse Mercator, 82–85
trigonometry, 8
true airpeed (TAS), 107
turn and slip, 171–7
turn co-ordinator, 174–6
turning errors, 127, 168, 264–9
twilight, 292
    tables, 301–2

UTC (co-ordinated universal time), 289

variation, 222, 277
vertical soft iron (vsi), 225, 231
vertical speed indicator (VSI and IVSI), 124–9
V_{MO}, 135
V-NAV, 203
V_{NE}, 105, 136

wander, 144, 154
warning flags, 120, 129, 135, 212